Images of Nations and International Public Relations

LEA'S COMMUNICATION SERIES
Jennings Bryant/Dolf Zillmann, General Editors

Images of Nations and International Public Relations

—◇—

Michael Kunczik

LAWRENCE ERLBAUM ASSOCIATES, PUBLISHERS
1997   Mahwah, New Jersey

Lawrence Erlbaum Associates, Inc., Publishers
10 Industrial Avenue
Mahwah, New Jersey 07430-2262

Cover design by Semadar Megged

Library of Congress Cataloging-in-Publication Data

Kunczik, Michael, 1946–
    Images of nations and international public relations /
Michael Kunczik.
        p. cm.
    Includes bibliographical references and indexes.
    ISBN 0-8058-1713-1 (cloth : alk. paper). — ISBN
0-8058-1714-x (pbk. : alk. paper)
    1. Government publicity. 2. Propaganda, International.
3. International relations. 4. Discourse analysis. I. Title
JF1525.P8K83   1996
659.2'935—dc20   96-19393
                                                       CIP

Books published by Lawrence Erlbaum Associates are printed on acid-free paper, and their bindings are chosen for strength and durability.

Printed in the United States of America
10 9 8 7 6 5 4 3 2 1

Contents

Foreword   ix

1   **Introduction to the Problems of
International Image Cultivation**   1

Preliminary Remarks   1
Status of Research in the Field of
International Public Relations   12

2   **Problems of International Image Cultivation**   18

Domestic Public Opinion and World Public Opinion   18
The Structural Necessity of Public Relations for States   20
Actors in the Field of International Public Relations   27
Image and the International System   37

The World of Literary Images: Some Examples   52
Image and Reality: Self-Fulfilling Prophecy   58
Some Examples of Image Polishing by States   61
The Country of Origin Effect   68
The Main Aim of International PR:
Establishment of Trust   74
Terrorism as International Public Relations   80

3   Mediation of Foreign Policy   **85**

Theoretical Considerations   85
The Media and Politics: Some Examples of Mediation   87
CNN, Mediation of Foreign Policy, and the Gulf War   96

4   Observations on Image Changes   **102**

Image Changes and Selective Perception   102
Research Findings and Tricks of the Trade   109
Examples of Enemy-Images   120
    The Red Menace   120
    The Jewish-Bolshevist Conspiracy   126
    The Fabulous Orient   129
    The New Scapegoat: Japan   134
Propaganda and Stability of Images   144

**5   Short Historical Outline of Image Cultivation
      by Governments**   **152**

Early Examples of Image Manipulation   152
Developments in Germany and France   158

The Birth of Professional Image Cultivation:
The Fight for America's Neutrality During World War I   169
   British Activities   169
   German Propaganda in the United States   180
   The Creel Committee   186
   Resume - The Birth of Professional Image Cultivation   188

6   Selected Cases of International Public Relations   191

Ivy Lee and PR for Nazi Germany   191
Nazi Propaganda to Foreign Nations   193
Edward L. Bernays: Gaining Goodwill for India   198
The Tactic of Withdrawal: PR in the United States for
Developing Countries   201
The Big Rip-Off: Image Cultivation by
General Chiang Kai-shek   205
Muldergate: Apartheid and Image Policy of South Africa   212

**7   International Image Cultivation During
Cold War Times   227**

Image Cultivation by the United States   227
   Image Cultivation by the USIA   230
   Image Cultivation by the CIA   240
   United Fruit and the CIA: The Coup in Guatemala   246
Image Policy of the Soviet Union   252
   A Short History of Soviet Propaganda   252
   Disinformation Campaigns of the KGB   256
   Gorbachev's PR Offensive   263

**8   Image Policy During Wartimes:
      Theoretical Considerations and the Gulf War   270**

      Carl von Clausewitz and Paradoxical Communication:
      The Necessity of Censorship   270
      Public Opinion in Wartime   273
      Public Relations in Wartime: The Gulf War II   277

9   Consequences for Image Polishing   283

      References   286

      Index   318

Foreword

This book addresses the importance of images of nations in international relations. One fundamental assumption is that the behavior of states is not the same as that of individuals. States are social systems whose behavior as a rule directly corresponds neither to the motives of their respective leaders nor to those of their populations. Self-evidently, however, international activities always depend, too, on personal relationships; for example it is indubitably important whether the U.S. president and the leader of Russia get on well with each other at a personal level.

The book also presents studies which relate to more or less deliberate attempts to induce change in images. There is no need to fear that this is a kind of Machiavellian manipulation manual to enable dictatorships trampling on human rights suddenly to appear in the purest shining light of innocence. Fears of the alleged omnipotence of the image producers, which are still widely spread in public, are also to be countered, which is not to be equated, however, with making the might of the "captains of consciousness" appear harmless. Obviously, one of the main objectives of advertising and public relations agencies must be to convince clients and prospective clients of the effectiveness of their work. And it must already be said here that active and planned inducement of image change is a long and demanding process. A positive image cannot be forced nor bought, and once it has been built it needs continuous cultivation. Image building can go on at many levels, starting with sport. Artists and scientists may travel abroad or the mass media might be used. Such activities will be briefly touched on here, too, but because of the breadth of the theme the emphasis will be clearly on image building or influencing by the mass media. Given the interdisciplinary nature of the subject matter, findings made in the public relations, advertising research, prejudice research and other fields will also be taken into account. One difficulty is the drawing of boundaries concerning the actors influencing the images of nations. Very often it is impossible to distinguish between the image of the nation-state and the images of big enterprises like Krupp, Ford or Coca Cola. For this reason the country of origin effect is also discussed here.

Public relations is also the art of camouflaging and deceiving, successful PR also means above all that the target group (those to be influenced and those who have the money to pay for such attempts) do not notice that they have become the "victims" of a PR activity.

Publication of this book is made possible by the Friedrich Ebert Foundation. My special thanks for suggestions and criticism in this research project carried out for the Friedrich Ebert Foundation are due to (in alphabetical order): Dr. Dieter Bauer, Reinhard Keune and Gunther Lehrke of the foundation. My special thanks are due to Claudia Peters who provided secretarial assistance and to Dr. Alexander Heintzel who not only offered helpful criticism but also provided administrative assistance.

CHAPTER 1

Introduction to the Problems of International Image Cultivation

PRELIMINARY REMARKS

The first time one visits a new country, regardless of how thorough his or her preparation, it is always different from the way he or she imagined it would be. Not all Scots are tightfisted and frugal, and they do not all run around in kilts and play bagpipes. Not all the Swiss are bankers, nor do they spend their time yodeling from the mountains. And the Viennese have other things to do besides dancing waltzes. At the same time, one discovers that the inhabitants of the host country often have the most peculiar, largely inaccurate, perceptions of one's own country. The question is, what kind of information has created such images, and can they be changed?

Images of certain nations, however right or wrong they might be, seem to form, fundamentally, through a very complex communication process involving varied information sources. The process starts with one's experiences in very early life; in school; in children's books, fairytales and other leisure literature; the theater and so on, and may include accounts by relatives, acquaintances, and friends. But radio and TV transmissions of international programs, newspapers and magazines, cultural exchange programs, sports, books, news services, and so on are probably the strongest image shapers. The various communication sources are responsible for the image or images of another nation in all strata of a

1

population. Education and travel -- that is the degree of personal experience of foreign cultures -- are also of extraordinary importance to image building.

Practically anything can contribute to our forming an image of another nation: the fact that a bottle of Italian wine tastes of cork; that the highways in Russia are awful; that the consular official has bad breath; that yet another product made in Germany doesn't work; that the opposing national team plays more unfairly than our own ever would or, rather, than we perceive it ever would, which is the more likely of the two, for in observing a very physical game, like soccer, the supporters of each team, as a rule, see two completely different games, with one's own players the heroes and the opposing players the villains. Third parties may be affected altogether differently again by the match. During the Grenoble winter Olympics in 1968, the West German ice hockey team brawled with the United States team. According to the German public relations (PR) practitioner, Rainer Fabian (1970), this earned the Germans considerable empathy from the French, who are not enthusiastic fans of the United States.

As to what public relations could do to remove prejudices between peoples, Fabian (1970) responded: "They present one's own nation to the other as being as likeable as possible. They exchange ambassadors and arrange state visits, they put on art shows and transport warm blankets to the locality of a disaster, they print brochures and invite students to a language course, they do all they can and they hope that at the next soccer international there is no brawling between the players of the two teams. Then all the work was for nothing. Public relations between nations is the most difficult variety of public relations work" (p. 29). von Studnitz (1950) put it this way: "In the old days one could win over an empire by marrying, today you can win over peoples by a leading article" (p. 299).

However, one cannot wholly agree with such assortions with respect to the imputed fluctuation of nation-images from the point of view of research. Thus, social psychologists M. Sherif and C. W.

Sherif (1956) observed that "once established in a group, stereotypes tend to persist" (p. 653). Similarly, Deutsch and Merritt (1965) in their analysis of research findings on the effects of events on national and international images, came to the conclusion that "human thinking and imagining" is very resistant to "sudden environmental pressure": "Almost nothing in the world seems to be able to shift the images of 40 percent of the population even within one or two decades" (p. 183).

With respect to the entire field of image building, it can be said that there has not been enough research on the historical dimension. So called "classical" literature also transports images. Thus, objections were raised in the United States against using Shakespeare's "The Merchant of Venice" in school lessons on the grounds that the character of Shylock would prejudice youngsters against Jews. Similar objections were raised against Pinocchio as allegedly featuring "Italians and 'assassins' in close association" (G. W. Allport, 1954/58, p. 196). Many prejudices about nations are carried forward through the generations, so that historical events of long ago remain decisive in a nation's image.

This is so with the Germans' perception of Russia, for example, shaped decisively in the 16th century by reports about the despotic czar, Ivan IV ("the Terrible", 1533 - 1584). Since then, Germans' predominant image of Russians has been that they are cruel, naive, and servile. The misdeeds and horrors perpetrated by Ivan have not been perceived as those of a pathological individual, but as a trait in the Russian or, more precisely, the Muscovite national character. Thus, in 1706, Christian Stieff characterized the Russians as a people born to be slaves: "Their nature is so corrupted that they will do nothing voluntarily; only the harshest and most cruel beatings can make them do anything at all". Just before World War I, the German Kaiser Wilhelm II expressed to the Austrian foreign minister, Count Leopold Berchtold, the opinion that "Slavs were not born to rule, but to serve; this had to be brought home to them". Conversely, an old Russian adage says, "The Germans have invented the devil."

Even Czar Peter the Great (1689 - 1725), the "master craftsman on the czarist throne", who tried to reform Russia and open it to Europe, was not able to change decisively the Germans' notions of Russia, although his efforts were very positively assessed in Germany. The German philosopher Gottfried Wilhelm Freiherr von Leibniz (1646 - 1716), for example, saw Russia as a kind of clean slate under Peter the Great. It had a chance, he observed, to avoid many mistakes made elsewhere and to adopt the best from both Europe and China. As late as the 19th century the Berliner Albert Lortzing wrote his very popular opera, "Zar und Zimmermann" ("Czar and Carpenter"), in which Peter's deeds are positively depicted. Peter the Great himself, in fact, already pursued image cultivation for Russia. His diplomats were instructed no longer to use the terms <u>Muscovites</u> or <u>Muscovia</u>, because they were associated with Ivan the Terrible; instead they were to use <u>Russians</u> and <u>Russia</u>. In other words, a positive image of a "changed" Russia was to be built up. Russia urgently needed at the time to make specialists from Europe want to go there to work.

Someone who became famous for image cultivation by deception was Prince Grigory Aleksandrovich Potemkin, who wanted to show his empress, Catherine II, how successfully he was colonizing New Russia, the Ukrainian steppes, although he was, in fact, overreaching himself. In 1787, accompanied by a splendid retinue and the ambassadors of foreign powers, the empress traveled via Smolensk to Kiev and then down the River Dnepr on a lavishly appointed fleet of galleys. The journey proceeded through a world of villages with garlands, triumphal arches, and make-believe buildings -- the fantasy world of the Potemkian villages. An entire sham world of people busy at their work, of trade, and of change had been staged all along the Dnepr. The supposedly flourishing villages on the banks and beyond were wooden backdrops. The cheering crowds were comprised of serfs breathlessly hurrying ahead of the royal route to play their jubilation role over and over again.

Fidel Castro used much the same ruse to make his guerrilla force appear bigger than it was. Some authors (e.g., Ratliff, 1987) suggest that Castro got his job through The New York Times that is, through the help of Times correspondent and editorial writer Herbert Matthews, who had visited Fidel Castro, his brother Raúl, Ché Guevara, and others in the Sierra Maestra on February 17, 1957. The famous article "Cuban Rebel Is Visited in Hideout" appeared on the front page of the paper on February 24, 1957, with the subhead "Castro Is Still Alive and Still Fighting in the Mountains." The Times article was of central importance to Castro's further career and made Castro an international figure. The overestimate of the size of Castro's forces was the result of Castro's enormous skill in handling journalists and his extreme adroitness in manipulation. Castro only had about fifteen men with him: "And while the interview was going on . . . Raúl would march in a group of ten men, and then they would be marched off stage, they would change hats, and be marched on stage again. Castro was so successful that Matthews's three lengthy articles were laced full of references to Castro, with about three hundred troops, [and to] our other camp where the rest of our troops are" (Wallach, 1987, p. 149 - 150).

In his famous book, Public Opinion, Walter Lippmann (1922) wrote: "Man . . . is learning to see with his mind vast portions of the world that he could never see, touch, smell, hear, or remember. Gradually he makes for himself a trustworthy picture inside his head of the world beyond his reach" (p. 181). The mass media are, in fact, continuously offering images of nations. Take this random selection of cover story topics in Time magazine: Super Japan; Panama's Noriega, with the cover headline "The Drug Thugs: Panama's Noriega Proves They're a Law Unto Themselves"; Colombia, "Can Colombia Break Free From the Drug Lords?". But the image of the United States is also drawn, and not only positively: "Drugs in the United States: Kids Who Sell Crack." The image of the United States abroad was also the subject of a Time cover story: "A Candid Look at How The Rest of the World Views

America Today" (March 27, 1989). These reports in Time, without a doubt, affect the images of the respective countries. After publishing a cover story "Gun Crazy" (August 2, 1993), reporting on violence in the United States, a German reader wrote: "I have never visited the United States, and after reading your report will not. I hope that our youth in Europe will be spared the terrible gun habit." (This letter to the editor was published in Time on August 23, 1994; the cover story was titled "America the Violent: Crime Is Spreading and Patience Is Running out.")

In the weekly German news magazine, Der Spiegel, the Bahamas, Belize, Bolivia, Burma, Haiti, Lebanon, and Panama were described as states that have been bought by the worldwide drug cartel so that they could run their drug business undisturbed. Cutlip (1994) gave an account of unethical public relations connected with the image of the Bahamas: In 1955 public relations firm Hill & Knowlton acquired the Bahamas tourist account. During the 1960s, there were rumors of a close connection between the gambling house and gangsters. In 1965, Allan W. Witwer, a former reporter then in charge of Hill & Knowlton's Bahamas account quit his job and started to write a book, The Ugly Bahamas, in which he made use of his confidential information. Witwer could not find a publisher. Cutlip (1994) wrote: "Then with an obvious motive, he took the chapters to Hill and Knowlton and not so subtly suggested that Sir Stafford Sands, Minister of Bahamian Tourism, might be interested to know about his proposed book. According to Fortune, Bill Durbin, H & K's vice president for foreign accounts, read the book and hurried down to Nassau" (p. 451). According to Cutlip, Durbin convinced Sands that the publication of the book would damage the Bahama's image. H & K arranged for the manuscript to be bought by a dummy publisher.

Mexico, too, has an image associated with drug corruption. The drug dealers are said to have an ideal situation in Mexico: They do not sit in the President's palace, but they control political decisions without anyone beein able to prove it. This negative image of Mexico became even more pronounced after the assassination of

José Francisco Ruiz Massieu in 1994, General Secretary of the ruling Institutional Revolutionary Party, because the brother of the victim was Mexico's deputy attorney general in charge of the war against narcotraffickers. Mexico is now regarded by many people as a narco-democracy. The image of Mexico has been further damaged by the 1994 peasant revolt in Chiapas.

This bad image caused Enrique Krauze, a Mexican journalist, to write an article about the image of Mexico, *"Violence: Legend and Reality"* (1994). Krauze argued: "In 1994 Mexico seems destined to confirm all the old stereotypes, after all, it *is* the land of Pancho Villa, where men with handlebar mustaches and wide-brimmed sombreros whip out pistols at the slightest provocation, making it a perennial theater of human sacrifice" (p. 39). Krauze maintained that Mexican history is the stuff of legend, but some of the legends are far from true. He characterized Mexico as a peaceful country that from 1930 to 1994, was "a haven of stability in a region that oscillated between anarchy and dictatorship". But "at least for the moment, the legend of a barbarous, violent, unstable Mexico has become a reality". Whether Krauze was correct or not, Mexico no longer has the image Marie Robinson Wright described in *Picturesque Mexico* (1897): "Mexico, land of mystery and romance; land of mingled tradition and history; land of vast forests and fruitful valleys; of snow-capped mountains and inexhaustible mines; land of sapphire skies and unrivalled climate; land of tropic luxuriance and noble patriotic hearts; of thee would I sing; thy praises would I carry to the farthest end of the broad green earth" (p. 15). Mexico's bad image may have been the reason for an elaborate campaign: In pursuit of congressional approval of the North American Free Trade Agreement, Mexico spent more than $25 million between 1989 and 1993 for public relations and lobbying (Manheim, 1994, p. 34).

There can be no doubt that the mass media influence the way a country's people form their images of the people and governments of other countries, because it is the mass media that disseminate the greater part of the information about foreign countries, but, in the context addressed here, I must note that into the 1970s, the thesis was widespread in communication science that mass media had no effects at all. This empirically untenable claim has never been valid with respect to the forming of images of other nations.

Hollywood, the dream factory, disseminated images of nations from the outset. Thus, according to Richards (1973) in the 1920s and 1930s, a completely stylized and mythic England was created, "where nothing ever changed, where everyone knew his place and where civilized dramas of life and love could be played out. This became even more important with the outbreak of the Second World War. For the projection of this image as an ideal world reinforced the British in their struggle to preserve it and convinced the Americans that it might be worth fighting for, too" (p. 107). This presumed effect cannot be sustained by quantitative data, however.

Woll (1980) traced the evolution of the portrayal of Latin American men, women, and locales as shown on the American screen from the birth of the motion picture until the 1980s, and concluded that the Latin has remained a rapacious bandit or an object of ridicule: "Americans . . . receive a dominant picture of Latin society populated by murderous *banditos* and submissive, but sensual, pleasant women" (p. 2). Films influenced and continue to influence fashion, language, and foreign images. In a study sponsored by the American Commission for Freedom of the Press and News Exchange, "Peoples Speaking to Peoples", L. White and R. D. Leigh (1948) pointed out that among the many examples of false perceptions of America that surfaced during World War II, the most incredible were not found among the jungle inhabitants of Borneo, but among West Europeans, who had seen dozens of Hollywood films.

The influence of novels, films, and youth literature in forming images of foreign nations and countries should not be underestimated. One of the most important British writers of youth literature to spread the vision of the British empire was George Alfred Henty (Huttenback, 1970). Henty's writings dealt with events in the history of British imperialism. His heroes were gentlemen and adventurers. They were of modest and brave character. In his books the beneficial aspects of British imperialism were emphasized. Not much store was put in intellectual abilities. In With Clive in India, one reads, "What do the natives care for our learning? It is pluck and fighting power that have made us their masters". Sheer imperial racism probably emerges most clearly in The Tiger of Mysore. The Rajah of Tripataly tells his sons, "We in India have courage; but it is because our princes are brought up in indolence and luxury that the English, though but a handful in point of numbers, have become masters of such wide territories . . . Your grandmother was an Englishwoman, and I want to see that, with white blood in your veins, you have some of the vigour and energy of Englishmen". In By Sheer Pluck Henty described "African natives" as follows: "They are just like children . . . clever up to a certain point, densely stupid beyond it . . . absolutely without originality, absolutely without inventive power. Living among white men, their imitative faculties enable them to attain a considerable amount of civilization. Left alone to their own devices they retrograde into a state a little above their native savagery".

Huttenback (1970) described the readers of Henty's writings: "He was read by virtually all boys who grew up at the turn of the century and by most in the generation that followed; his works gained a significance as social commentary that they do not merit as literature" (p. 47). One can only speculate about the effects of such books on their youthful readers. Richards (1973) quoted the following statement of the Amalgamated Press, one of the leading publishers of "boys' papers": "These boys' journals aimed from the first at the encouragement of physical strength and patriotism, of interest in travel and exploration and of pride in our empire. It has been said that boys' papers of the Amalgamated Press have done more to provide recruits for our Navy and Army and to keep up esteem of the sister services than anything else" (p. 41).

Rudyard Kipling was the writer who best represented the ideology of British supremacy and imperialism in, for example,"The

White Man's Burden" (1899), subtitled "The United States and the Philippine Islands":

> Take up the White Man's burden--
> Send forth the best ye breed--
> Go bind your sons to exile
> To serve your captives' need;
> To wait in heavy harness
> On fluttered folk and wild--
> Your new-caught, sullen peoples,
> Half-devil and half-child.

For Kipling, colonialism meant advantages for the "natives" (e.g., Indians) and disadvantages for the British. Although the Indians enjoyed the advantages of effective British administration, the British had to "carry the White Man's burden" -- hard-working, noble, and selfless, being aware that "East is East, and West is West, and never the twain shall meet" ("The Ballad of East and West").

Richards (1973) characterized the British imperial archetype in the following way: "He is tall, thin, square-jawed, keen-eyed and almost always equipped with pipe and moustache" (p. 64). Edgar Wallace created his hero, Mr. Commissioner Sanders, who was to typify the classical British district officer as "stern but just, all-wise and all-knowing, keeping himself at a distance from the people he rules, but knowing their languages and their customs and able to pass amongst them in disguise without detection" (Richards, 1973, p. 28). Wallace wrote 102 stories about this colonial official. To quote a passage from "Sanders of the River", published in 1919, "By Sander's code, you trusted all natives up to the same point as you trust children with a few notable exceptions. The Zulu were men, the Basuto were men, yet childlike in their grave faith. The black men who wore the fez were subtle but trustworthy; but the browny men of the Gold Coast who talked English, wore English clothes and called each other 'Mr.' were Sander's pet abomination" (Richards, 1973, p. 30).

The synonym for the "Yellow Peril," Dr. Fu-Manchu, was the creation of Sax Rohmer. The first of a total of 13 Fu-Manchu novels appeared in book form in 1913. A great number of films followed. In The Mystery of Dr. Fu-Manchu, Rohmer wrote: "Imagine a person tall, lean and feline, high shouldered, with a brow like Shakespeare and a face like Satan, close shaven skull and long magnetic eyes of the true cat-green. Invest him with all the cruel cunning of an entire Eastern race, accumulated with all the resources of a wealthy government -- which however, has already denied all knowledge of his existence. Imagine that awful being and you have a mental picture of the yellow peril incarnate in one man" (Richards, 1973, p. 31). Ian Fleming's Doctor No, however, was an even more sinister mixture, the son of a German missionary and a Chinese woman, with two metal hands and a striving to rule the world.

World fame was also achieved by Edgar Rice Burrough's Tarzan of the Apes, although one needs to distinguish carefully between the Tarzan of the novel and the Tarzan of film. Tarzan, a figure strongly reminiscent of Kipling's Mowgli (The Jungle Book), is the son of John Clayton, Lord Greystoke, who in 1888, while on a ship voyage to Africa, is put ashore with his wife and son because of a mutiny. The parents die, and Tarzan grows up among the apes. After his discovery and rescue, he eventually becomes a member of the House of Lords. The message is clear: Heredity overcomes environment. (This statement implies that, in most cases, being reared by apes does not qualify one to take a seat in the House of Lords, but that remains to be proved.) In the film, Tarzan is the noble half-savage; despite his obvious speech difficulties ("Me Tarzan, you Jane") he is clearly superior in intelligence to the natives. Richards (1973) characterized Tarzan as a hero of the empire who helps the British against the Germans in East Africa, leads by the nose communist agents who want to finance the world revolution with the gold of Opar, and fights in World War II against the Japanese in Sumatra as a colonel in the Royal Air Force.

Clearly, fiction can influence the images of foreign countries, because most people depend on second hand experiences or information for what they know about foreign countries. And for most of them, this information is not important to shaping their lives, so there is usually no need to try to obtain first hand information. Because most people's scope of experience is naturally very limited and their knowledge of complex social processes in foreign countries comes mainly from the mass media, there is always the danger of manipulation.

STATUS OF RESEARCH IN THE FIELD OF INTERNATIONAL PUBLIC RELATIONS

The world (i.e., the international system) can be understood as a large and complex communication network, in which the mass media cannot be treated in isolation. Other transaction streams, trade relations; the exchange of people (e.g., tourism, student exchanges, business travel, immigration, etc.) and other communication relations (e.g., letter exchanges, telephone traffic, telex, internet, books, etc.); attempts at one-sided influencing (international advertising, international public relations, propaganda), diplomatic contacts and secret services; newer forms of international communication, such as transborder data flow, satellite communication, and so on, must also be taken into account. A great many events at the international level also have a primarily symbolic communicative character, be it a kind of gunboat diplomacy or a sports event that can be selectively used to cultivate a certain image; one need only recall the Olympics in Nazi Germany in 1936 or in Korea in 1988.

For the nation-state, PR means the planned and continuous distribution of interest-bound information by a state aimed (mostly) at improving the country's image abroad. Trying to distinguish among advertising, PR, and propaganda in foreign image cultivation is merely a semantic game. In Lasswell's (1942) definition of propaganda as "the manipulation of symbols as a means of influencing attitudes on controversial matters" (p. 106), one could easily substitute PR for propaganda. Throughout this book, I treat propaganda and PR as synonyms. This means, following the tradition of one of the founding fathers of PR, Edward L. Bernays (1923), that "The only difference between 'propaganda' and 'education', really, is the point of view. The advocacy of what we believe in is education. The advocacy of what we don't believe in is propaganda" (p. 212). So, PR for the nation-state comprises persuasive communicative acts of a government, directed at a foreign audience.

The Latin word *propagare* means to multiply by offshoots. In 1622, Pope Gregor XV founded the Sacra Congregatio de Propaganda Fide, which had the task of spreading the Christian (Catholic) faith by persuasion and teaching and not by fire and the sword. (It was at this time that witchhunts, which cost hundreds of thousands people, mainly women, their lives, were spreading terror in Europe. The high point of the witchhunts was from about 1500 to about 1650. The last official witch trial in Europe took place in 1782 in the Canton of Glarus in Switzerland.) In the Bull LVIII, "Inscrutabili Divinae Providentiae", of June 22, 1622, Pope Gregor defined his main pastoral task as leading the lost sheep back to Christ's herd so they could recognize their master and shepherd. In 1627, Pope Urban VIII set up a training center, Collegium Urbanum de Propaganda Fide. In addition to museums and a library, the Collegium Urbanum had its own printing works. Here, the propagandists were trained in various languages and then sent out to missionize for Catholicism. For the church, propaganda was a benign process because those persuaded by propaganda came to enjoy the true faith and divine mercy. (Propanda also had no negative connotation for the communists. Agitation and propaganda were seen as instruments for spreading the scientific ideas of Marxism-Leninism and for fighting the ideology of imperialism.)

On the eve of World War II, A. M. Lee and E. B. Lee (1939) recognized international propaganda as an instrument of aggression, "a new means for rendering a country defenseless in the face of an invading army. While it has been used in a halting way for centuries, within the past few years we have seen it prepare the way for Hitler to seize the Saar, Austria, the Sudetenland and Czechoslovakia" (p. 14). It was in 1936, against this background of perceiving propaganda as a surrogate for fighting on the battlefield, that an international agreement was reached about the use of broadcasting in the interest of peace. The aim of the agreement was to eliminate radio broadcasts that could strain good relations between nations and to use radio to promote a spirit of understanding and cooperation. But radio and other mass media are still being used to attack other countries: The People's Republic of China and Taiwan have insulted each other continuously over the airwaves, and in the 1950s, Middle Eastern states hectored each other with boundless hate: "Egyptian radios call on the Jordans to murder their own King, and spread false news reports leading to violent riots in Baghdad" (Whitton & Larson, 1964, p. 4). At the same time, the Arabs were jointly attacking Israel.

Although "old style" propaganda was executed by zealous propagandists, most modern propagandists are coolly distant from their subject matter. The modern professional propagandist does not have to believe what he or she is propagating. McCann (1976), for many years the PR chief of United Fruit, reported that he was astounded that Eli M. Black, who had bought the company in the late 1960s, ultimately believed the illusion spread by his PR department that his company was one of the most socially minded enterprises in the Western hemisphere. (This is further discussed in chap. 7, section 7.1.3) Ellul (1965) wrote, "The true propagandist must be as cold as a surgeon. There are subjects and objects. A propagandist who believes in what he says and lets himself become the victim of his own game will have the same weakness as a surgeon who operates on a loved one or a judge who presides at a trial of a member of his own family" (p. 241). The principles laid down by Joseph Goebbels, Hitler's chief propagandist, at the Nazis' national party congress in Nuremberg on September 6, 1934 were similar: "Propaganda by its nature is neither good nor evil. The moral value is decisively determined by the height of the aim it tries to achieve" (Stephan, 1949, p. 65).

Literature distinguishes three forms of propaganda: black, grey and white. In black propaganda, the identity of the propagandist is not revealed, and so it is used to covers all attempts at deceit. Jowett and O'Donnell (1986/1992) reported on one of the most successful pieces of black propanda. They maintained that Radio Free Hungary, the station regarded in the West as the voice of the rebels during the 1956 Hungarian uprising against the Soviet Union, was, in fact, operated by the KGB:

> Radio Free Hungary's fervent pleas for help from the United States aroused sympathy from the free world. The atrocities of the Russians were described in hideous detail, and the Russians were cursed and denounced in every transmission. The station was actually a totally brilliant fake operated by the KGB with the intention of embarrassing the United States. There was little chance that the United States would send troops to Hungary, even though Radio Free Europe had suggested that Americans would support a popular uprising in Hungary. Russia used Radio Free Hungary to demonstrate that the United States could not be relied upon to help a country in revolt. Radio Free Hungary was so effective that the United States Central Intelligence Agency did not know it was a Russian propaganda device until after it ceased broadcasting. (p. 18)

Black propaganda involves the attribution of allegations to a third party. Grey propaganda consists of allegations of doubtful quality or validity, with sourcing deliberately avoided. White propaganda is basically the open spreading of information as "true". The United States Information Agency (USIA), for example, claims to disseminate only white propaganda, if any -- hardly a convincing claim in view of its Vietnam propaganda (see chap. 7, section 7.1.1).

Governments have always tried to manipulate media reporting abroad, and many members of governments and high officials build their images of foreign countries, to a large extent, on the basis of mass media reporting. One of the first to use the term <u>national PR</u> explicitly was Israel's ambassador to the United Nations, Chaim Herzog, when he commented in 1978 that from the point of view of national public relations, the Israeli policy of settling the occupied territories won in wars with the Arabs had done more damage than had anything else.

Taking the quantity of publications as an indicator, it is clear that the body of research on international communication has moved increasingly into the center of research interest. This does not, however, apply to image cultivation by states, an area that still has large gaps. Kelman (1965), in what is still a definite work in the area, wrote, "Very little if anything was written before 1950 attempting to link images and attitudes to the interaction between nations -- in other words, to assess how such images and attitudes develop out of the relationships between two nations, and what role they play in the foreign policy process" (p. 5).

The main reason for this gap in research can be seen in the highly sophisticated methods to influence world opinion, in which the secret services play a decisive role, in activities that take place far from the light of day. Because credibility is a decisive variable in the communication process, attempts are forever being made to influence media reporting by covert means to avoid the impression of manipulation. The aim of such activities is chameleonlike: to adapt to the surroundings and remain submerged. The attempt to identify the instigators of national public relations is like trying to nail pudding to a wall. Therefore, the accessibility of literature on this theme is quite poor. One cannot, after all, do a representative survey of the KGB or the USIA, although the USIA has been the subject of a published empirical study (Bogart, 1976). The borders between secret services and news agencies are often fudged, as the example of TASS, the former main Soviet agency, shows (Kruglak, 1962).

Most industrial and many developing countries either have created special organizations to improve their country's image or have commissioned PR organizations to do so. Among the best known of these state-run organizations is the USIA, but the biggest spender on international image making was the Soviet Union. In 1987, the U. S. Department of State reported that the Soviet Union had spent $ 4 billion dollars on foreign propaganda in 1982.

CHAPTER 2

Problems of International Image Cultivation

DOMESTIC PUBLIC OPINION AND WORLD PUBLIC OPINION

Public opinion is perceived as an ill-defined, fluid, unmeasurable phenomenon, as a social process tied to certain objects, temporal circumstances, and persons. Public opinion comes about when many persons take the same view of a given issue and are aware of this sameness of view. This knowledge that others think like one does oneself is created in most cases by public statements, including those of the mass media. The statements made in the mass media generally have two functions. One is to enable the groups and/or political elites participating in the political process to communicate with each other, that is to create a focused public opinion. The other is to establish themes that may become subjects of public discussion by selecting the topics they consider worth reporting and reporting on them in leading articles, commentaries, and so forth.

It makes sense to speak of public opinion only if there is a certain readiness on the part of political decision makers to take views shared by large population groups into account in their decision making. One can take the view that in modern pluralistic societies it is not existing public opinion that influences the behavior of politicians, but the fear of possible changes in public opinion as a result of political decisions. But Abraham Lincoln already had a problem with that. It was his will, he said, that what the people wanted, should happen, but the question was how one could find out just what it was they wanted. Lincoln already knew about the relationships between PR and politics: "Public sentiment is everything. With public sentiment nothing can fail. Without it, nothing can succeed. Consequently, he who molds public sentiment goes deeper than he who enacts statutes or pronounces decisions. He makes statutes and decision possible or impossible to be executed" (Reagan, 1971, p. 141).

There is controversy over whether there is any such thing as world public opinion, but without a doubt the international public is becoming an ever more important factor in international politics. Davison (1973) suggested that there are three prerequisites to an international public opinion becoming an important political factor: "People in several countries must give their attention to a given issue; they must have sufficient means of interacting so that common and mutually reinforcing attitudes can form; and there must be some mechanism through which shared attitudes can be transmitted into action" (p. 874). These prerequisites are met in only exceptional cases. However, there is a certain consensus in the selection of top stories by the world's leading daily newspapers (Davison, 1973). Certain private and international organizations (e.g., Amnesty International, Greenpeace, the United Nations, and UN subsidiary agencies) assume considerable importance. Environmental activists working all over the world (e.g., World Wide Fund for Nature [WWF] and Greenpeace) were responsible for getting political leaders to attend the 1992 Earth Summit in Rio. There are also certain media that rank as international opinion leaders, such as Time and Newsweek. According to S. Peterson (1981) The Times of London is "one of the world's great cosmopolitan newspapers, a leading figure among the 'elite press' as judged by repeated surveys of world leaders and scholars" (p. 143).

The international public does address itself to concrete political authorities and has achieved narrowly defined political aims by pressure through the media and through the formation of committees and the like (e.g., the release of political prisoners or a ban on seal killing). So, regardless of whether there is such a force as world public opinion and how we define it, activities mounted to influence it do remain centrally important as long as politicians take them into account in their decision making.

THE STRUCTURAL NECESSITY OF PUBLIC RELATIONS FOR STATES

Mass media reporting of foreign affairs often governs what kind of image of a country or a culture predominates. Galtung and Ruge (1965) argued that the world comprises individual and collective actors whose actions are determined by their particular images of reality. International actions are based on the image of international reality. Although these are not shaped by the news media alone, their ubiquity and perseverance would certainly make them first-rate competitors for the number-one position as international imageformer. Especially in democracies, which are based on competitive willformation and in which, at least theoretically, the individual can participate in the socially relevant decision-making processes, the mass media can exercise considerable indirect influence on a country's policies by the images they help to create with their foreign reporting. There are no data as yet, however, on how, say, foreign policy might be influenced by images so shaped. In this field, discussion consists almost totally of plausibility arguments.

Foreign reporting operates as follows: The mass media selectively perceive events in the world and, as they propagate them, distortions occur. The media image thus created is then perceived by individuals selectively and, hence, distorted further. Galtung and Ruge (1965) examined the reporting about crisis in the Congo, Cuba, and Cyprus. Overall they found that the cynical journalists' adage, "Bad news is good news," applied to the reporting they examined. Östgaard (1965), who comes from the Scandinavian tradition of peace research, took the view that international behavior (i.e., the actions of states) depended on the images they held about the international situation and/or the relationships between individual states. Östgaard concluded that media reporting strengthens the status quo, that the world is depicted as more conflict-loaded than it really is, that politics is made to appear as the actions of influential persons, and that the categorization of the world into states with high and low status is thereby perpetuated.

News values, the criteria by which journalists select from the flood of information what to publish, are basically nothing but intuitive assumptions about what interests their respective publics. Day-topical media concentrate on short-lived events relevant to a given circle of recipients making locally or ethnocentristically oriented news choices of events, publishable with minimum delay. The widespread neglect of ongoing social processes can be explained by an analogy to perception theory. Such processes occur slowly and almost unnoticeably, functioning as part of the background. They attain attention value only when they turn into unusual events (e.g., hunger to mass dying, tensions between nations to war, social tensions to revolutions or revolts) or when everyday events are summarized in such things as annual reports. The unusual, the deviation from the norm, has particular news value. The inattention by the media to sociostructural contexts or complex motives for actions is often due mainly to reporters simply not having the time to uncover or "dig" for such phenomena. Moreover, the journalist's prejudices and world view influence their reporting, so that certain phenomena are simply taken as cultural characteristics.

International news is selected by criteria similar to those used for national news or local news: Higher ranking (superpower) or geographically and/or culturally close states are most likely to be reported on. Economic, alliance, and ideological relations also generate more intensive coverage of another country. In the Foreign Images Study for the United Nations Educational, Scientific, and Cultural Organization (UNESC0), the selection of international news in 29 countries was examined (Sreberny-Mohammadi, 1980, 1984, 1985). According to this study, selection is done by universally valid criteria, with particular emphasis on the unusual: disasters, unrest, coups, and so forth. Regionalism is particularly pronounced in all media systems. Hence, one cannot speak of a clear predominance of the world centers over the periphery. Thus a study of "foreign news flow in Africa" found a principle of news selection that can be described, at best, as a village pump perspective (Ume-Nwagbo, 1982). But negativism (civil war, natural disasters, debt crisis, human rights violations, electoral frauds, etc.) often remains the only important news factor dominating the coverage of developing countries in the North. Aside from this aspect, the media of the Third World do not themselves measure up to the demands made by their representatives at the international level, for they select news according to the same criteria as the Western media. Accordingly, the media of the Third World are noted for using a high proportion of nonpolitical bad news from the industrialized nations. The crisis-oriented reporting on the Third World by the Western media corresponds to the bad picture of the Western nations in the press of those developing countries.

In addition, the transnational news agencies have greatly regionalized their services and, in their news gathering, depend largely on national agencies. For the correspondents of the large news agencies, the press in the countries they are reporting from is the most important source of information. Boyd-Barrett (1980) suggested that because of this, "the global agencies are partly in the business of relaying national journalistic definitions of news on an international level" (p. 96). The Foreign Images Study did not find "that Western media and news agencies ignore the Third World. It does not show that they single out the Third World for unfair negative coverage. It does not show that they see the Third World through a filter of cultural bias. It does not show that Third World media are hostages to Western news monopoly. It does not show that the socialist media and Third World media systems which claim to represent an alternative model operate much differently than their Western counterparts" (Sreberny-Mohammadi 1984, p. 134). The Foreign Images Study also found a marked reciprocity of indifference between individual media systems. Each region gives greatest attention to its own region. Secondary attention was given by all media systems to Western Europe, followed by the Middle East and North America. The least attention was given to Latin America and Eastern Europe. The African and Latin American media systems, for example, take practically no notice of each other.

Lara (1968), then director of the Institute of Information and Culture of Venezuela in Washington, complained about news selection with regard to the image of Latin America in the United States news media as "groups of natives unfit to govern themselves" (p. 31). A Danish foreign correspondent (Lee, 1968) made similar observations, although he inferred neglect rather than negativism: "Denmark has made page one of the American newspapers only twice in the last quarter-century -- once when Germany invaded her, and once when the little mermaid lost her head" (p. XIV). A communist bloc press attache complained (Lee, 1968), "You can talk about the iron curtain or the silk curtain or the bamboo curtain all you want. It can be just as difficult breaking through the democratic curtain" (p. XIII). There is no shortage of attacks on the way the media select news and thereby influence the images of nations. Cooper (1942), in criticizing the reporting about the United States by the Reuters news agency, said the world at large was being told about Indians on the warpath in the Wild West, about lynching justice in the South, and about bizarre crimes in the North. For decades, accusations have been made that nothing positive is reported about the United States.

Regarding the structure of the international flow of information in recent years, the major changes have taken place in the sphere of international exchange of news. Until now, the news offerings of the alternative Third World agencies, in comparison with the "big four" Western agencies (Associated Press [AP], Agence France-Presse, Reuters, and United Press International [UPI]) have continued to find relatively few takers. Stevenson (1985) concluded that the pool of the nonaligned countries' news teams distributes primarily official or "protocol" news. A crucial question here concerns the credibility of the agencies: The rule of thumb is the less the state can exert influence, the greater the credibility of the news.

A particularly effective alternative is Inter-Press Service (IPS). Keune (1985) wrote, "IPS has become the sixth-largest news-and-information enterprise on the world market (measured by the extent of its transmission network and the number of correspondents, not by turnover). This success certainly finds its rationale in the fact that the dedicated IPS journalists also own the agency" (p. 24). IPS deals with in-depth accounts of news. Recently, the Spanish news agency EFE has had remarkable success in Latin America. When UPI was bought by Saudi Arabia in June 1992 (for $ 3.95 million), Asharq al-Aswat, a newspaper published in London, but under control of Saudi-Arabia, commented that the Arab world now had the opportunity to present its point of view to the world.

The quality of the future communication structure is expected to benefit from the development of the television news exchange in the Third World, which, until now, has been dominated by Anglo-American companies, like Reuters TV, Worldwide Television News (WTN), and CBS News. In general, the poorer a television station, the more likely it is to depend on agency news, thereby presenting a picture of the world from the point of view of foreigners. In French-speaking West Africa, for example, television stations receive daily news transmissions from Paris via satellite for retransmission. Only about 10% of this telecast is news film footage from Africa itself (Keune, 1981); ironically the French complain about American cultural imperialism: In 1982, the French Minister of Culture, Jacques Lang, voiced fears with regard to American cultural imperialism, which "no longer grabs territory, or rarely, but grabs consciousness, ways of thinking, ways of living" (Cantor & Cantor, 1985, p. 511), yet France has always had a forceful policy of spreading the French language and culture.

Given the structural conditions of the international flow of news, countries with economic or political interests in having a positive image in a certain region, including those that are at a disadvantage from the outset because of the standard processes of gathering and selecting information, must mount active publicity campaigns. Although by definition, PR for states is always interest-bound communication, it can, however, offset communication deficits due to structures. This form of PR for states, meant primarily to compensate for structural communication deficits, aims mainly to adapt the image to news values by trying to influence mass media reporting. Structural international PR aims at correcting the "false" images previously created by the mass media. Manipulative PR, on the other hand, tries to create a positive image that, in most cases, does not reflect reality, including lying and disinformation. The AIDS campaign of the KGB (cf. chap. 7, section 7.2.2) and the disinformation campaign of the Reagan administration against Muammar Qaddafi (cf. chap. 7, section 7.1.2) are good examples of this.

I believe it is useful to adapt some hypotheses that have been developed in news research to guide research on PR for states. For example, the hypothesis could be put forward that, the more a country depends on exportation, the more likely and the more intensely it will mount campaigns of image cultivation. Further, a state may be more likely to mount a PR campaign in another region if the reporting there is biased due to the structures of news selection. Another hypothesis could be: The more important (economically and/or politically) an entity (whether country or union, e.g. the European Community [EC]), the more likely it is that foreign countries will undertake campaigns there (e.g., most campaigns are waged in the US and Western industrialized countries).

One way to get oneself presented in the media of another country is to buy news space and time in the mass media (through radio commercials or print advertising). Such a procedure is appropriate when a broad foreign public (e.g., the tourist industry) or certain target groups (such as opinion leaders or decision makers in politics and economics) are to be influenced. According to Lobsenz (1984), the major goal of countries whose interests are being represented by PR firms in the United States is the improvement of tourism, trade, investment, industrial development, and, above all, image cultivation. Until now, PR and/or advertising campaigns for tourism have represent the focal point of activities in the area of international PR (Kunczik & Weber, 1994).

Amaize and Faber (1983) analyzed the amount of advertising by national governments in leading United States, Indian, and British newspapers and found significantly more ads placed by developing nations than by developed ones. The authors concluded, "Developing nations can use advertising to promote their products and services to large markets in industrialized countries in order to improve their balance of payment. Additionally, advertising by governments can provide a means for developing nations to inform citizens of other countries about their beliefs and values" (p. 99). Kunczik and Weber (1994), on the other hand, did not find such a relationship in the leading German newspapers, revealing that sometimes developing countries, which can benefit most through the use of PR techniques to correct negative images of their societies, avail themselves of these techniques less often than do developed countries, for whom this is not as crucial. One possible explanation is that they are limited financially. The poorest countries of the Third World thus see themselves confronted with a twofold structural barrier: They are underrepresented because of prevailing routines in the selection of news in the western media (where the factor dominating news selection is negativism), and, lacking financial resources, they are unable to correct these deficits using PR.

ACTORS IN THE FIELD OF INTERNATIONAL PUBLIC RELATIONS

It is almost impossible to differentiate clearly between international PR of nation-states, of international social/economic organizations (e.g., UNESCO, the World Bank), of international political organizations (e.g., Greenpeace, Amnesty International, World Wildlife Fund [WWF]), and of multinational corporations (MNCs). Furthermore, the same PR agency can work for states and MNCs. The following discussion proceeds from the premise that the economy cannot be regarded as a subsystem equal in importance to others. Rather, economics is assumed to be a basic social factor that also decisively influences other subsystems; in particular I argue that economy and policy cannot be separated. Consequently, PR of MNCs will be at least partly taken into account. All too often, people overlook the fact that MNCs are quite active in foreign policy and interact with states: I need refer here only to the oil crisis (of the 1970s) or the worldwide bribing by Lockheed. E. L. Bernays (1965), working as PR counselor to United Fruit, wrote, "I was struck by the thought that although I was advising a banana company, I was actually fighting in the Cold War." (p. 766; cf. chap. 7, section 7.1.3).

Nations' worry over their image gives power to such organizations as Amnesty International. Founded in 1961 by the British jurist, Peter Benenson, its aim is obtaining the release of political and religious "prisoners of conscience" through international protest. Benenson was moved to act in 1961 when two Portuguese students were sentenced to 7 years' imprisonment each for uttering a toast to freedom. Benenson announced his campaign on May 28, 1961 in a full-page article in The Observer. Amnesty's aim is to stir up moral outrage. Lia Dover of the organization put it like this to Time (October 17, 1988, p. 23) "The fact that a crime is known and publicized has an effect on decision makers. They care about their image. Torturers go to great lengths to ensure that they are not identified, so putting them in the spotlight helps ensure it doesn't happen again". In January 1989, Amnesty International focused on violations of human rights in Turkey. This may be one of the reasons why, in June 1989, the Turkish government hired Saatchi & Saatchi, an advertising agency known throughout the world, to improve its country's image.

A simple classification of those who use international PR can be developed using two dimensions: for-profit versus nonprofit and public versus private.

	public	private
for-profit	state-owned airlines	MNCs
nonprofit	governments, ministries, UNESCO	foundations

This is only a rough classification however. Other actors are also in the field such as international influence brokers as individuals (e.g., Henry Kissinger) and international PR agencies (e.g., Hamilton Wright, Hill & Knowlton, and Saatchi & Saatchi), which often give advice to influence, or at least try to influence, world politics. Isaacson (1992) argued that Kissinger's comments on the crackdown of the democratic movement in China in June 1989 were based on commercial interests, because Kissinger had clients with strong business involvements in China (among them, Atlantic Richfield, ITT, and an investment partnership called China Ventures). After the Tiananmen Square crackdown, Kissinger recommended in a television interview on ABC, that the United States should maintain good relations instead of imposing economic sanctions, as an indication of political maturity. Isaacson maintained, that "if the American reaction to the Tiananmen had been mild, as Kissinger urged, China Ventures would have proceeded, and Kissinger would have made a significant amount of money" (p. 749). According to Isaacson Kissinger's trip to China in November 1989 was staged to show the world that the time for ostracism was over. Kissinger met Deng Xiaoping and later reported on his meeting and the atmosphere within China to President Bush and top American leaders.

There are also voluntaristic campaigners who fight for certain goals or against certain institutions without having well-established organizational structures. Tocqueville emphasized in 1835 in his famous <u>Democracy in America</u> (1835/1945), "Americans of all ages, all conditions, and all dispositions constantly form associations . . . If it be proposed to advance some truth, or to foster some feeling by the encouragement of a great example, they form a society" (p. 114). Tocqueville believed the Americans to be˙ perfect campaigners, noting: "the extreme skill which the inhabitants of the United States succeed in proposing a common object to the exertion of a great many men, and in getting them voluntary to pursue it" (p. 114).

Olasky (1985) gave two examples of this kind of nonprofessional, spontaneous PR in 19th century United States: the visit of Lafayette and the campaign for Pope Pius IX. Lafayette, a hero of the American Revolution, visited the United States in 1824 to 1825. According to Olasky Americans in those days tried to emphasize the revolutionary roots of their history and to demonstrate to European monarchs that they had developed their own cultural identity. Americans invited Lafayette to demonstrate that a republic can show respect for a man who had made history. If Olasky is correct, we have a case of image polishing for a nation-state by means of spontaneous, voluntaristic PR. Lafayette was invited without there being a central coordinating institution. Each community invited and hosted Lafayette separately. Judge Toomer from Fayetteville, Virginia, pointed out: "We are plain republicans and cannot greet you with the pomp common on such occasions. Instead of pageantry we offer you cordiality [and in this way show that] ingratitude is no longer the reproach of republics" (Olasky, 1985, p. 5). As Olasky put it, "In short, throughout the year of Lafayette's 'pilgrimage of liberty' throughout the United States, arrangements were made, speeches were written, the press was used artfully, brochures were produced, funds were collected and distributed, public opinion was sounded, and 'a good time was had by all', without professional public relations counsel" (p. 5).

Olasky's (1985) second example is the New York citizens' campaign for Pope Pius IX. In 1846 he succeeded Pope Gregor XVI, who had a somewhat negative reputation in the United States. The American public knew that Gregor had filled the Vatican dungeon with political prisoners. Pius immediately abolished all secret tribunals and announced an amnesty for political prisoners. As a consequence a group of New York citizens met in 1847 and discussed how the new politics of the Pope could be publicly supported. A committee, established to organized meetings and so on, wrote letter to the Pope: "We address you not as a Sovereign Pontiff, but as a wise human ruler of a once oppressed and discontented, now well-governed and gratefully happy people. We unite in this tribute, not as Catholics, which some of us are while the great number are not, but as lovers of Constitutional Freedom" (Olasky, 1985). Copies of the letter were distributed throughout the United States.

A more recent example of voluntaristic international PR occurred when, in September 1994, the World Bank and the International Monetary Fund (IMF) celebrated their 50th anniversary. In the German weekly Die Zeit (September 23, 1994) an advertisement by a public interest group *Entwicklung braucht Entschuldung* (development needs freedom from encumbrance) was published. It declared that there was nothing to celebrate, that the managers of the World Bank and IMF failed to control the debt explosion in the South, resulting in economic conditions in Africa worse than 15 years earlier. For instance, many of the projects supported by IMF and the World Bank resulted in ecological and social disasters (especially building of dams). The committee urged the German government to attempt to change the policy of the World Bank/IMF, that is, to control the projects of the World Bank/IMF, contending that the focus of the World Bank's activities should be the fight against poverty. They also demanded that all debts be paid.

The close interconnections between states and MNCs are demonstrated by the Mobil Corporation. In October 1981 an advertisement was published in The New York Times: "Saudi Arabia: Far More Than Oil" (Grunig & Hunt, 1984, p. 521). In 1986 Mobil waged a campaign in the United States for the sale of missiles to Saudi Arabia, which, Mobil argued, would serve America's interests: "This week, the Senate will attempt to override President Reagan's veto [President Reagan had vetoed the resolution of the Congress to block the sale of missiles to Saudi Arabia], and kill the sale. When the crucial roll call is taken, members should remember a simple fact: They aren't voting on just an arms bill for Saudi Arabia. They are voting on an arms bill for American interests. Against such a yardstick, we trust the presidential veto will be sustained" (Onkvisit & Shaw, 1989, p. 148). Mobil also referred to the Red Menace (cf. chap. 4, section 4.3.1) emphasizing the Soviet interest in the turmoil in the Middle East.

The Ford Company also fought against communism. In 1951 Henry Ford took part in the Crusade for Freedom. According to Cutlip (1994) Henry Ford II identified himself with that crusade "making an imaginative, constructive and dramatic effort to fight Communism. Uses of Ford-Lincoln-Mercury dealerships throughout the United States as focal points for Crusade collections magnified this identity" (p. 698). In 1953, near the 50th anniversary of Ford, the film *The American Road* was produced to show that Henry Ford was an American success story. Furthermore, a 50th anniversary book was published with a foreword from Henry Ford II written by the PR agency of Earl Newsom, saying, among other things, that "the growth and achievements of Ford Motor Company have been made possible by the kind of world we live in, by American democracy, and the economic opportunity to seek change and progress freely" (Cutlip, 1994, p. 698).

The German Demag, which built the steel works in Rourkela, India, waged a 3-year campaign in which the politics of industrialization of the Indian government were praised and the efficiency of German industry was emphasized. During this time, the Soviet Union built another steel works. The Soviets then waged a campaign against Germany and its industry, alleging that Germans were capitalists and exploiters trying to colonize India, and that German products were of poor quality. This fight for Indian public opinion was called "West German-Russian steel battle" (Darrow et al., 1967, p. 523). Demag countered with its own campaign: Pamphlets were distributed to journalists, to members of the congress, to teachers and professors at universities; 20,000 diagrams explaining the production of steel and its further processing were donated to schools and universities; Radio Ceylon aired programs sponsored by Demag; advertisements were published in Indian newspapers; journalists of the most important Indian dailies were visited by the press secretary of Demag.

In recent years, Russia started its own PR activities in cooperation with capitalist companies. On April 20, 1992, an advertisement was published in Time for a conference to convene on April 25 and 26 in the Hotel Intercontinental in Geneva:

MEET THE NEW GOVERNMENT OF RUSSIA

The New Business Environment -- Industries for sale -- Foreign trade -- Countertrade -- Privatisation

Sponsors of the conference were Time and Volvo. Swissair was the official carrier, and the organizer of the conference was listed as the "Academy of National Economy in Russia, Management Network, and the Multimarketing group in cooperation with Time magazine". Speakers were, among others: Petr O. Aven, Minister of Foreign Economic Relations; Yegor E. Gaydar, First Prime Minister; Sergey M. Shakry, Vice Prime Minister of the government of Russia; the mayor of St. Petersburg, and the director of the Trade Department of the Economic Commisssion Europe.

The close interconnections between state and business were also evident in the Bank of Credit & Commerce International (BCCI) scandal. The most important shareholders in BCCI were the government of Abu Dhabi, the Abu Dhabi Investment Authority, and the Department of Private Affairs of H. H. Shaikh Zayed bin Sultan al-Nahyan. On March 9, 1992, they advertised in Time that they found out about the difficulties of the bank only after they had already bought their shares. Their aim was "to ensure that the bank should be run properly and that it should operate successfully"; the amount of losses suffered by BCCI "were revealed by the investigations instigated by us", and when liquidation of BCCI was unavoidable, a plan was immediately made "to improve and speed up the overall return to creditors worldwide".

Even rates of exchange can become the target of PR campaigns waged by MNCs. This was the case with Eastman Kodak (Dilenschneider & Forrestal, 1989). The company knew that its competitive position in the world marketplace was hurt by the then strength of the United States dollar. Kodak's communication division suggested they run a PR program targeted at this issue. Fact-finding meetings with President Reagan, high-level administration officials, and key national economic and trade groups were arranged. According to Dilenschneider and Forrestal the company funded a $150,000 study by the American Enterprise Institute, a conservative think tank (18 members of the Institute joined the Reagan Administration in 1981), to research the relationships between the strength of the dollar and the federal budget deficits. The Institute found a relationship between high interest rates required to finance the huge deficits and the dollar's strength. Dilenschneider and Forrestal wrote:

> Kodak believed a public affairs program could play a major role in persuading the government to pass legislation to eliminate federal budget deficit and intervene in currency exchange markets to stabilize the overvalued dollar. Kodak developed a 12-month communications program to reach members of Congress, the administration, and others in a position to influence economic policy. The message was that the overvalued

dollar and escalating budget deficits were so damaging to
manufacturers that a decisive action was needed. (p. 679).

The program, which received a Silver Anvil Award in the 1986
competition of the Public Relations Society of America, included a
mailing to Kodak's shareholders, a "Write to Congress" campaign,
consultations with leading politicians including Treasury Secretary
Baker, and visits by Kodak executives to members of Congress and
Cabinet members. According to Dilenschneider and Forrester the
campaign played a direct role in changing the government's position
and furthermore set the stage for two historic events: the September
1985 Group of Five communiqué pledging dollar stabilization, and
the Gramm-Rudman-Hollings Act, aimed at eliminating federal
budget deficits by 1991.

Organized labor, too, can become active in the field of
international PR. For example, the United Steelworkers of America
AFL-CIO ran an advertisement in which they stated, "America's
economy is like a row of dominoes. If the steel domino falls, other
will also fall" (Onkvisit & Shaw, 1989, p. 26). According to the ad,
despite a remarkable rise in productivity, the steel industry was
being drowned in a flood of cheap, subsidized foreign imports. The
advertisement closed with the following words: "Solutions require
the joint efforts of labor, industry, government and financial
institutions. It's now or never".

Some MNCs try to keep a low profile in order not to become a
target of political activists. Kerry King, former PR senior vice-
president of Texaco, said to the German Wirtschaftswoche in 1984
that Texaco's PR strategy was keeping a low profile. When a
journalist asked for an interview, Texaco declined. Texaco is not
unique. A study by Blake and Toros (1976) found that most of 38
American MNCs surveyed did not carry out a systematically
planned international communications policy: "In addition to the
failure to adopt a managerial approach to external affairs, many
MNCs seek a low profile in the face of challenges from political,
social and government sectors" (p. 11). On the other hand, a study

by Strenski (1975), based on interviews of the PR directors of the 55 largest American companies, discovered an urgent need to protect corporate interests abroad from rising nationalism, monetary fluctuations, political upheavals, and destructive tariff and/or trade restrictions.

A remarkable example of the close connections between privatly held companies and international policy are the attempts of the French Panama Canal Co. to mold public opinion in the United States (Spellman, 1994). Count Ferdinand de Lesseps, the builder of the Suez Canal, wanted to build a canal across the isthmus of Panama. His *Compagnie Universelle du Canal Interoceanique de Panama* in 1879 had obtained permission from Colombia to dig the canal. But, according to the French ambassador in Washington, the American press and other opponents considered the activities of the French firm to be a violation of the Monroe Doctrine (1823), which declared that America belonged to the Americans and that no foreign power should be allowed to intervene in the Western Hemisphere. Lesseps waged a PR campaign in response: He edited the *Bulletin du Canal Interoceanique,* a widely distributed source of news favorable to his endeavor; made trips to the United States to argue that the digging of the canal by a French company was not a disadvantage to the United States; he testified before Congress, emphasizing the private nature of the company; and he toured America, addressing people in New York, Boston, Philadelphia, and other cities. But Lesseps could not convince President Hayes to go forward. The most important PR activity was the creation of the American Committee. During the 1880s this organization influenced public opinion in the United States and carried out political lobbying. According to Spellman (1994) the Panama Canal Co. spent $2.4 million on the American Committee. Three American banking houses served the Committee and its first chairman was the former Secretary of the Navy, Richard W. Thompson. The American Committee, which provided information about the Panama project, wrote articles for magazines, and provided trips to Panama for journalists and decision makers, "did no more than engage in conventional public relations efforts with newspapers and magazines. It helped friendly journalists research their stories and issued statements to counteract unfavorable stories. It requested and sometimes persuaded editors to publish favourable stories" (Spellman, 1994, p. 186).

Many countries make considerable efforts to cultivate their images abroad, especially in the United States and Europe. It was Chaim Herzog of Israel who said in 1975: "The main battlefield now is the theater of opinion in the United States" (Newsweek, April 4, 1975). According to Manheim and Albritton (1984), the major service offered by American PR firms is to improve the respective governments' access to American journalists. In addition, they write press releases, do direct mailings, and send out newsletters and brochures; they train embassy personnel how to speak about sensitive issues such as terrorism or human rights; they organize field trips for the press, visits with editors, and lunches with business groups. As a rule, according to Manheim and Albritton, no precise linkage between commissioned PR activities and what appears in the mass media can be traced. Typically one can do little more than guess at what suggestions were made, which were accepted, and how they were implemented. The precise nature of the intervention remains something of a mystery.

Nevertheless, some of the emphases of the PR activities can be illustrated (see, e.g., Cutlip, 1994; Kunczik 1990; Manheim 1994; Manheim & Albritton 1984), such as visits by heads of state, invitations to presidents or vice-presidents of the United States to make state visits, the release of political prisoners, trips for journalists organized by the respective governments or by transnational corporations like United Fruit, establishment of information offices, cosmetic redistribution of power within a country, scheduling of elections, sporting events, and so on. Generally, it is extremely difficult to quantify the influence the activities of PR agencies have or may have on the images of nations. Furthermore, it is difficult to distinguish between PR activities done by the states themselves and activities initiated by PR firms. The discussion here focuses on PR activities directed at the mass media.

IMAGE AND THE INTERNATIONAL SYSTEM

In their definite book <u>National Character and National Stereotypes</u>, Duijker and Frijda (1960) discussed the problems connected with the idea of national character. The authors offered different concepts of national character, which all based on the assumption that there is actually such a thing as a national character, an assumption that is not necessarily valid. Is there such a thing as "the" American, "the" Indonesian, "the" Indian, or "the" Frenchman? In fact, the phenomenon of national character may exist only in societies that are relatively small and easily overviewed, that is, societies in which over a long time one or several characteristic(s) valid for all members of that society has (have) crystallized. So it is quite possible that many scientists have made great efforts to research a phenomenon that at the end of the day does not exist. As Deutsch (1969) wrote, quoting a European saying, "A nation is a group of persons united by a common error about their ancestry and a common dislike of their neighbors" (p. 3). Prejudices and/or images often are spread in the guise of scholarship. Thus it has been alleged that certain peoples are incapable of a stable political order because of their national character. For instance, the all-encompassing disqualification of entire races or peoples as inferior to the European-North American culture has a long tradition.

But, whether or not there are national characters, the issue here is images of nations, and these images do exist. The question is might there be a "kernel of truth" in a nation's notions about other nations. We know that conflicting characteristics are ascribed to other nations, making it easy to confirm the validity of one or another prejudice. That most prejudices about other nations are gross exaggerations or completely irrelevant, does not necessarily refute the theory of the kernel of truth in prejudices. Secord and Backman (1974) pointed out that such a kernel probably existed if two nations possessed the same characteristics but each described themself in flattering terms and the other in derogatory terms. For example, the British perceive themselves as reserved and respecting the private sphere of others, but regard Americans as obtrusive, brash, and pretentious. Conversely, Americans describe the English as cold, snobbish, and unfriendly, while seeing themselves as friendly, open-hearted, and gregarious. Nations seem to "understand" each other better (a) the more similar their autostereotypes (commonality of normative expectations), (b) the closer their image of the other is to their image of themselves, and (c) the greater the similarity between the images two nations have of a third nation (Hofstätter, 1957).

It was Lippmann (1922) who coined the concept of stereotype, a term borrowed from the language of printing. Lippmann saw stereotypes as routine judgments, simple and frequently inadequately founded. Most stereotypes are imprecise, yet are defended by many people with great conviction. All of us, to one degree or another, structure our perception by categories, because no one can ever perceive or consider everything to the last detail. Stereotypes, that is, statements in simplified categories (categorical statements), are not negative per se. In fact, the stereotype about stereotypes is that all stereotypes are bad, and this stereotype, like all other stereotypes, is too great a simplification. No one lives without such prejudices or presuppositions; they close information gaps and supply orientation aids. Basically, we all overestimate our own level of knowledge; indeed, many of our attitudes and behaviors are based on prejudices.

No one is able always to perceive other people in their entire, always unique individualities. We all typecast, be it by occupation, age, gender, color of hair, race, or nationality. This belonging to a category (e.g., Indian) can suffice to impute to that person all the attributes ascribed to that category. Most stereotypes about other nations include both negative and positive attributes. If one "knows" that the Germans are coarse and tactless or military-minded or scientifically educated, then one knows how to deal with them. Significant here is that such black-and-white depiction, like conflicts, where one is either right or wrong, has an integrative function: Negative images of other groups strengthen the cohesion in one's own group.

In literature there is no clear definitive delimitation between such concepts as attitude, stereotype, prejudices, or image. Often the terms overlap or are used differently from author to author. The term image became popular in the 1950s, especially in the United States, and was used to describe the aura of a person in public life, a party, a product, a nation, a people, and so forth. The image is something created and cultivated by its possessor, that is, something that can be actively influenced by PR activities. By contrast, prejudices and/or stereotypes are created by the environment and are ascribed. In this sense, in the following discussion image always contains an active component. But images of nations, at least partly, can be understood as hardened prejudices; these are not suddenly there but often have grown in long historical processes. Such social prejudices can be defined as expressed convictions of a particular group (or its members) about an alien group (or individuals because of actual or assumed membership of the alien group) without consideration of their correctness.

A theoretical frame of reference to explain the function of prejudices is the differentiation between ingroups -- that is, groups of which a person is a member or would like to be a member (reference groups) -- and outgroups, those to which a person does not nor wants to belong. This quite simple division makes clear that the social differentiation of groups affects the relationship of groups to each other because people's thinking and actions are also governed group specifically. Because we strive for personal security, for certainty, as a general rule we put our own group in the center and make it the yardstick for measuring other groups. The positive prejudice toward our own group is often linked with negative prejudice toward the others, the strangers. Perception is polarized, as it were. The others form the counterpole. Negative perception of the other group and positive perception of our own reduces insecurity and removes possible fears. (There are, however, positive prejudices between nations, such as the special relationship between Great Britain and the United States.) Common language, religion, and race can quite readily contribute to evaluating other peoples positively.

Sumner, who coined the term ethnocentrism in his book Folkways (1906), pointed out that people tend to use their own values, customs, and norms as the yardstick for evaluating other cultures. Because most people are ethnocentrically oriented, they generally regard themselves as superior to other peoples. In Sumner's definition ethnocentrism is the technical term for seeing things in a way in which one's own group is the center of everything and all others are judged by its standards. Each group feeds its pride and its vanity, Sumner argued, boasts of being superior, glorifies its own gods, and looks with contempt on outsiders. Each group considers its own folkways as the only right ones. For instance, in 1910 the French advocate of colonialism, Jules Harmand, advocated the "fact" that there is a hierarchy of races and civilization: "The basic legitimation of conquest over native people is the conviction of our superiority, not merely our mechanical, economic, and military superiority, but our moral superiority. Our dignity rests on that quality, and it underlies our right to direct the rest of humanity" (Said, 1993/1994, p. 17).

In its most extreme form, ethnocentrism is racism. A. Montagu (1942/1974) characterized racism as "man's most dangerous myth". The first attempt at a "scientific" theory of racial inequality was Arthur de Gobineau's "Essai sur l'Inegalité des Races Humaines" of 1853, which laid the foundations of racist thinking. The Briton H. S. Chamberlain (1900/1925), son-in-law of composer Richard Wagner and admirer of Adolf Hitler, argued that racism was the great hope of mankind. He interpreted world history as the struggle between good (the Germanic race) and evil (the Jewish race). If the evil could be destroyed, there would be paradise on earth. By contrast, I emphasize that the premise of this discussion is that there is no connection between membership of a race and the level of culture or intelligence of individual people. In other words, people of different races are equal with regard to their cultural abilities. To quote anthropologist Mead (1958), "Extensive effort to demonstrate the genetic superiority of one racial group of men over another has so far failed, so that the present working assumption is that, as far as their capacity to learn, maintain, transmit and transform culture is concerned, different groups of Homo sapiens must be regarded as equally competent" (p. 481).

LeVine (1965) argued that most human populations are hostile to some outgroups and carry negative images of them. This tendency to devalue others, especially where there is little knowledge about them, can extend so far as to deny their very humanness. Again, very often the evaluation of foreign peoples is made through contrasts: we human beings, those barbarians; we the faithful, those infidels; we of the Christian West, those natives; we Whites, those Blacks, and so forth. Even history is interpreted to fit such contrasts. Greek civilization, for instance, had its roots in African and Semitic cultures, yet it was stylized by European philologists into pure European culture, the other cultures being more or less barbaric. Such polarizing labels are also used for political systems: democracy and dictatorship; communism and capitalism; individualism and collectivism, and so on. For example, a brochure published (in German) in 1994 by the Croatian Tourism Office says that even today Croatia is trying to defend the splendid achievements of Western civilization against the barbarian aggression from the Orient.

Very often there are differences between autostereotypes (prejudices about one's own group) and heterostereotypes (prejudices other groups have about one's own group). A good example can be found in the preface to Made in France -- Why the Whole World Envies Us, a compendium of foreigners' complaints about the French: "Our much-loved country sometimes has a tendency to overestimate its fame. Foreigners describe us as frightful, dirty and nasty, greedy gobblers rather than gourmets, drooling sex fiends rather than good lovers, inveterate complainers who neglect their toothbrushes" (<u>Newsweek</u>, July 26, 1993, p. 9). Markedly negative autostereotypes indicate grave cultural identity crises. For instance, the Germans, according to a 1994 study of the Universities of Enschede and Münster, seem to dislike themselves: They regarded themselves as conservative, domineering, arrogant, and dogmatic; furthermore they considered themselves to be not very friendly, not very tolerant, and not sympathetic.

Fundamentally, stereotypes and images of nations are relatively inflexible and often, apart from the kernel of truth, have nothing to do with the people judged. Such images exist without the "users" of them running the risk of confrontation with reality, thereby having to change their views. Further, the laws of logic do not apply to the world of images. The criterion of "correctness" or "truth" of images is not their correspondence with objective reality, but the successful coping with the environment in which those images exist. If everyone regards a "false" image of another nation as "true", there is then no compelling reason to subject oneself to the pressure of public opinion and express a view deviating from that of the majority.

As stated earlier, images of nations and stereotypes often appear in the form of contrasts. For example, the Germans are said to be cozy, scientific, and on the one hand, but hard, authoritarian militarists on the other hand. Such contrarily paired stereotypes fundamentally allow each new "fact" to be interpreted as understandable and natural, as well as confirm one's prejudices. Ithiel de Sola Pool (1973) wrote: "People are seldom sufficiently self-critical to force themselves to think about the disconfirmed part of the stereotype and worry about reconciling it" (p. 785). In other words, the prerequisites of a change of attitude, namely awareness of an inconsistency, are not given. Duijker and Frijda (1960) observed that some of these contradictions are due more or less to the situations in which stereotypes are measured:

> If a person objects to the Jews on the ground that they are too
> clannish, too exclusive, and a few moments later states that they
> always are seeking admission to Christian groups, there is
> clearly a contradiction between these two statements. In each
> case his attention is directed to different phenomena. In the
> former statement he focusses on the strong intragroup solidarity
> of the Jews, in the latter on their attempts at integration in a
> society which is predominantly non-Jewish. So for him there is
> no contradiction. It exists only for us, who interpret his sayings
> as manifestations of a general ill-feeling towards Jewish people
> (p. 117).

In surveys, most people tend to express views without being at all able to substantiate them. Almond and Verba (1963) in their international study, characterized the Germans, Mexicans, Americans, and Britons they polled as follows: "The willingness to express opinions is widespread, affecting even the uninformed . . . even the cognitively incompetent feel free to express opinions" (p. 98). In other words, the image of a certain nation exists in many people purely as affect with no knowledge basis whatsoever. Possibly also some images belong in the realm of cultural truisms, that is, beliefs that are so widely shared within a person's social milieu that he or she would not have them attacked and indeed would doubt that an attack were possible. Just as people used to be sure that the sun revolves around the earth and that the earth is flat, one "knows" that the "natives" are lazy, the Italians a nation of papagalli, the Jews rapacious, the Blacks musical, and so on.

Of course, it is possible that when the question of images is posed often something is measured that does not even exist. Many respondents answer only to hide their own nonknowledge or to do the interviewers a favor. When asked about a foreign nation, for instance, what might be measured as an attitude is instead merely a momentary reaction. Foreign nations, especially if one has never had contact with them, represent an extremely unclear, ambiguous stimulus. And, though there is some public interest in international affairs, the vast majority are basically disinterested majority. Robinson (1967) concluded that a third of Americans are actually cut off from information about world happenings and that there is only a small "hard core of know-it-alls". There are "dark areas of ignorance" (Kriesberg, 1949). Considine (1994) observed that, in the case of the Vietnam War, the knowledge base of most young Americans has not come from social studies or history classes but from the television world of "China Beach" and from motion pictures like Platoon, Full Metal Jacket, and the Rambo saga.

Milbrath (1965) wrote: "About one third of the American adult population can be characterized as politically apathetic or passive; in most cases, they are unaware, literally, of the political part of the world around them. Another 60 percent play largely spectator roles in the political process; they watch, they cheer, they vote, but they do not battle. In the purest sense of the word, probably only 1 to 2 percent could be called gladiators" (p. 21). Considine (1994) pointed out that in the United States coverage of overseas news has actually diminished. In 1971, for example, 10% of editorial space in the nation's 10 leading newspapers was dedicated to foreign news. By 1986, it had dropped to 2.6%. Considine cited Dan Rather's argument that, "at the very time that it has become indisputably clear that America's future depends upon our having a better understanding of that great big world beyond our shores . . . we have by and large accepted the proposition that people don't care about foreign news" (p. 10). Maybe the view of the world of most Americans is akin to the dominant view of the world in Lupupa, Zaire, in the 1950s as reported by Merriam (1961):

> The earth is conceptualized as a round, flat platter; if one approaches the edge . . . and is not careful, he will tumble off and into a limitless sea beyond which is only the unknown. In the exact center of this platter is Lupupa and, by extension, the Congo, while somewhere around the rim are placed America, Belgium, and Portugal . . . The most sophisticated person in the village knew that this picture of the world was untrue, and told us so. He had learned the truth in school, he said, and the world, far from being a flat platter, was in reality a flat triangle, with Lupupa in the center, and Belgium, Portugal, and America at the various angles of the figure (p. 176).

Prejudices as a rule do not form before the age of 4 or 5 and, when they begin to, contacts with people who have prejudices, such as parents, kindergarten staff, teachers, and so forth are of decisive importance. During this period the child develops an awareness of his or her own ethnic identity. Sears and Whitney (1973) concluded that group-related predispositions seem to be acquired rather early in life, with heavy affective loading and little informational content. These predispositions seem to be relatively stable. They wrote: "There is now convincing evidence of the early acquisition of racial attitudes, nationalism, and political partisanship . . . they seem to be simple affects and commitments, with little informational content" (p. 263). It follows them, that the changing of images is a long-term process. If prejudices about other groups become firmer as one develops and thereby ever less changeable through additional information, then the influence of, say, television on such attitudes is greatest among younger children. For instance, in a study of English children (Himmelweit, Oppenheimer & Vince, 1958) those who watched TV described the French as gay and witty, reflecting the fact that nearly all the French people they saw on television were cabaret artistes. Younger viewers saw the Germans as arrogant and vicious -- again a reflection of television drama, where Germans were presented mainly in the role of Nazis. Again, if no other sources of information are available, the greatest influence on the image of foreign nations is the mass media.

Different social groupings may have very different images of a certain nation. The image of the Germans as "metaphysical builders of systems" probably dominated more in Anglo-Saxon academic circles, whereas the image of Germans as "Huns" was more prevalent among journalists who produced propaganda in World War I. Lippmann (1922) observed: "A pattern of stereotypes is not neutral . . . It is not merely a short cut . . . It is a guarantee of our self respect, it is a projection upon the world of our own value, our own position, and our own rights . . . They are the fortress of our own tradition and behind its defenses we can continue to feel ourselves safe in the position we occupy" (p. 96). In this sense, the categorization of another nation as, say, domineering may indicate dissatisfaction with the political role one's own nation plays. Thus, when Buchanan and Cantril (1953) found that the French were the only nation that classified the United States as domineering, this could quite legitimately be interpreted as an indication that those questioned were dissatisfied with the role France played in the world system.

Similarly to Boulding (1956), it is assumed here that the conception of an image means not only the conception of the image at present, but also aspects of its past and future expectations. National image, then, can be defined as the cognitive representation that a person holds of a given country, what a person believes to be true about a nation and its people. Of special importance to political action is the benevolence or malevolence imputed to other nations in the images, as well as the historical component of the image. This last takes on special meaning in the context of political figures who assert that they are supported by history, whether one incants the course of history (Yasser Arafat, e.g., said the following in 1988: "The current of history is not on their [the Israelis'] side. We are with the current of history," Time, November 7, 1988), one talks of destiny (e.g., Adolf Hitler), or one claims, that like the communists the scientifically recognizable law of history was moving toward a victory for socialism or communism and the demise of capitalism.

Feelings about a country's future are important, too. Giovanni Agnelli (1994), chairman of the Fiat Group, assessed Italy's future in an article titled, "Quo Vadis, Italy?". His premise was that no other Western nation has ever had to address a simultaneous political upheaval and economic crisis as overwhelming as the Italian crisis. An explosion of corruption scandals created the impression that Italy's entire economy depended solely on political favor. Agnelli concluded: "What the economy desperately needs is a political renaissance. Confidence is the decisive factor" (Time, March 7, 1994). And confidence depends on having visions of a bright future, that is, a positive image.

References to the past, often artificially created by "historians", are crucial to the creation of a national identity. Appeals to the past, as Said (1993/1994) pointed out, are among the most common strategies used in interpreting the present. Said emphasized the mobilizing power of images and traditions and their fictional, or at least romantically colored, fantastic quality. For example, William Butler Yeats (1865 - 1939), gave the Irish nationalist struggle something to revive and admire, an Irish past. Lord Byron was of equal importance for Greek independence. Said maintained that during the Algerian War of Independence decolonization encouraged Algerians and Muslims "to create images of what they supposed themselves to have been prior to French colonization" (p. 17).

The purpose of the 1983 renaming of Upper Volta to Burkina Faso after a revolution was to change its image from a former French colony to a country of incorruptibility. A Ghanaian diplomat explained why the Gold Coast took the name of Ghana, although the old kingdom was not located on the territory of the present Ghana: "We know perfectly well where the old kingdom of Ghana was situated. We chose it because much of the gold worked in the old Ghana was traded in our territories. Furthermore, it was a glorious civilization, of which all Africans can be proud" (Time, June 12, 1989). Creating a positive image sometimes means getting rid of a negative image, like that of the Dark Continent or The White Man's Grave (a 19th century expression for the Dark Continent). Despite the fact that the latitude and longitude of most of Africa's coast had been fairly accurately fixed by the 19th century, as Macnair (1954) pointed out in Livingstone's Travels, details of the interior were drawn from hearsay and imagination rather than fact. In 1971, as part of Mobutu's *authenticité* campaign trying to erase traces of colonialism, the river Congo was renamed Zaire. According to Forbath (1977) the change from *Congo*, an authentically African word, to *Zaire* meant adopting "a clumsy mispronunciation of the ancient Kikongo *nzadi* or *nzere*, meaning the river that swallow all rivers" (p. XI). Forbath cited a young

Zairois government veterenarian interpreting the meaning of the new name: "You will understand me . . . when I say that *Congo* is a very heavy word. It is a word far too heavy for a people like ourselves to bear in this modern age. When I was a student in Europe, I never liked to say I was Congolese. I pretended I was Guinean. Because there in Europe and also in . . . America and, yes, even here in Africa, *Congo* has become to stand for all the things we are now struggling so hard to leave behind, for all the savage and primitive things of our past" (p. XI).

Often images to foster cultural identity are created by focussing on what one doesn't want to be. For example, Ayatullah Ruhollah Khomeini declared in March 1979 in the holy city of Qum: "What the nation wants is an Islamic republic. Not just a republic, not a democratic republic, not a democratic Islamic republic. Just an Islamic republic. Do not use the word *democratic*. That is Western, and we don't want it" (Time, March 12, 1979, p. 12). Furthermore, he declared that the reshaping of Iran "in the image of Muhammad" would be done by the purge of every vestige of Western culture from the land: "We will amend the newspapers. We will amend the radio, the television, the cinemas. All of these should follow the Islamic pattern".

Boulding (1969) defined image as "total cognitive, affective, and evaluative structure of the behavior unit, or its internal view of itself and the universe" (p. 423). The problem of what is reality or fiction in our various perceptions of the world usually plays no large part in our daily lives. One behaves as if one's perception of the world were "true". Moreover, in everyday behavior there are mechanisms leading to the discovery and remedy of mistakes. There is the possibility of moving to "near reality", as feedback leads to the elimination of errors. As Boulding (1956, 1967) argued both in science and in the area of "common beliefs" advances in recognition come from the disappointment of hopes because only through mistakes could anything new be learned; successes only confirmed existing perceptions. In this respect there are by and large, no differences between scientific learning and folk learning.

Experiences that do not fit into one's perceptions can, but need not, lead to modifications of those perceptions. As Boulding (1967) wrote: "Disappointment, unfortunately, does not always force a revision in this image, for it can cause us to deny either the image of the past or the inference that gave rise to the future" (p. 3).

Between the world of folk learning and the folk images derived from it and the world of scientific learning and scientific images, Boulding (1967) localized another image sphere, which he described as a "world of literary images" (p. 5). In this world the test of reality is the least pronounced; that is, the elimination of errors either does not take place at all or occurs only at enormous cost. It is in this world that the images of the international system are localized and in which the international decision makers mainly move. Indeed Boulding regarded the international system as by far the most pathological and costly part of the world system (e.g., costs of military, foreign ministries, diplomatic corps, secret services, and wars). In fact, decision makers are usually aware that they are living in a world of images. As the famous French statesman Talleyrand pointed out, in politics what is believed to be true is more important than truth itself. Ronald Reagan knew that "Facts are stupid things" (Time, August 29, 1988, p. 52). Knorr (1980) quoted Dorothy L. Sayers: "My lord, facts are like cows. If you look them in the face hard enough, they generally run away" (p. 226). Kissinger (1969) stated: "Deterrence above all depends on psychological criteria" (p. 61).

According to Boulding there are two main reasons for the pathology of the international system. First, neither folk learning nor science can shape adequate images of it. The simple feedback mechanisms that work in everyday life do not help in understanding the complexity of the international system. And scientists currently are unable to provide the information needed to build a realistic image of the international system, although there have been repeated efforts to that end. Further, as a rule, political decision makers are highly mistrustful of research findings in the social sciences. Boulding wrote (1967):

> On the whole the images of the international system in the
> minds of its decision makers are derived by a process that I have
> described as "literary" -- a melange of narrative history,
> memories of past events, stories and conversations, etc., plus an
> enormous amount of usually ill-digested and carelessly collected
> current information. When we add to this the fact that the
> system produces strong hates, loves, loyalties, disloyalties, and
> so on, it would be surprising if any images were formed that
> even remotely resembled the most loosely defined realities of the
> case (p. 9).

Manheim (1991) took the same position, arguing that for top
decision makers in the United States, "the likelihod is that most
people in our government and others, even at the highest level,
received at least as much information about the June 1989 massacre
in Beijing's Tiananmen Square from media reports as from
diplomatic or intelligence sources. They know little more than we
know. We are vulnerable" (p. 130). For politicians like foreign
ministers, for example, the success of their career has not been
dependent on the ability to estimate correctly the images of foreign
nations but to meet the demands and stereotypes of their voters: If
the people believe that the Russia is the evil empire, one can win
elections only if one is of the same opinion or at least gives at
impression.

The high price of misperception in government decision making
was discussed by Fisher (1987) who maintained that most decisions
in international politics are based on misperceptions and distorted
images:

> [T]hose dealing with foreign affairs problems tend to rely
> staunchly on their own "common sense" observational and
> judgement skills despite the warning signals that they are
> venturing onto unfamiliar ground where more specialized
> experience and even scientific help should be sought. It is the
> mentality that will use computer cross-checking to extend the
> capacities of the mind in order to manipulate data for making
> airline reservations or to diagnose a disease, but seeking no

objective means to check the accuracy of perceptions of foreign events or to verify an image of another nation's pattern of behavior (p. 127).

The American intervention in Vietnam is a good example. Former secretary of defense, Robert McNamara (1995), has admitted that the Vietnam War was wrong. The image of Vietnam did not correspond with reality.

The pathology of the international system is particularly evident when compared with science. The sciences are concerned with the gathering and processing of information as well as tests in relation to reality. Whereas secrecy in the sciences is condemned and love of truth is the highest virtue -- the spreading of lies and the falsification of data is a scientific deadly sin -- in the international system, under the pretext of national interest or national security all secrecy and every lie can be legitimated. Diplomats and statesmen, says an old European adage, are paid, after all, to lie for their country. Or, as Josef Stalin said, "With a diplomat words must diverge from acts -- what kind of diplomat would he otherwise be? Words are one thing and acts something different. Good words are masks for bad deeds. A sincere diplomat would equal dry water, wooden iron" (Leites, 1953, p. 358). Trying to influence foreign politicians/sovereigns by lies, rumors, and so forth to gain political advantage is old diplomatic practice.

Plato (c. 428 B.C. - c. 347 B.C.) addressed problems of image building. He spoke of the relationship between reality and appearance, comparing people to prisoners who from childhood on live in an underground cave and are tied up so they cannot turn around. All they ever see are the shadows cast on the cave wall in front of them by things passing that exist in the world of the sun. People living so would regard the shadow world on the cave wall as the real world and, were they released from their cave, would be unable to believe that the outside world was the true reality. Boorstin (1961) offered a similar notion regarding the perception of reality by modern American society, as shaped by mass media: "We risk being the first people in history to have been able to make their illusions so vivid, so persuasive, so 'realistic', that they can live in them. We are the most illusioned people on earth. Yet we dare not become disillusioned, because our illusions are the very house in which we live; they are our news, our heroes, our adventure, our forms of art, our very experience" (p. 240).

THE WORLD OF LITERARY IMAGES: SOME EXAMPLES

Isaacs (1958) examined the attitudes of a sample (N = 181) of influential Americans -- opinion leaders and policy determiners -- toward China and India to demonstrate how their world of literary images is structured. In response to the question "When you think of Asia, what comes to your mind?" for 80% an "image of an undifferentiated crush of humanity was summoned up instantly . . . and for many this is the 'Asia' that carries with it a dread blur of mystery and fearfulness, associated with vast numbers, with barbarism, with disease". A total of 129 of the respondents saw in Asia a future danger to the United States. The American image of China has fluctuated greatly over the course of history, from Marco Polo to Pearl S. Buck, from Genghis Khan (though Mongolian, not Chinese) to Mao Tse Tung. Almost every American schoolchild knows the name of Marco Polo. Linked to him is the image of a great old Chinese civilization, characterized by art and wisdom. This China image is as follows: The Chinese are intelligent, hard-working, peace-loving, and characterized by stoicism and strong family ties. Genghis Khan and his Mongolian hordes, who were in fact enemies of the Chinese, stand for the other China image: cruel, barbarian and inhuman, a faceless, overwhelming mass of people that, once it has begun to move, is unstoppable. Linked with this image are notions of Chinese tortures (variously described as devilishly ingenious methods of inflicting pain and death), the Yellow Peril (often also including the Japanese), the murder of female babies, and so forth. Especially at the time of Mao Tse Tung the Chinese were perceived as a mass of barbarians, armed with artillery, tanks, and fighter planes instead of the bow and arrow. Isaacs wrote: "China occupies a special place in a great many American minds. It is remote, strange, little familiar, full of sharp images and associations, and uniquely capable of arousing intense emotion" (p. 66). With respect to the China image, there is again a division into good and bad, into superior and inferior. The image of China as a superior country encompasses such aspects as philosophy (Confucius and Lao-tzu) and its old and great culture, that is, its art, science, and architecture. On the other hand, there is the image of the Chinese as inferior (Isaacs, 1958) -- as weaklings, as nonaggressive, submissive, servile people who passively accept things and are incapable of solving problems.

Isaacs (1958) found that the American image of India is much less marked than that of China, and has been shaped in particular by the works of Rudyard Kipling, especially The Jungle Books, which was written for children. Thus Indians are seen as creatures of fable ("fabulous Indians") living in an exotic world of maharajas, jewels, wealth, snakes, elephants, tigers, cobras, and so on. This image has also been bolstered by mass media, especially films. Isaacs collected examples of stereotypes about India in the American mass media in 1957:

- The New York Times, November 23: "A new Indian movie, a great success in the land of rope tricks and fakirs"
- Longines Symphonette, CBS-Radio, November 27: Announcer: "We shall now take you to the land of temples and tigers with the playing of 'India Caravan'"
- Time, December 5: About its New Delhi correspondent: "At his New Delhi home sacred cows browse in the flower beds, snake charmers with their cobras, fortune-tellers and holy men with begging bowls crowd the veranda, push in on him. 'I feel them at my shoulder as I work,' says Campbell." (p. 264)

India also possesses an image as a country of religions, philosophers, gurus, and Eastern mysticism. Isaacs wrote: "The image of the very benighted heathen Hindu is perhaps the strongest of all that come to us out of India from the past and it retains its full sharpness up to the present day. It appeared, vivid, clear, and particularized, in the mind of a large majority of our interviewees, 137 out of 181. It was evoked from distant memory or from the last week's issue of <u>Time</u>, from pictures and captions in the <u>National Geographic</u>" (p. 259).

Like China, the picture of India is one of masses of humanity: a cruel, fanatical, and violent mob likely to massacre. Kipling, who influenced the image of India like no other, characterized the Indians as "new caught, sullen . . . half-devil and half-child" (Isaacs, 1958, p. 274). By contrast, the image of India has also been decisively shaped by Mahatma Gandhi, the famous pacifist. In scholarship, too, there remains a certain stereotype of India stemming from Max Weber's analyses of Hinduism made at the beginning of the 20th century. These still are used by many authors as the basis for their assessments of Indian society, and in fact, as M. Singer (1972) maintained, serve as the foundation for present-day development policy measures.

According to Isaacs' (1958) data, 54% (N = 98) of American opinion leaders questioned had more or less sharply defined negative notions of India, whereas 70% (N = 123) had a mainly positive image of China. It must be assumed that such images will also influence political decision making. In view of his findings, Isaacs felt justified in concluding that the images of Asia and of Asian-Western relationships persisting in the minds of men educated and conditioned primarily to an Atlantic-Western-white view of the world certainly have a major place in the slowness and pain with which major American policy makers have reacted to the new realities in Asia since 1945.

An example of a top decision maker's stereotyping India is Winston Churchill, who in 1896 told his mother that India was a "godless land of snobs and bores" (Gilbert, 1991, p. 65). On March

18, 1931, he called the British policy of negotiations with Gandhi and Nehru "a crazy dream with a terrible awakening" (p. 500). If British authority were destroyed India would break down: Medical, legal, and administrative services would perish; profiteering and corruption would flourish; nepotism and graft would be the handmaidens of a Brahmin domination; and the Hindus would tyrannize the Untouchables (Gilbert, 1991, p. 500). In 1933 another leading British politician, Lord Hailsham, characterized the Indians as very clever, but not good administrators and often corrupt, as their own religion compelled them to look after their own relations (Gilbert, 1991, p. 517).

India's image was seriously damaged in the fall of 1994 when the Black Death broke out, causing not only mass hysteria within India but also worldwide concern that "the most terrible of all terrors" (Time, October 10, 1994) might spread to other countries as well. Neighboring countries closed their borders and some countries even discontinued their air connections with India. An Indian federal minister maintained that "plague in India is being spread not by rats but by the media". Vijay Kalantri, president of the All-India Association of Industries, lamented: "All this has really created a bad image for India" (Time, October 10, 1994). Again India was seen as a country where rats not only are rife but even worshipped by people living in slums and governed by corrupt and inefficient politicians. In response to the crisis, Air India offered about 500 foreign journalists free tickets to give them a chance to see with their own eyes that everything was in order again. The tourism industry alone anticipated losses of about $20 million. India herself in 1992/1993 waged an image campaign in Europe titled "Jewels of India". The advertisements told European readers that the North glitters with Mogul tradition and with the pearl-encrusted Taj Mahal, that there are mysterious mountaintop sites, and that every region of India shines with palaces, temples, festivals, and resorts.

Although they often refuse to believe it of themselves, politicians are as prone to distorted perceptions as anyone else. When such distorted perceptions flow into political decision making, there can be very negative consequences. Say that in peace or disarmament negotiations one or both sides assume that the other is malicious and intent on foul play: Whatever the other side does will be perceived as underhanded. If United States politicians branded the Soviet Union an "empire of evil" (as did Ronald Reagan) and vice versa, any suggestion to completely disarm could have been interpreted as a communist ruse. Spanier and Nogee (1962) showed how hardened the negotiating fronts were in the Soviet-American disarmament talks: "Each side probably wants disarmament on its own terms. But since this would improve the power position of the proponent, such disarmament is unacceptable to the other side. And in the absence of agreement, each side is determined to maintain its strength while blaming the opponent for the failure of the negotiations and the continued tensions in the world" (p. 55).

There is especially good documentation of the way John Foster Dulles, former United States secretary of state, perceived matters during the Cold War. An analysis of the speeches and writing of Dulles (Holsti, 1962) reveals that both truculent and conciliatory messages from the Soviet Union were reinterpreted to fit into the image of an aggressive, hostile, evil, and dynamically monolithic dictatorship. Holsti (1967) analyzed all publicly available statements made by Dulles during the years 1953 - 1959, including 122 press conferences, 70 addresses, 67 appearances at Congressional hearings, and 166 other documents according to which Dulles considered Soviet policy within a framework of three contrasting pairs of concepts: ideology vs. national interest, party vs. state, and rulers vs. people. Dulles was convinced that Soviet policy was a manifestation of the communist ideology, and regarded the communist party as aggressive and the state as a tool of the party. Dulles told the Senate Committee on Foreign Relations and Armed Services on January 15, 1957:

> Russian foreign policy is an instrument of international communism. . . . International communism is a conspiracy composed of a certain number of people, all of whose names I do not know, and many of whom I suppose are secret. They have

> gotten control of one government after another. They first got control of Russia after the first World War. They have gone on getting control of one country after another until finally they were stopped. But they have not gone out of existence. (Holsti 1967, p. 259)

The Bay of Pigs disaster was caused by the fact that decision makers had a distorted image of Cuba, believing that the people were dissatisfied with Castro's rule and would help the invaders. Russia's war against Chechenya, begun in 1995, is another example of mishandling foreign policy due to distorted images. In fact, the "liberation" of Grozny has been a disaster for Russia. Top decision makers in foreign policy tend to be specialized in certain fields (e.g., law of the sea). As Fisher (1987) observed, "Their interest in any particular country is thus narrow, and the effort that be required their special interest through its full context of meaning for all the countries with which they must deal would be considerable. When the need arises they too typically have to rely on 'what I have read in the newspapers'" (p. 130). Very often decision makers see what they want to see. If they have a black-and-white dichotomy of the world (e.g., during the Cold War, it was we the good vs. they the communists) cultural differences are ignored -- for example, either they are communist or they are on our side.

An extreme example of hate-filled distortion of perception and cognitive constriction, i.e. the simple black-and-white explanation, is Tarik Asis', the Iraqi foreign minister, 1988 characterization of the Iranians as "backward barbarians": "The Iranian brain suffers from schizophrenia. If we read history properly, Persia for a long time was part of Babylonia or Assyria or the Abbasidic caliphate. And those periods were longer than those in which Iraq was part of Persia. It is alien to us for a foreign minister of an Islamic republic to speak such language. On the one hand he regards himself as a good Moslem, then suddenly he changes his colour and talks like a chauvinistic Persian. The Iranians are expansionist to their very roots. One of the reasons why the Shah fell in 1979 was his imperial madness. Now the Iranians no longer wear the crown of the Shah but hide under an Islamic cap. But the sickness is the same. Under Hitler, too, the Germans were afflicted by the disease of expansionism. Only after they had lost the war they became normal, peaceful people again who got on with their neighbours. Iran is still in the acute phase of this illness. We hope it heals soon." (Der Spiegel, No. 46, 1988).

IMAGE AND REALITY: SELF-FULFILLING PROPHECY

W.I. Thomas and D.S. Thomas' (1928) famous comment is still valid: "If men define situations as real they are real in their consequences" (p. 572). The image of a country in permanent crisis or as economically unreliable, generated perhaps by continuous negative reporting, can influence economic decision-making processes and discourage investment, which in turn can exacerbate future crises. For example, the Prime Minister of Slovakia, Vladimir Meciar (1993), complained in an interview that due to negative reporting investments had declined. Meciar said that foreign investors didn't know much about Slovakia, but from the newspapers they learned that communist dictator Meciar was ruling and that the country was not known for its stability. If he had only this distorted information about his country, allowed Meciar, he would not invest there either. Similar complaints have been heard from Malaysia (in October 1983, e.g.) and the Philippines.

The impact of a self-fulfilling prophecy is evident when, for instance, political decision makers in developed countries consider whether or not to give aid to a developing country. If mass media reporting convinces them that the developing country had only itself to blame for its poverty because the people living there were lazy or incapable, and/or the government was corrupt and incapable, giving development aid would be tantamount to squandering money. Reduced aid or no aid at all leads to greater, poverty which in turn reinforces the decision maker's prejudices or images of the developing country regarding future aid. And the cycle continues.

It doesn't necessarily have to happen that way, however. When, for example, representatives of the Indian firm, Tata Brothers, sought capital and technical assistance from British steel companies to build a steel mill southwest of Calcutta, the British maintained that, because of religious differences and the caste system, it was impossible to find suitable labor. Tata Brothers ultimately raised the capital in India and engaged an American, John Keenan, as manager. Keenan stayed for 20 years; when he gave up the job the Tata steel plant was the biggest throughout the British empire (Keenan, 1943). Similarly, during the Suez crisis in 1956, the Western mass media took the view that the Egyptians were incapable of operating the canal. And the Japanese for a long time were regarded in the West as clever imitators who could copy Western designs but lacked originality. Deutsch (1969) summarized the essence of such examples as follows: "In short, the alleged incapability of non-Western peoples to perform the delicate and demanding operations of science, technology and human organization is simply a myth" (p. 81).

Processes of self-fulfilling prophecy can occur even at the global level. Entire regions or continents can be stigmatized if, say, the term developing country is interpreted as hopeless backwardness, corruption, and waste of money. For example, in an article entitled "Africa's Woes: Coups, Conflicts and Corruption", Senegal's president, Abdou Diouf (1984) is quoted as saying: "To Africa's sickness, pestilence and disease, add corruption. It is endemic to this continent" (Time, January 16, 1984). P. J. O'Rourke said in an essay "Africa's Uphill Battle", "Man developed in Africa, he has not continued to do so there" (Time, August 15, 1994). However, the article also pointed to a role model for Africa: Botswana, an established democracy and economic miracle on a par with the four Asian tigers (South Korea, Taiwan, Singapore, and Hong Kong).

In 1994 General Olusegun Obasanjo of Nigeria, one of the few African heads of state to voluntarily cede power, emphasized the dangerous consequences of the negative image of Africa for the whole continent. The image of Africa, distributed worldwide via television, was that of a continent without hope, characterized by bloody conflicts, hunger, refugees, power-thirsty dictators, and children dying from malnutrition. With slow economic growth and a population explosion, Africa has been labeled a continent with no hope, destined to receive development aid and, due to its inefficency, unable to pay its debts.

There are countless examples of deterioration and corruption in Africa. As Desmond Tutu observed in 1990, "There is less freedom in Africa than during colonial times" (Time, October 14, 1991, p. 27). Zaire's Mobuto Sese Seko is one of the richest men in the world (experts estimate Mobutu's fortune at $4 billion), but he exploited his country. When the Belgian Congo became independent in 1960 it had about 58,000 miles of good road; in 1984 only 6,200 miles were passable. In Uganda, which under British rule was one of the most prosperous countries in Africa, there is a saying referring to the quality of the infrastructure: "When you see a man driving in a straight line along Kampala road, he must be drunk!" (Mazrui, 1986, p. 202). The country was terrorized by Idi Amin and his lumpen-militariat (Mazrui, 1986). And then President-for-Life Jean-Bédel Bokassa of the Central African Republic declared himself Emperor in 1976 and staged a $20-million ceremony, crowning himself with a $2-million gold-and-diamond diadem. One of the most prestigious symbols of status in Africa are Mercedes-Benz limousines; wabenzi, a new Swahili word, was coined to describe the new elite, the men of the Mercedes-Benz.

Many African politicians blame African backwardness on former colonialism, which destroyed traditional social structures and created boundaries that ignored tribal loyalities. Many contemporary leading African politicians and intellectuals believe that Africa has no bright future. Edem Kodjo (1984), former Secretary-General of the Organization for African Unity, said: "Our ancient continent is now on the brink of disaster, hurtling towards the abyss of confrontation, caught in the grip of violence. Gone are the smiles, the joys of life" (Time, January 16, 1984, p. 10). Whether this image of Africa is correct or not does not matter; the danger is that such an image is defined as reality.

On the other hand, African societies are trying to construct a positive self-image, a workable common identity. Leopold Senghor, a proponent of *negritude*, turned Descartes' famous "I think, therefore I am" upside-down ("I feel, therefore I am") and argued: "Emotion is Black . . . Reason is Greek" (Mazrui, 1986, p. 73). Mazrui asserted that Europe's supreme gift to Africa is neither Christianity nor Western civilization but a new African identity, quoting Nyerere when he said that the colonization of Africa had one significant result: "A sentiment was created on the African continent -- a sentiment of oneness" (p. 108). He went on to give some examples of African attempts to create a new identity, a proud image of itself:

> Under the presidency of Kwame Nkrumah in Ghana, romantic gloriana sometimes sought to trace almost all the ingredients of literature, culture and written science to some African origin. I have a collection of postcard reproductions of paintings. These were issued from the archives of Accra during Nkrumah's reign. One postcard shows Tyro, an African secretary of Cicero, and attributes to Tyro the invention of shorthand writing in the year 63 B.C.. Another postcard shows Egyptian figures, and points to the African origins of paper. Yet another postcard claims that the science of law originated in Africa and was practised in the ancient empire of Ghana. Yet another portraits an African teaching mathematics to the Greeks. Also in the collection is a painting of an African teaching the alphabet to the Greeks. (p. 74)

SOME EXAMPLES FOR IMAGE POLISHING BY STATES

In 1978 Lesly noted that "virtually all nations now conduct international public relations programs. Sophistication varies greatly, depending on awareness among the nation's leaders of the effect on their goals of attitudes abroad . . . Programs among smaller nations tend to be directed toward tangible goals, such as tourism, investment in local industry, and marketing of local products" (p. 352). As far back as 1981, Adelman took the view that in the United States "public diplomacy", that is, the disseminating of America's message abroad, is expected to "become Washington's major growth industry over the coming years" (p. 913). Manheim (1994) characterized the representation of foreign interests in Washington as "political campaigns whose objective is not the election of a candidate to office, but the advancement of some policy of interest to the client government or corporation" (p. VIII). This development is evidenced by the steady replacement of lobbyists by firms with experience in managing domestic campaigns.

One might say that we live in an age of public diplomacy. Most embassies in the big industrial countries -- especially in the United States, Great Britain, France, and Germany -- have press attachés whose job is to cultivate their country's image. Yet often the press attachés are called instead something like "Second Secretary". The former (West) German chancellor, Helmut Schmidt, emphasized the "central importance" of public diplomacy in German foreign policy. German institutions serving image cultivation abroad include the Press and Information Office of the Federal Republic (attached to the chancellory), the foreign cultural policy section of the foreign office, the Goethe institutes, the German Academic Exchange Service, the Humboldt Foundation, foundations of the political parties, the Carl Duisberg Society, Deutschlandfunk radio, Radio Deutsche Welle, and Trans-Tel sells German television programs. According to Hansen (1984) both West Germany and France spend about 1% of their national budgets on information and cultural programs, whereas the United States spends only on tenth of a percent of its budget for such purposes. In 1980 France spent about $1 billion on information and cultural activities. For France, too, this form of public diplomacy is an essential instrument of foreign policy. And in 1977, the Paris government funded 70% of the budget of the Agence France Press (AFP) news agency (all data from Hansen, 1984).

Great Britain has at its disposal the instrument of the British Council (language teaching, cultural exchanges and presentations, and libraries). It was founded in November 1934 "to make the life and thought of the British people more widely known abroad and to cooperate with the Dominions and Crown Colonies in strengthening the common cultural traditions in the British Commonwealth". During Nazi times, the Germans argued that the British Council was an instrument of political and cultural encirclement of Germany (Thierfelder, 1940). The Prince of Wales remarked on July 2, 1935, "Of all the Great Powers, this country is the last in the field in setting up a proper organisation to spread knowledge and appreciation of language, literature, art, science and education" (Foster, 1939, p. 267). This was a princely misjudgment. As early as May 1919, Lord Curzon signed a circular dispatch, transmitted to all diplomatic missions abroad (except Washington, D.C.), informing the diplomats about propaganda in peacetime: "[A] complete and contemptuous silence, however gratifying to our self-respect, is no longer a profitable policy in times when advertisement -- whether of past achievement or future aims -- is, perhaps unfortunately, almost a universal practice of nations as of individuals" (Taylor 1981, p. 53).

Even before World War I the British had experience in the field of international PR. Imperialistic international propaganda was motivated mainly by commercial interests. August (1985) reported: "Long before World War I the dominions saw the advantage in establishing agencies (Canada House, Australia House, etc.) in central London" (p. 73). Other colonies, like the Gold Coast, the East African Dependencies Trade and Information Office, the Ceylon Office, the Cyprus Information Office, and the Malayan Information Agency, also established offices in London. Their task was image polishing and establishing and maintaining good relationships with relevant target groups. According to August, the Gold Coast placed numerous advertisements and articles in the mass press. Governor Slater wrote in a letter on March 23, 1928:

> With the commercial gain that has accrued to the Colony by the
> institution of the Bureau [Commercial Intelligence Bureau of the
> Gold Coast] cannot be measured in terms of actual figures, I am
> satisfied that the Bureau fulfills very useful functions. Apart
> from proving a most convenient agency in the United Kingdom
> and abroad, it disseminates up-to-date knowledge about the
> colony in quarters where such information is likely to be useful,
> and by replies to enquiries, it saves much of time in placing the
> enquirers in early touch with the appropriate local authorities
> (August, 1985, p. 73).

Some French colonies established publicity offices in Paris, for example, Indo-China and Afrique Occidentale. As August observed, "Through continuous propaganda, constructive imperialists endeavored to create the widest possible consensus about the future direction of the nation. Even before World War I, the press has been used for this purpose" (p. 104). Exhibitions were one of the most common PR instruments (cf. August, 1985, chap. 4, "The Circus Comes to Town"). For example, Great Britain participated in the 1939 New York World's Fair with the motto "Building the World of Tomorrow" (Ainsworth, 1939; Taylor, 1983).

As August (1985) explained, "During the 1920s and 1930s the imperialist movement in Britain and France waged a systematic propaganda campaign at home and overseas" (p. 69). For instance, in 1929 the "Travel and Industrial Association of Great Britain and Ireland" was established. Its task was "to increase the number of visitors to Great Britain; to stimulate the demand for British goods and services and to promote international understanding by every means, and particularly by the stimulation abroad of interest in Great Britain" (Taylor, 1978, p. 250). But the British avoided using the word propaganda, preferring instead euphemisms like education, information, imperial studies, or commercial intelligence. PR campaigns in the UK emphasized the economic importance of colonies and the need to invest there. And during the 1930s, campaigns were waged like "Buy British", "Empire Shopping Week", and "Eat More Fruit". As the Imperial Economic

Committee pointed out: "The housewife must be let to realize that, in buying Empire produce, she is building up employment for her husbands and sons . . ." (August, 1985, p. 64).

PR activities by colonies in their respective mother countries were not unusual. Hamilton Mercer Wright's international PR agency, founded in San Francisco by in 1905, secured as its first project the promotion of the Philippine Islands on behalf of United States business interests. As Cutlip (1994) observed, "Wright's output of propaganda, glorifying United States occupation and touting the Philippines' assets was prolific; a check of the _Reader's Guide to Periodical Literature_ finds titles such as 'The Forrests of the Philippines', 'Philippine Prospects', 'Philippines in Prosperity', 'Tobacco Raising in the Philippines', and so forth" (p. 77). In 1906 Wright even served as the commander of the United States Army in the Philippines in order to promote understanding between the Philippines and the United States. In 1907 he published _A Handbook of the Philippines,_ which according to Cutlip is still useful.

For small countries in particular, cultivating their national image abroad is often crucial to their economy. For example, in 1957 Belgium initiated a PR campaign in the United States designed to boost sales of Belgian products there (Ross, 1959). The aim of the PR firm, Communication Counsellors, Inc. (CCI), was to put Belgium on the map for the American public. CCI, a subsidiary of the transnational United States advertising agency McCann Erickson, had enjoyed earlier success getting American women to buy more hats. As apparently there is not much difference between PR for hats and PR for Belgium, the firm was hired and, according to the client, worked satisfactorily. Surveys had revealed that the American business community was poorly informed about possibilities of investing in or trading with Belgium and that ordinary people knew practically nothing about Belgium. CCI used as many communication channels as possible to increase awareness of Belgium: The business press was supplied with information materials; key businesspeople and newspaper publishers were sent a newsletter with "facts and figures" about Belgium; and Belgian products were advertised in publications for women, on the radio, and on television.

In fact, events were organized just to get them reported. For example, in 1957 Charles van Doren, the longstanding champion of the American TV quiz show, was unable to name the Belgian king. Quiz programs were so popular that van Doren's failure made front-page news nationwide. CCI seized the opportunity, inviting van Doren to Belgium and distributing a press handout headlined "The King Who Dethroned van Doren". Then there were the press reports of the presentation to film star Elizabeth Taylor of a crystal vase, a Belgian luxury product. CCI helped The Wall Street Journal with research for a report about Belgian atomic energy, and they advised Belgium to take part in the San Diego County Fair. Of course, certain subjects had to be avoided, such as reports that Belgian structural steel was selling successfully in New York, because of feared opposition from the American steel industry.

The PR campaign generated 704 reports in newspapers, 145 articles in the technical and trade press, 1,251 TV stories, and 6,906 positive radio reports. Although, as mentioned earlier, the client was satisfied, plans for follow-up activities by the PR firm were dropped for budget reasons. Among the CCI activities dropped was a plan to influence select American businesspeople and journalists at the Brussels trade fair. The state-owned Belgian airline, Sabena, was to give free flights to the 25 most important business and finance journalists and the Belgian government was to pay the other costs. CCI argued that the money would be well spent because it has been CCI's experience that after special trips of this kind the editors concerned usually do feel a sense of obligation and invariably reciprocate with favorable stories and features. They also wanted to publish a special supplement about Belgium in The New York Times. CCI described the procedure as follows: "The government concerned buys this supplement for $10,200 (two pages) and, through its public relations counsel, controls what is printed on various aspects of trade, commerce and industry". Of course, the

Times would have headed each page of the supplement with the word *Advertisement*, a flaw from an advertising perspective.

Sweden, another small country, was ranked far behind the United States, Great Britain, West Germany, and Switzerland in technical know-how according to an opinion survey in Japan, so it decided to take part in the Osaka trade fair. A Swedish official concerned with international information observed, "[I]t is of the greatest importance that there be a not too limited information activity about Sweden in those countries where we would like to be understood and find customers" (Davison, 1971, p. 12). Sweden has established several organizations to polish its image in foreign countries. For example, the Swedish Institute fosters cultural exchange and cultivates contacts with foreign institutions and persons (Kunczik, Heintzel & Malmström, 1995). According to a brochure published in 1992, the Institute distributes information materials to "many recipients -- decision makers, opinion molders and journalists, experts, writers, artists, students and scholars, companies and private citizens." The task of the Swedish Travel & Tourism Council is to project the touristic image. In 1993 Sweden conducted an image survey in Europe (Styrelsen för Sverigebilden: Image of Sweden in Europe, Stockholm, 1993, unpublished). Whereas people from central Europe associated mostly nature and scenery (lakes) and cold climate with Sweden, Italians most often mentioned the cold with "beautiful blond women" coming second. The most prominent persons associated with Sweden's image were the King and tennis player Björn Borg, followed by Queen Silvia, the pop group Abba, and another tennis player, Stefan Edberg. The Swedish King Carl XVI Gustaf defined his role as a kind of advertising manager of Sweden incorporated, as a "combination of doing PR for Sweden and unifying symbol for the Swedish nation" (Kunczik, Heintzel & Malmström, 1995, p. 36).

THE COUNTRY OF ORIGIN EFFECT

The *country of origin effect* refers to close interconnections between the image of a nation and its economy. Companies often have tried to create an image transfer between the products produced or the name of the company itself and the (positive) image of the nation-state. The opposite is also possible, whereby the images of products are transferred onto their country. According to Nagashima (1970) the image of the United States in Japan was built up by products like Coca-Cola, Ford automobiles, and IBM computers. Pendergrast (1993) quoted one Coca-Cola executive remarking to a colleague in 1950: "Apparently some of our friends overseas have difficulty distinguishing between the United States and Coca-Cola. Perhaps we should not complain too much about this" (p. 237). Kuwait made use of the country of origin effect in 1986 when Kuwait Petroleum bought most of the European distribution net of Gulf Oil and changed the name into Q8.

The country of origin effect may also negatively affect exportation, as with the Republic of South Africa under apartheid. In Western Europe, especially Germany, South African products were boycotted. The image of a company can also be used to create or strengthen existing negative images of a nation, for example, the German company Krupp, whereby Krupp was labeled a merchant of death and a warmonger.

The British were the first to regulate by law the close connections between the image of a nation and its economy. Paragraph 16 of the Act to Consolidate and Amend the Law Relating to Fraudulent Marks on Merchandise, August 23, 1887 (Merchandise Marks Act), prescribed: "[A]ll goods of foreign manufacture bearing any name or trade mark being or purporting to be the name or trade mark of any manufacturer, dealer, or trader in the United Kingdom, unless such name or trade mark is accompanied by a definte indication of the country in which the goods were made or produced, are hereby prohibited to be imported into the United Kingdom . . ." (Head, 1992, p. 29) The aim was to hinder the sale of foreign knock-offs of British products. Henceforth, German products, for instance, had to be marked "Made in Germany". In the long run, the Act had a boomerang effect, because all over the world "Made in Germany" became synonymous with excellent quality. James (1989) even maintained that Germany's identity was coined by a kind of fixation on economic success.

British companies used the country of origin effect for a long time, employing John Bull, Britannia, the British Lion, and the Royal Family (Dresser, 1989; Opie, 1985; Surel, 1989). During the 19th and 20th centuries patriotic and martial themes were utilized; great warriors decorated products like "The Baden-Powell Scottish Whisky" (around 1905) and "The Kitchener Stove Polish" (1910). A 1904 advertisement for Schweitzer's Cocoatina refered to the Russian-Japanese war. It depicted a Japanese soldier kneeling on a tin box shooting dead the Russian bear in Manchuria; sitting before the box was John Bull. The advertisement's slogan was: "The secret of his [Japanese soldier] strength. John Bull's moral support." (Opie, 1985, p. 33) A 1902 advertisement by Dunlop (Tyres) also used the country of origin effect. Below a Union Jack inscribed with Dunlop Tyres, the text read: "Where the British flag flies, Dunlop Tyres are paramount. A BRITISH invention, made by BRITISH workpeople, with BRITISH capital, for BRITISH cyclists. Avoid all imitations -- Foreign or otherwise" (Opie, 1985, p. 53). The Empire Marketing Board distributed a poster that said: "Follow the flag in all your purchases" (Opie 1985, p. 19). During World War I "buying British" was a kind of patriotic duty. Sometimes "Buy British" involuntarily was exposed to ridicule. An tin sign (ca. 1905) not only stated "Strike out foreign competition by buying England's Glory Matches" but also portrayed a British boxer, his trousers depicting the Union Jack, knocking out a German boxer looking like Bismarck. Upon the boxing gloves of the German was written "Made in Germany". (Opie, 1985, p. 16)

The Royal Family was used mostly to attract consumers within Great Britain and later the British Empire. The first Royal licence was granted in 1155 by Henry II to the Weaver's Company. At the end of Queen Victoria's reign, 1,080 companies had the right to utilize the royal coat of arms; in 1985 850 companies still had this right (Opie, 1985). A typical advertisement, for Rowland's Macassar Oil in 1830, informed consumers they were: "Under the august patronage of His Most Gracious Majesty, Their Royal Highness The Dukes of York and Sussex, The Royal Family, Their Imperial Majesties The Emperor and Empress of Russia, and the Nobility and Gentry." Queen Victoria illustrated sewing boxes and drank Cadbury's Cocoa. Edward VII helped market Horniman's Tea. Even foreign competitors labeled their goods with patriotic British trade names. The Britannia Box of Slate Pencils, with portrayals of Britannia, the Union Jack, British ships, and British soldiers, was made in Germany; the label "Made in Germany" was inconspicious on the box. In fact, Punch in 1911 warned: "Patriotic purchasers are cautioned against buying goods of any sort marked BRITISH MADE" (Opie, 1985, p. 8).

During World War I the country of origin was emphasized by showing warriors. A Sunlight Soap advertisement portrayed a soldier taking aim at the enemy with his rifle, a second soldier with a white bandage around his head, and a third soldier washing himself. The slogan read: "The CLEANEST fighter in the world -- the British Tommy". The text continued: "The clean, chivalrous fighting instincts of our gallant soldiers reflect the ideal of our business life. The same characteristics which stamp the British Tommy as the CLEANEST FIGHTER IN THE WORLD HAVE WON EQUAL REPUTE FOR British Goods. SUNLIGHT SOAP is typically British . . ." (Opie, 1985, p. 68). Lux advertisements tried to catch the eye of consumers by asserting that Lux could whiten the dirty shirts of stokers on warships (Opie, 1985). Johnnie Walker talked with an aviator. Car producer HUMBER stated: "When the War Birds Return -- those who have risked their lives at the Front will find peace, comfort and solace once more in touring the country roads of England in a post-war HUMBER car." Ovaltine, with their slogan "Builds up Brain, Nerve & Body," depicted a R.A.F. pilot drinking Ovaltine. The text read: "Nerve Force & Sustenance. Taken just before and after fight nothing can sustain Nerve and Body like a cup of Ovaltine. This is the opinion of many flyingmen and is the opinion of the highest medical authorities in the Air Service" (Opie, 1985, p. 72).

According to Campbell (1978), the German Werkbund was formed in 1907 by artists and manufacturers in response to a widespread feeling that the rapid industrialization and modernization of Germany posed a threat to the national culture. One of its founders, architect Hermann Muthesius, probably coined the phrase that the Werkbund would revitalize the applied arts "from the sofa cushion to urban planning" (Campbell, 1978, p. 5). The Werkbund fought against "cultural despair" (Campbell, 1978, p. 5). Its founders wanted to create a harmonious national style in tune with the spirit of the modern age. Campbell observed: "The immediate task before the new association would be to improve the design and quality of German consumer goods" (p. 10). Fritz Schumacher, professor of architecture at the Technische Hochschule in Dresden, according to Campbell, "sought to enlist the moral and patriotic sentiments of his auditors in support of the ideal of quality, arguing that quality work would strengthen the nation's competitive position in the markets of the world and foster social peace at home" (p. 10). The importance of good design to the success of German export trade was emphasized by the Werkbund's founders.

From 1896 to 1903 Muthesius was posted to England as a Germany's attaché for architecture in order to find out why England was so successful on the world market (according to Emperor Wilhelm II, competition on the world market was a fight to the death). At the 1876 world's fair in Philadelphia, German products had been labeled by the press as trash. In his 1907 inaugural address at the Berliner Handelshochschule, Muthesius argued that, by ceasing to produce shoddy goods, German industry would not only reap great profits but at the same time Germany would redeem her reputation on the world market (Campbell, 1978): "Instead of seeking desperately -- and ineffectually -- to adapt their designs to foreign tastes and predictions, German producers . . . might one day dictate good taste to the world, while enriching themselves. The rewards of a change of heart seemed plain: profits, power, and freedom from the stylistic tyranny of the French, then still dominant in the realm of fashion and design" (p. 15).

The Werkbund also tried to convince the German government that the Werkbund ideals had to be propagated abroad: "By 1914, the German Foreign Office had accepted the idea that consulates and embassies should serve as showcases for quality work in the new style, and requested the Werkbund to organize a series of lectures for the benefit of consular and diplomatic officials, in conjunction with the Cologne exhibition" (Campbell, 1978, p. 46). Cologne was chosen because of its proximity to France. The Werkbund believed that artistic style was closely connected with national character and appealed to the patriotism of the artists. Muthesius was convinced that Germany -- encircled by her competitors, poor in colonies and resources -- had no choice but to exploit the spiritual and intellectual gifts of her people commercially. Germany needed to overcome her stylistic dependence on England and shatter the artistic primacy of France. The Werkbund was determined to polish the German image abroad. After the outbreak of World War I the Werkbund office initiated a concerted propaganda campaign on behalf of the German government. Using its contacts abroad, it attempted to influence opinion in Germany's favor. British and French atrocity propaganda during World War I led to Werkbund's close cooperation with the German Foreign Office, which subsidized Werkbund arts and crafts exhibitions in Bern, Winterthur, and Basel in 1917, and in Copenhagen in 1918 in order to defend of Germany against the charge of barbarism.

Recent research has revealed that German-made products have an excellent image in most parts of the world; engineering and technical products especially are highly esteemed (Schweiger, 1992). The less information the consumer has about a product and the more similar are competitive products to each other, the greater the influence of the image of a nation-state on the sale of those products. In such cases the "made-in" designation often is the decisive factor on whether or not to buy. Schweiger (1992) compared the images of Germany, Austria, and Switzerland. On a global level Austria is perceived as a country of culture. That Austria is considered the "world champion of classical music" may be due to its 1991 global campaign for its Mozart year. The waltz is the most pronounced component of Austria's image: An Austrian exporter wanting to use the country of origin effect thus should advertise the products by means of waltz music. Altogether the Austrians have the image of being friendly and romantic, charming and pleasant. The image of Switzerland is characterized by economic strength and beautiful landscape (the idyllic Alps). Germany's image is centered around its industry, its technical products and high-tech know-how. The Germans are perceived as intelligent, hardworking, and having the most beautiful women.

In the United States the image of Canada is blue skies, snowcapped mountains, sparkling brooks, and green forrests, and is used frequently by Canadian breweries. One brewery advertises that its beer is brewed "on the fringes of Canadian wilderness." Lowenbrau by contrast lost its image as prestigious German or Bavarian beer when it became known that Lowenbrau was not genuine Löwenbräu but was brewed in the United States (Onkvisit & Shaw, 1989). Onkvisit and Shaw pointed out that consumers not only have general images about certain countries, but also form specific attitudes about products made in those countries. A consumer survey conducted in 1979 in France, West Germany, and Belgium revealed that German goods were evaluated as comparatively excellent (Onkvist & Shaw, 1989). On the other hand, British goods were evaluated as less technically advanced, lower in quality, and poor value for the money. Onkvisit and Shaw concluded: "In general, engineering and technical products from West Germany, electronics products from Japan, fashion products from France, and tobacco products from the United States are favorably received in most parts of the world" (p. 287). An international poll sample in 1994 rated the quality of various goods produced by the 12 largest exporters. Favorable responses by percentage resulted in the following ranking: 1. Japan (38.5%), 2. Germany (36.0%), 3. United States (34.3%), 4. United Kingdom (21.9%), 5. France (20.6%), 6. Canada (18.3%), 7. Italy (16.0%), 8. Spain (10.3%), 9. China (9.3%), 10. Taiwan (9.0), 11. Mexico (6.2%), 12. Russia (5.8%) (Bozell-Gallup Worldwide Quality Poll, Newsweek, March 14, 1994, p. 3).

Of course, it must be taken into account that consumers from different countries perceive products from a certain country differently. So Italians may believe that some or all Italian goods are better than some or all German products whereas Germans may believe just the opposite. Furthermore, consumers from different countries may use different criteria for the evaluation of a certain product. In many cases, therefore, the marketing strategy "one product, one message, worldwide" is inadequate.

THE MAIN AIM OF INTERNATIONAL PR: ESTABLISHMENT OF TRUST

The main objective of international PR is to establish (or maintain an already existing) positive image of one's own nation, that is, to appear trustworthy to other actors in the world system. Trust is no abstract concept. In the field of international policy, trust is an important factor in mobilizing resources, for examples, in receiving political and/or material support from other nations. In other words, if other actors in the world system place their trust in one's nation, in her future because of her reliability, trust becomes the equivalent of money. Put simply: Trust is money and money is trust. The positive image of a country's currency reflects confidence in that country's future. International business and currency exchange rates are not determined simply by pure economic facts (like currency reserves and gold reserves, deficit or surplus in balance of trade or balance of payment). The image of a nation-state, the rating of its business as solvent, the credibility of its politicians (i.e., can they be relied on to tame inflation by tight fiscal and monetary policies?), and so on are of decisive importance. Indeed, a country's reputation for solvency is more important to the stability of her currency than some short-term economic fluctuations.

In 1926 the French economist Albert Aftalion published his theory (Théorie psychologique du change) based on the hypothesis that the exchange rate of a country's currency is determined mainly by trust in the future of that country. A deficit of the balance of payments will not cause a devaluation of the currency as long as the belief in the future of this currency will attract foreign capital and balance the deficit. There is one main reason for the use of a certain currency as key currency: trust in the respective currency. Monetary policy is image policy. Money is an illusion, nothing more than the trust people have in their respective currency.

The collapse of the United States dollar in March 1995 and the rush to the German mark and the Japanese yen at least partly reflected a loss of trust in the world's (former?) major reserve currency. The flight from the dollar will certainly have consequences for the American economy. Due to the loss of trust and prestige the United States will likely no longer be able to run up foreign debts and trade deficits at least to the extent it had in the past. A German banker, Ulrich Beckmann (1995), explained the rush to the mark: "It's not the D mark's strength. It's the weakness of all other currencies. The mark is at the moment the one-eyed king in the world of the blind. People find the Mexican or the Canadian or the Spanish situation so confusing that, psychologically, they feel more comfortable in the D mark" (Time, March 20, 1995, p. 26).

Ivy Ledbetter Lee certainly was aware of the importance of trust: "Those who handle a loan must create an atmosphere . . ." (Hiebert, 1966, p. 266). Lee knew that simple statistics were not enough to market a loan. Lee handled loans for Poland, Rumania, France, and other countries, but considered Hungary a difficult case because too many people in America "had a mental picture of the [Hungarian] people as a wild, Bohemian lot, instead of the agricultural, sane, and highly cultivated people that they really are" (Hiebert, 1966, p. 267).

His advice to Hungary was to create the image that their country was stable and civilized. Argentina had problems attracting investors because of its image of social instability. Lee advised to them to send a polo team to the United States to compete with American teams, arguing, "The vital idea is that polo is not played except where there is a very high degree of civilization and a stable society . . . The galloping gentleman would tell the story more convincingly than any amount of statistics or mere statements as to the true conditions" (Hiebert 1966, p. 267).

The following are some recent examples of various countries' attempts to gain trust in the international community:

1. On July, 1, 1994 Banco do Brasil advertised in the leading German daily <u>Frankfurter Allgemeine Zeitung</u> that Brazil now had a new and stable currency: the <u>real</u>. This monetary reform was called the most decisive turning point in the history of Brazil's economy, an unparalleled enterprise. Brazil now offered investors more opportunities than ever before. It urged investors to have confidence in the new currency of a country, which in former times was plagued by inflation. The advertisement closed with the slogan: "BANCO DO BRAZIL. Good for you. Good for Brazil."

2. Estonia published in <u>Time</u> (July 4, 1994) a country profile/advertisement: "ESTONIA: Rebirth of a Nation". According to the advertisement after years of quiet opposition to Soviet rule, Estonia seized the opportunity of the failed coup of August 1991 in Moscow to declare full independence: "Swift and decisive actions underwrote this move: a new constitution was drawn up, free elections held, monetary reform (including a new currency) was initiated, and a fast-track policy of economic renewal was implemented." The advertisement pointed out that the change was without friction and caused ripples of consternation, but Estonia in the meantime had developed into a stable democracy with a strong currency (kroon exchange rate linked to the German mark). Estonia characterized itself as throwing open the doors to trade and being confidently braced for the shock of competition.

Knowing that years of Soviet central planning distorted Estonian economy, "the imperatives of a military/industrial ideology gave rise to monolithic, uneconomic and inflexible industries." Information about the economic climate and new opportunities in the Baltics was provided, especially concerning the progress of privatization: "New ownership structures are the single most important aspect of the marketization of economic life."

3. Malaysia published in Time (August 1994) a special advertising section of 20 pages "MALAYSIA. Looking to the future." It described the remarkable success of the beautiful and friendly people of Malaysia. 25 years ago, in 1969, there was a much different Malaysia. Half the people were living below the poverty line, proper education and health care were beyond the reach of many people, and cities were rocked by race riots: "And most people had a very weak national identity -- they called themselves Malay, Chinese or Indian -- but certainly not Malaysian." But, according to the advertisement, things had changed. The poverty rate had been reduced to less than 17% and there was a network of health care facilities and schools. Yet the best gauge of development according to the advertisement was the fact "that Malay, Chinese, Indians and people from smaller ethnic groups now call themselves Malaysian. This is especially remarkable when you consider the ethnic strife and secessionist tendencies that persist in much of southern Asia." The advertisement pointed out that the government brought the country back from the brink of disaster, not by means of harsh military crackdown, but by years of domestic diplomacy. Attention was drawn to the balancing of progress with conservation. The complex ecosystem of the tropical rainforrest was called "a heritage, much valued and cherished." According to the advertisement a systematic approach to forest management had evolved that required the fulfillment of environmental needs as well as the achievement of rational economic production. The success of Malaysia's capital market was explained by the strength of the economy, political stability, and the good results shown by Malaysian companies. Immediate problems in the economic sector were characterized as being on the mend. Anxiety about inflation had largely eased behind an effort to

curb excess liquidity and currency speculation. The Deputy Prime Minister and Finance Minister emphasized that the government is determined to broaden and deepen the capital market as a reliable source of long-term capital. Tourism and the tourism industry also were presented in the advertisement.

4. Peru, which had a worldwide bad image due to the outbreak of cholera in 1991 and the guerrilla movement Shining Path, in 1993 published a special advertising section in the International Herald Tribune (November 24). President Alberto Fujimori emphasized in an interview the "dramatic moves his government has made to improve the country's economic and business climate." One article dealt with the economic comeback of the country. Privatization was described as generating cash and competition. Peru was characterized not only as a country of ancient culture but also as a whole world of opportunities.

5. Egypt, which has troubles with Islamic fundamentalist terrorists, also wages campaigns to maintain/create the image of being a safe country. The Ministry of Tourism had the tourist offices distribute press releases maintaining that the government was in control of the situation, that most of the terrorists were already imprisoned. On October 23, 1993, Minister of Tourism Mamdough Beltagui stated: "The reality is that Egypt remains one of the safest destinations in the world, but there is no where that is totally safe from such isolated acts."

A long list of nations have published similar advertisements. One of the first advertisements of this kind appeared in Time, June 28, 1976. A special presentation by the State of Qatar was published to mark the staging of the Fourth Gulf Football Tournament in its capital, Doha. The special advertising section was also used to present to an international public Qatar's internal and external affairs, oil and gas resources, industrial diversification, education opportunities, social services, public works and infrastructure, finance and investment, commerce, and telecommunications.

Sometimes nations are interested in projecting a negative image, at least to a target group. Mexico became the first country to practically declare itself insolvent by an ad in the <u>International Herald Tribune</u> (June 8, 1989). Luis Tellez, general director of financial planning in the Mexican ministry of finance, signed the text, in which the chairman of the Citicorp bank, John Reed, is attacked. The banker is accused of having too restricted a view of things:

> For Mexico, the debt crisis is much more than a discussion of swaps or of the return of flight capital. It is a story of adjustment, of an extraordinary effort to transform an economy and of the hopes of millions of Mexicans for an opportunity to increase their standards of living. All parties involved should begin to look at the situation from both sides. We created the debt problem together; therefore it is up to both debtors and creditors to find a way out . . . We should all realize that there is much to gain by acting together. If banks insist on keeping their eyes closed to economic realities there will be no winners.

Worth mentioning is that Henry Kissinger, one of the most effective influence brokers in Washington, published columns on Mexico and its debt problem. The issue was of specific concern for some of his clients, including American Express and Chase Manhattan Bank. Isaacson (1992) documented that Kissinger wrote a column for the <u>Los Angeles Times/Washington Post</u> syndicate after the election of Carlos Salinas as President of Mexico. Kissinger evoked the enemy image of the international communist threat, praised Salinas, and argued that "the United States can play a major role in encouraging democracy and economic reform" (p. 746). He proposed an easing of the debt problem, recommending that some of the burdens of relief should be borne by creditor governments.

In 1991 Austria's Home Secretary, Franz Löschnack, published an advertisement in the Romanian newspaper <u>Romania Libera</u>. Romanians wanting to emigrate to Austria were warned against trying to enter Austria. Foreigners were not allowed to work in Austria without official permission and for Romanians no permission would be given. Romanians also had no prospects for asylum in Austria: "There are no more shelters for people asking for asylum". The last sentence of the advertisement was: "You don't have the slightest chance". The compositor of Romania Libera protested in a subtle way: Below the Austrian ad was placed an ad for the Bucharest center for disinfection, which fought against rat infestations and rounded up stray dogs.

TERRORISM AS INTERNATIONAL PUBLIC RELATIONS

Attracting attention is another aim of international PR. Certain forms of terrorism, namely those designed to reach the public through media coverage, are specifically staged for the mass media (Schmid & de Graaf, 1982; Weimann, 1990). Terrorists or freedom fighters know that journalists tend to regard dramatic and violent events as news. Weimann (1990) quoted a Palestinian terrorist/freedom fighter after the 1972 Munich Olympic Games (Palestinian terrorists captured Israeli competitors, and nine Israelis and five Palestinians were killed): "We knew that people in England and America would switch their television sets from any programme about the plight of the Palestinians if there was a sporting event on another channel. . . . From Munich onwards nobody could ignore the Palestinians or their cause" (p. 16). The "theatre of terror" (Weimann, 1990) evolved by adjustment to the modes of news selection; international terrorism became a media event, became public relations. Concerning the stigmatization as terrorist, Yasser Arafat argued in a 1988 interview: "George Washington was called a terrorist by the British. DeGaulle was called a terrorist by the Nazis. What can they say about the P.L.O., except to repeat this slogan? We are freedom fighters, and we are proud of it. According to international law and the United Nations Charter, I have the right to resist Israeli occupation. I don't want to harm anybody. But look how they are treating my people. These savage, barbarian, fascist practices against our children, our women!" (Time, November 7, 1988).

In the Algerian War, which began in 1954 and lasted 8 years, the Algerian insurgents used the media instrumentally. Abane Ramdane, the FLN liberation movement leader, asked rhetorically: "Is it better for our cause to kill ten of the enemy in the countryside of Telergma, where no-one will speak of it, or one in Algiers that will be mentioned the next day in the American press?" (Schmid & de Graaf, 1982, p. 19). In this interplay symbiotic relationships developed between the freedom fighters and the mass media. Robert Kleinmann of CBS, reporting on the final phase of the Algerian War, said: "If the photographer wanted to be sure to get a picture, it was very useful for him to find out when an assassination was going to take place. Many of the most startling pictures of assassinations in Algeria were obtained in that fashion . . . There is a very fine line here between reporting and instigating murder . . . There are competitive pressures on reporters and cameramen in the field" (Schmid & de Graaf, 1982, p. 141).

A good example of successful instrumentalizing the mass media is the Greek-Cypriots' war of liberation from British rules. This small group, who fought a hit-and-run guerilla war against the British banked on the power of world public opinion (Grivas, 1962). In their heyday the partisans had at most 100 heavy machine guns, Tommy guns, Sten guns, and rifles; 300 pistols; and a few hundred hunting weapons, mines, and grenades. In the beginning they were up against 20,000 well-equipped British troops whose numbers were doubled to 40,000 as the insurgency progressed. Given those circumstances, practically the only possibility left to the Cypriots was to wage a psychological struggle, the major aim of which was to win over world opinion for their cause. From the outset this was part of the plan of Colonel Georgios Grivas, the leader of the rebellion. Grivas, a Greek army officer and Cypriot by birth, founded the Ethniki Organosis Kypriakou Agonos (National Organization of Cypriot Struggle, EOKA) in Cyprus in 1954, which favored union with Greece. In the original "Preliminary General Plan of Insurrectionary Action in Cyprus", drawn up in Greece, "deeds of heroism and self-sacrifice" were called for "to draw the attention of international public opinion, especially among the allies of Greece" (Grivas, 1962, p. 91) to the Cyprus question. "By continuously harassing the British in Cyprus, we must show that we are determined not to yield, whatever the sacrifice, but that on the contrary we are prepared to continue until our aim is attained" (Grivas, 1962, p. 91). The struggle would continue, the original master plan said, the United Nations, and the British in particular, were compelled to examine the Cyprus problem and reach a speedy settlement in accordance with the aspirations of the Cypriot people and the whole Greek nation.

Grivas (1962) wrote that passive resistance by the population was a powerful weapon that reinforced and supplemented the armed struggle:

> I know of no other case in which this method was used on such a wide scale and with so effective an organization, except in India under Mahatma Gandhi. Unfortunately, few people attach due importance to it -- perhaps because they are not in a position to appreciate its value, or because they feel that it demands a big organizational effort and has great difficulties in the way of its success. . . . In Cyprus passive resistance assumed a special form. Its aim, as I saw it, was to arouse the interest of international public opinion in the Cyprus struggle which would be seen as a well organized movement embracing the whole population. It would show once more the Cypriot people's irrevocable determination to do their utmost to win freedom (p. 18).

Grivas claimed that as a result of the passive resistance the Cyprus government went bankrupt. There was also an administrative boycott which, he maintained, "put the government machinery completely out of gear. For instance, nearly all village mayors and elders resigned, thereby reducing administrative contact between the people and the government to nil" (p. 18). On public enlightenment and propaganda, Grivas (1962) wrote:

Our aims were: first, to enlighten public opinion, at home and abroad, about the justice of our cause as well as to draw attention to those acts of our opponent which were likely to discredit him internationally; second, to keep morale on the home front at a high level of endurance.   . . .   The enlightenment of international public opinion was bound to play an important part in bringing home to all concerned the Cypriot people's demand for self-determination. It is a fact that there were many foreigners and even United Nations representatives who were completely ignorant of why we were demanding our freedom" (p. 19).

Because of his limited resources, Grivas went on, he had to leave the work in the international arena to "those who were handling the political and diplomatic side of the question, namely the Greek Government and [Cypriot] Archbishop Makarios, to take care of things abroad" (p. 19). Grivas (1962) described the propaganda work as follows:

Firstly, leaflets which we published and which were distributed all over the island with marvelous success. The Greek Cypriot Press, which was censored and subject to very severe penalties if it published information that might help our cause, was not in a position to help us outright. As we had no printing press at our disposal, our pamphlets were mimeographed. The service which dealt with the issue and distribution was organized by sectors. Despite the efforts made by the authorities to discover where the pamphlets were printed and attempts to prevent their circulation, and notwithstanding the severe penalties enacted against those who distributed or read them, the pamphlets continued to be issued and circulated freely, thanks to the great care and precaution with which the whole service was organized. It was the young people who undertook the dangerous task of distributing the leaflets and they carried out their task admirably. Special plans were drawn up to enable our young distributors to escape the attention of the police and soldiers of whom the streets were full. They invariably succeeded in scattering the pamphlets about the streets or delivering them at houses without being caught. The police were obliged to go round the streets picking up the pamphlets under the mocking eyes of the inhabitants. This pamphlet propaganda must be accounted a major success . . . Secondly, there was propaganda by word of mouth. This was as effective as the pamphlets. When well-organized, a whispering campaign yields first-rate results. But such propaganda had its dangers [because it could be] . . . overheard by enemy agents who were lurking everywhere. In our propaganda, whether by pamphlet or word of mouth, we had one valuable advantage which the other side lacked -- truth. Our opponents, unlike ourselves, used lies. The people had ample opportunity of judging between the two and in the end would only believe what we said, never the British propaganda, even on the rare occasions when it did speak the truth. The moral of the fable of the shepherd who always cried "Wolf!" applies here (p. 20).

The world press reported the struggle as if David had taken on Goliath. While the British combed the island for guerillas in large-scale search actions, Grivas-Dighenis (Grivas became publicly known as Dighenis in 1955) had news circulated about the consequences of these searches: Reports of British repression, the forced evacuation of villages, and so on plainly caused the British huge image losses. Although not quantifiable, it is indisputable that by skillful information policy the Greek Cypriots managed to win over world opinion and to gain empathy for their cause even among the British public. There are no reliable data, however, to assess how great an influence the PR policy had on the British decision to withdraw from Cyprus.

CHAPTER 3

Mediation of Foreign Policy

THEORETICAL CONSIDERATIONS

Public relations for states is closely connected to mediation of foreign policy. Hertz (1982) asserted: "It is perhaps no exaggeration to say that today half of power politics consists of image making. With the rising importance of publics in foreign affairs, image making has steadily increased. Today, hardly anything remains in the open conduct of foreign policy that does not have a propaganda or public relations aspect . . ." (p. 187). Kepplinger (1983) concluded that the mass media, originally located outside the political system, have taken over a place within the political system. The media have become a political force that no longer just reacts, but also acts, and essentially -- because the media, as an autonomous force, define the extent of the political possible -- cogoverns. The functional dependencies of political institutions and the mass media in parliamentary democracies are seen as a matter of both domestic and foreign politics. Through their mediating function the mass media hold a key position in the political process. The media have the power to put themes on the agenda hitherto ignored by politics, they can help to establish contacts not possible at the level of diplomacy, and they can be used as instruments of foreign policy.

On the significance of the mass media in foreign policy, Karl (1982) wrote: "The media are increasingly a part of the process (if not the entire process) in the communication between governments and publics about international politics" (p. 144). Indeed, governments can come under pressure from what is already on media record. Thus, in the event of a potential or actual conflict, negotiated solutions could become more difficult if it seemed that such a new, conciliatory approach might, because of an earlier media-expressed hard line, involve a loss of face. To quote Karl again: "In an age of media diplomacy, statecraft may have become the hostage -- if not the victim -- of stagecraft. Only the media have a first-strike capability on both national and international levels" (p. 155).

The mass media of communication have broken into the traditionally exclusive sphere of diplomacy, and have themselves become an instrument of international conciliation, and mediation -- and also of conflict. The mass media, by serving in the diplomatic sphere as a source of international information, can contribute to international orientation, for example by establishing a common fund of knowledge that enables or facilitates negotiations. But as to the quality of this common basis of information, many countries (especially developing countries) believe that their positions -- because of the current structure of the global information system -- are not receiving due attention in the world or in a certain region. Such a situation can be defined as an image crisis: The political elite of a state believes that they do not have a fair and adequate image in a foreign country; that is, they believe that they are not given adequate and unbiased media attention.

According to Signitzer and Coombs (1992), the field of diplomacy is shifting from traditional diplomacy toward public diplomacy: "[T]he actors in public diplomacy can no longer be confined to the profession of diplomats but include various individuals, groups, and institutions who engage in international and intercultural communication activities which do have a bearing on the political relationship between two or more countries" (p. 139). Signitzer and Coombs made a distinction between the tough-minded and the tender-minded schools in public diplomacy: "The tough-minded hold that the purpose of public diplomacy is to exert an influence on attitudes of foreign audiences using persuasion and propaganda. . . . The tender-minded school argues that information and cultural programs must bypass current foreign policy goals to concentrate on the highest long-range national objectives. The goal is to create a climate of mutal understanding" (p. 140).The authors argued that neither school is correct, but have to be synthesized. The authors furthermore made a distinction between political information, usually administered by a section of the foreign ministry or by an embassy, and cultural communication, usually administered by a cultural section of the foreign ministry and/or cultural institutes abroad and/or some semiautonomous body (e.g., the British Council). Two types of cultural communication are identified: Cultural diplomacy, the creation of cultural agreements in a formal sense, aims at presenting a favorable image of one's own culture. Cultural relations do not have unilateral advantage in mind but have the goal of information exchange in order to present "an honest picture of each country rather than a beautified one" (p. 140).

THE MEDIA AND POLITICS: SOME EXAMPLES OF MEDIATION

Empirical evidence of a modification of "classical" diplomacy through international communication can be found in Davison (1974, 1975), who questioned diplomats and foreign correspondents for a study. The correspondents were so-called diplomatic correspondents -- that is, journalists who by definition regularly write on international affairs, often taking part in international conferences and reporting on them. Such journalists are granted sufficient time for thorough research; their output is recognized by members of the diplomatic network. They belong to the "foreign affairs community". The diplomatic correspondents, thanks to the information that comes to them from all sides, are also an important source of information for the diplomats. As a United States State Department staff member put it: "They [the correspondents] can give you more information than you can give them. Their job is to know everybody; and some of them keep excellent files" (Davison, 1975, p. 141). There exists a "diplomatic reporting network", which is characterized by Davison (1975) as a network of mutual dependencies that draws diplomats and correspondents into an elite community of foreign affairs specialists.

A lot can be learned from the way American politicians handle journalists. President Kennedy's information policy was criticized because he leaked news to favored reporters or gave them exclusive interviews or inside stories (Bateman, 1963). Kissinger was a master of the game with the press. Secretary of State under Presidents Nixon and Ford, he regularly supplied journalists with information, who quoted him as "a senior State Department official". Kissinger remarked on this:

> Everybody really knew that I was the senior official. The advantage of doing it in this manner was that it enabled foreign governments not to have to take a formal position about what I had said, and not to force me to take a formal position. Since everybody in the negotiations was, theoretically, pledged to secrecy, but at the same time, since everybody was giving a briefing on their own version, I felt it was important that the American version also available, so we all, played this complicated game. (J. Blyskal & M. Blyskal, 1985, p. 62)

The practice of passing on information "off the record", that is, unattributed and under a pledge of secrecy, is widespread in the United States. There is a high proportion of anonymous attributions in American media reports. As far as newspapers and magazines are concerned, their readers perceive fact or opinion stories to be as believable and accurate when unnamed sources are quoted as when named sources are quoted (Wulfemeyer & McFadden, 1986). Washington reporters revealed that more than one fourth of their interviews are off the record (Hess, 1981). This "necessary evil" can have positive, confidence-building consequences. A symbiotic relationship may form between the source of information and the journalist, so journalists obtain access to otherwise unavailable, confidential information. But the negative consequences should not be overlooked. Sigal (1973) wrote: "Reporters pay a price for access: they become dependent on their official source. Dependence combines three elements: some reluctance to offend news sources in the stories they write, considerable willingness to print whatever their sources tell them, and little or no insistence that officials take responsibility for the information they pass along" (p. 54).

The confidential passing on of information is actually a variant of the policy of withholding information. Journalists feel like they are taking part in important decision making and/or that they possess otherwise secret background information, so their possible motivation to "rake muck" is taken away. Leaking is the ideal complement to keeping information scarce, which is argued as necessary for reasons of state. However, it is those in power who decide what the security of a nation permits. According to an article in Time (October 13, 1986) a new FBI team was to track down anyone leaking classified information to the press. This move was in reaction to the exposure of the disinformation campaign of the Reagan Administration against Qaddafi (cf. chap. 7, section 7.1.2). In foreign policy there are also often conflicts of interest between politicians and journalists. Foreign policy makers want their specific definition of reality, their particular perception of the world, to spread, and will even prevent publication of certain foreign political happenings if they deem it appropriate.

Adaptation of foreign policy to the mass media means that politicians are accepting advices from PR. The dominating motive of political action is no longer the substantial quality of policy, but the creation of newsworthy events. To paraphrase Karl (1982), statecraft becomes stagecraft, and the PR practitioners know how news is selected by journalists. Bernays (1923) argued: "The counsel on public relations not only knows what news value is, but knowing it, he is in a position to make news happen. He is a creator of events" (p. 197). In his memoirs (1965) Bernays described how he advised the exiled Czech politician, Tomás Garrigue Masaryk, who had been elected president of the Czechoslovak National

Council, to issue his country's declaration of independence on a Sunday for PR reasons: because Sunday was a slow news day, so it would get more space in the world's newspapers. Bernays wrote:

> I had met Tomás Garrigue Masaryk, the Czech leader, some time before his assignment. At luncheon at the old Delmonico's, I had been much impressed with this teacher and philosopher for many years my senior. He fled Austria at the beginning of the war and became president of the Czechoslovak National Council. At lunch in 1914 I urged him to declare his country's independence on a Sunday. The slack news events of Sunday would give his declaration more space in the newspapers of the world. Masaryk was astounded. "That," he said, "would be making history for the cables." I answered that cables make history (p. 159).

Bernays (1965) emphasized the high symbolic value Masaryk possessed to the still-to-be-created Czechoslovakia. And Ignacy Paderewski, then a world famous pianist, later prime minister of the Republic of Poland, was equally valuable to Poland. At Bernays' suggestion, these two symbolic figures of the two oppressed nations joined together in 1918 to convene a mass meeting in Carnegie Hall "to protest Austrian domination" (p. 159). Masaryk and Paderewski stood shoulder to shoulder on the podium. Bernays said of the events: "Newspapers in this country [United States] gave the event some coverage -- we were still isolationist in our country -- but it made big news in Europe" (p. 159).

Manheim (1994) examined the head-of-state visits of Prime Minister Benazir Bhutto of Pakistan (1989) and of President Roh Tae Woo of Korea (1989) to the United States in the context of public diplomacy. He analyzed how each visit was planned, orchestrated, and conducted with United States and their home country media, elite, and public opinion in mind. Bhutto for instance, had signed a contract with lobbyist and political consultant Mark Siegel, who waged a campaign with the theme of democratic partnership. Siegel laid emphasis on the political elite and tried to create the impression that Bhutto was the guarantor for democracy.

Manheim wrote: "The centerpiece of the visit was Bhutto's address at the Harvard University commencement, where she called for the creation of an association of democratic nations, one in which the richest democracies would aid the poorest and through which economic and political sanctions might be applied against those nations moving away from the democratic ideal" (p. 85). According to Manheim the visit was a complete success.

Wooing the mass media, international and domestic, was the primary purpose of the 1994 visits to the beleaguered Bosnian city of Sarajevo by Benazir Bhutto and Turkish Prime Minister Tansu Ciller. The two leaders as "women, mothers and spouses," wanted to show their solidarity with the courageous women of Sarajevo. Before Bhutto went to Sarajevo her main political opponent, former prime minister Nawaz Sharif, had visited Bosnia and made a $3 million personal donation. The press in Pakistan glorified this as a heroic deed, so Bhutto was forced to counter in order to win the upcoming March 1994 elections.

President Reagan used foreign policy in the 1984 campaign to gain increased TV presence. He visited Buckingham Palace, participated in the Economic Summit in London, and attended the commemoration of D-Day in Normandy. This trip to Europe alone helped the President appear nearly irreplaceable. A month earlier Reagan had visited China. Hilton (1987) commented that while ". . . Mondale was campaigning at a bowling alley in Amarillo, Texas, Mr. Reagan has been appearing 'presidential' at the Great Wall of China in picture postcards for television -- thanks to a trailing press corps of 300 correspondents and technicians" (p. 176).

Important to image building are "pseudoevents" (Boorstin, 1961), events more or less deliberately staged to gain attention or create a certain impression. These make up much of media coverage. An example was the July 1983 action of Greenpeace in the Bering Sea. Members of Greenpeace deliberately violated Soviet territorial waters after having informed the mass media of their intention. Ostensibly, they were there to photograph illegal Soviet whaling, but in all probability their real aim was to be captured by the Soviets and thereby create a "news event". Greenpeace had earlier checked out the dangers of possible punishment by the Soviet Union. As Peter Dykstra of Greenpeace explained, "We consulted all available experts. If there had been any strong indication our people would actually have spent any time in harsh conditions of the prototypical Siberian labor camp, we'd never have taken that kind of chance" (Blyskal & Blyskal, 1985, p. 188). And, on the real objective of the PR stunt, Dykstra said, "Obviously, if the public supports what we did in the Soviet Union, they will support us [with funding]" (Blyskal & Blyskal, 1985, p. 188). Because of strong public opinion, clearly some countries actually feel threatened by Greenpeace actions. Grave damage to international image is done, at least in the short term, by such actions as the sinking of a Greenpeace ship by the French secret service or the subsequent treatment of those who committed the act. Relations between France and New Zealand were strained when, in 1985, French secret service agents attacked the ship _Rainbow Warrior_ in the port of Auckland. The ship has not yet left port to protest the French atomic bomb testing on Mururoa Atoll when it was sunk to prevent drawing world attention to the protest. France obviously felt that its policy was endangered and worried about its image as a "grand nation".

Gandhi staged pseudoevents in his struggle for liberation from the British. In 1930 he organized the march on the salt works of Dharasana and allowed police to batter several thousand demonstrators with long sticks with steel nails embedded in the end. More than 2,000 newspapers throughout the world reported this bloodbath. World public opinion condemned the British. An American senator read the report by a UPI correspondent in Congress. Physically, the police had been the victors, but morally they were beaten. E. Taylor (1947) pointed to another aspect of Gandhi's behavior as pseudoevent:

> When Gandhi mediates in public he is propagandizing with a nonverbal symbol, and the meaning of the symbol as intended by

Gandhi and understood by the crowd, can probably be most closely rendered in words by saying that it associates political and social action with the holiness which former generations of Indians ascribed to ascetic practices. . . . The symbol of withdrawal has become the symbol of struggle, but nobody could be expected to grasp this without understanding the revolutionary context of Gandhi (p. 225).

A smart way of coping with a pseudoevent was reported by Trento (1992). When the PR firm Gray and Company accepted the government of Angola as a client, the following occurred:

[Y]oung 'outraged' Savimbi backers picketed in front of Gray and Company's offices. First they tried to burn a hammer-and-sickle flag. Then they chained themselves to the railing's outside of Gray's new headquarters . . . This set up a showdown in which the best PR men got to battle it out. A Gray and Company senior vice president recalled a knockout blow with delight: "Frank Mankiewicz and I sent three Gray and Company employees down to the basement to get their car, and we gave them an empty video camera, and they drove around the corner and got out of the car . . . , and one of them had done a little bit of television work, and they walked up to the people who had chained themselves and said they were from Channel Five and they were doing a story. So we interviewed them -- lights, camera, the whole thing -- interviewed them for about ten minutes and then left. Frank said that as soon as we'd done the interview they'd leave, because all they were interested in was publicity. As soon as our people got in the car and drove around the corner, they all uncuffed themselves and left. So that's how we got rid of the demonstrators. We did a phony interview. I'm sure they're still turning on TV every night waiting for the six o'clock news." (p. 314)

Foreign policy is changed by television on another level, too. Leaders are in the center of public awareness before they have enough information to make rational decisions. Policymakers in democracies, being dependent on public support, are under permanent pressure to make decisions and are forced to decide immediately. If they delay decisions, which more often than not is the best course, the people may get the impression that politicians are refusing to meet their responsibilities. If under the influence of pictures disseminated by television (e.g., CNN) public opinion shifts all over the map and politicians are forced or believe themselves to be forced to follow these shifts, then the most important criterion of effective foreign policy is vanishing: the image of constancy and calculability. It can be argued, for instance, that the United States was drawn into the quagmire in Somalia under the influence of television. But television was also probably responsible for America's subsequent withdrawal from Somalia. As Considine (1994) put it, "The pictures of Michael Duran and other soldiers brutalized in Somalia set off a media and public clamour for American withdrawal. The frenzy prompted Secretary of State, Warren Christopher, to say that however useful television coverage was to national understanding, edited highlights and pictures taken out of context could not become the driving force for determining American foreign policy" (p. 11). But Considine maintained that "State Department sources had confirmed that news coverage was driving United States foreign policy" (p. 11). At least the quality of foreign policy has changed under the influence of television; possibly not a turn for the better.

There are indications that even warfare is being affected by media coverage. A NATO officer explained why the Allied forces declined to shoot down Serbian helicopters violating the no-fly zone: "Even if they were carrying arms, we worried that someone would stick civilian bodies in the wreckage just in time to be filmed by CNN" (Newsweek, March 14, 1994). Further, NATO commanders decided not to use napalm or cluster bombs, capable of clearing large swaths of terrain, in Bosnia because: "Bad TV. Napalm leaves it victims shrivelled and charred. Cluster bombs tear them into shreds. The West is worried how they might look on the nightly news" (Newsweek, April 25, 1994, p. 13).

Advertisements are even used to communicate between top politicians. In a country profile/advertisement, Lennart Meri (1994),

President of Estonia, emphasized that Estonia is not only sensitive to resurgent Russian nationalism, but also wary of the insensitivity of the West to some of Estonia's concerns. Then he attacked the German chancellor: "Mr. Kohl's recent comment that Russia was Germany's most important neighbour seemed to overlook some of us in between" (Time, July 4, 1994). Morocco, too, used Time as a diplomatic channel. In November 13, 1989 the weekly published a special advertising section: "Western Sahara: The Challenge of Peace", in which King Hassan's strategy against war was presented. The thrust of the advertisement was that Morocco guarantees Saharan prosperity. Within its defensive wall Morocco not only had kept Polisario at bay, but had also given the Sahara new economic life. Omar Hadrami, a founder and member of the Polisario, was presented as "The man who came home", and was quoted as saying: "Morocco has developed the Sahara. Our brothers in Morocco have prospered while we have been rotting away under tents. Total independence has now become impossible . . . The Saharan people must understand that Morocco, with its pluralist democracy and its policy of regionalization offers them every opportunity for self-fulfillment".

In the fall of 1994, during the conflict with Iraq, Hussein had concentrated troops at the Kuwaiti border. Kuwait's Foreign Secretary Sabbah el-Ahmed el-Sabbah used the German weekly Der Spiegel (No. 43, 1994, p. 181) as a channel of communication and publicly asked Iran's forgiveness for Kuwait's support of Iraq during the 1980 - 1988 Iran-Iraq War. The Foreign Secretary admitted that his country had made a great mistake.

A nation-state's international PR can be regarded as a kind of fifth column of foreign policy (fifth column was coined during the Spanish Civil War when General Franco, in 1936, attacked the Republicans with four columns and the fifth column was responsible for propaganda and espionage in the towns still under Republican control). Taken together, there are still few data about the precise role of public opinion in shaping the foreign policy of a country. But without a doubt there is a great awareness of the reporting about one's own country. It has become normal practice for embassies to try to correct mass-mediated images of their countries if they consider reports negative (e.g., via letters to the editor).

CNN, MEDIATION OF FOREIGN POLICY AND THE GULF WAR

The situation in the international media market has changed dramatically during the last few years with CNN (Cable News Network) entering the stage. During the Gulf crisis, CNN became known to a broad public worldwide through live transmissions of the press conferences of the American president, the addresses of Saddam Hussein, and its live reports from bombarded Baghdad. CNN, with its 24-hour news program, was already a way for governments to communicate directly with each other (e.g., the Soviet Union condemning the invasion in Panama). The most spectacular use of CNN, at least from my point of view, was made by ex-president Carter. In October 1993, television pictures of American soldiers brutalized in Mogadishu, Somalia, were seen by millions of viewers. American forces were hunting Somalian leader Aidid and President Clinton did not want to stop the chase. At the same time Carter communicated with Aidid via CNN. Aidid had let him know that he was watching CNN daily, hiding only in places in Mogadishu where he could receive CNN. Carter then invited CNN reporters to Plains, Georgia, where journalists asked Carter questions about Aidid and Somalia articulated in advance. Carter responded to the questions, General Aidid heard the answers on CNN, and, as a result, the United States flew Aidid to Adis Abbaba to start peace negotiations.

It is no secret among foreign correspondents that many of them, especially those working for newspapers, are no longer attending press conferences or locations where events are taking place, but instead are watching CNN in their hotel. Thus, a nation trying to polish its image will concentrate its efforts on getting CNN coverage. For example, in 1985 Morocco was being criticized for signing a treaty with Libya, Qaddafi then being the main scapegoat of the West. The PR firm Gray and Company, who was in charge of Morocco's image, organized and produced a PR package with a video news release. CNN (and Channel 5 in Washington) in March 1985 broadcast an exclusive interview with King Hassan II. Trento (1992) wrote: "In a standup outside the palace, a Gray correspondent warned viewers that the West should not react harshly to the treaty and that any criticism of Morocco should be 'tempered with the acknowledgement' of the country's strategic importance to the United States" (p. 20). Later, the Washington Post revealed that CNN was running video news releases as their own news stories.

During the Gulf War CNN's nickname became "Crisis News Network". The war was a media war, too, and CNN was an active combatant. The fighting started at television prime time: The first wave of attacks by Allied war planes reached Baghdad exactly at the time that the news was airing on the American East Coast. CNN correspondent, Peter Shaw, describing opening salvos of Desert Storm from al-Rasheed Hotel in the Iraqi capital, said, "You can hear the bombs now. This feels like . . . the center of hell" (Time, December 30, 1991). This kind of war reporting was new, and was the reason Time magazine named CNN's Ted Turner 1991's "Man of the Year": "The very definition of news was rewritten -- from something that *has happened* to something that *is happening* at the very moment you are hearing of it" (Time, January 6, 1992, p. 13).

Although CNN's reporting of the Gulf War was new, the control of information was the same as in most wars. Like Prince Albert during the Crimean War, the Americans wanted "No dead bodies". They were successful. The lack of information prompted journalists to focus on other journalists, like CNN's Peter Arnett. In Arnett, a new media hero was created and put on the media's agenda; reporters were reporting about a reporter. Never before did journalists deliver so little information with so many pictures and so many words. Later, reporters got only the information released by

General (Norman) Schwarzkopf, who presented his video show in battle fatigues. General Schwarzkopf even remarked to journalists that what they were about to be shown was no video game. Yet, what journalists in fact saw were as removed from reality as a video game -- war games with "smart bombs" in computer quality. As a Japanese saying so aptly puts it, war is the art of putting death in a favorable light (Virilio, 1986, p. 5).

According to MacArthur (1992) from the moment President Bush committed troops to Saudi Arabia in August 1991, the Administration never intended to allow the press to cover the war in any real sense. Ron Wildermuth, General Schwarzkopf's public relations man, drafted a secret memo (Annex Foxtrot) whose most important rule was: "News media representatives will be escorted at all times. Repeat, at all times" (MacArthur, 1992, p. 7). The flow of information was completely controlled: a perfect PR coup. The combat pool correspondent, William Boot (1991) remarked that he was " [. . .] one of the happy few who helped provide America with what Pentagon spokesman, Pete Williams, called 'the best war coverage we've ever had'" (p. 24). And The New York Times reporter Malcolm W. Browne, who was highly critical of the Pentagon's restrictions, said: "Each pool member is an unpaid employee of the Department of Defense, on whose behalf he or she prepares the news of the war for the outer world" (Manson, 1991, p. 23).

The media coverage of the Gulf War was totally different from that of the Vietnam War. For years on end television provided pictures of the fighting in Vietnam. In the Gulf War at first only the preparations for war were shown, a phase in which the enemy also got his say via CNN. In the preparatory phase there was information about how many dead were expected, but about the real war there was no uncensored reporting. CNN was also used by the White House to obtain war information. According to Time, whenever CIA Director William Webster received word via intelligence satellite that an Iraqi Scud missile had been launched, he would tell National Security Adviser Brent Snowcroft, "Turn on CNN to see where it lands" (Time, January 6, 1992). President Bush also watched CNN during the Gulf Crisis: "But as Bush followed the latest reports -- from C.I.A. and CNN television -- Iraqi tanks churned into the capital, forcing the royal family to flee" (Time, January 7, 1991). Schwarzkopf (1992) reported that one night early in February he turned on CNN and witnessed a live report from a pool correspondent saying that there had just been a major artillery duel in her location between the 82nd Airborne and the Iraqis. According to Schwarzkopf "any halfway competent Iraqi intelligence officer watching CNN could easily note the time and then canvas his forces to find out where precisely the exchange of fire had taken place. He would then discover the 82nd was positioned for a flanking attack, a fact we had taken great pains to conceal for the past three weeks" (p. 439).

Both sides in the war had instrumentalized the media -- particularly television -- for their strategic purposes, often without the correspondents on the spot or their home offices realizing it in time. Thus were the Allied Headquarters able to develop a refined system of disinformation, which deprived journalists of all self-control. On the other hand, Peter Arnett of CNN, the only correspondent from the West remaining in Iraq, became something like an involuntary ambassador for Saddam Hussein. He resisted this role as hard as he could but had to work within the limitations of censorship and deception of the Iraqi side. In the "war of images" (Time, February 25, 1991) waged in the mass media, Saddam Hussein was also a player, allowing reporting from Baghdad and Basra about the human side of the war, taking a line that had been recommended, as it were, by ABC's Ted Koppel, in a 1991 interview (Der Spiegel, No. 2, 1991). Koppel argued that if he were Saddam Hussein, he would invite American TV teams to Baghdad and tell them if they did not show their viewers what it looked like in Iraq, the Iraqis would show them. And he would, of course, try to give the news a certain twist, say by pictures of civilian bombing victims. Saddam Hussein did, indeed, try to use the emotional power of the television pictures by having pictures of civilian bombing casualties reach the American public. Saddam Hussein's assumptions, that America could not afford 10,000 dead whereas a million dead could not harm him, must be seen against the background of the different controls of the mass media.

Public relations and the media were at least partly responsible for the way the war ended. Schwarzkopf (1992) reported that after Kuwait City had been taken, his public affairs chief, Ron Wildermuth, informed him that: "All the reporters are heading for Kuwait City. It's the symbol they need for their stories and they're totally out of control" (p. 467). Schwarzkopf was phoned by General Colin Powell, chairman of the Joint Chiefs of Staff, who told him that "the doves are starting to complain about all the damage you're doing" (p. 468). Apparently, as soon as the area around Kuwait City had been liberated, reporters took pictures of Highway 6, where a convoy had been bombed earlier. It was a scene of utter devastation, referred to by reporters as the Highway of Death. Powell informed Schwarzkopf that the White House was getting nervous: "The reports make it look like a wanton killing" (p. 486). Schwarzkopf proposed to continue the war for another day, making it a "Five-Day War". Later that day, Powell called again. Schwarzkopf gave the following account of the conversation: "'I'm [Powell] at the White House. We've been batting around your idea about ending the war at five days.' He told me that in Washington the controversy over wanton killing had become uncomfortably intense -- even the French and the British had begun asking how long we intended to continue the war. 'The President is thinking about going on the air tonight at nine o'clock and announcing we're cutting it off. Would you have any problem with that?'" (p. 469). Schwarzkopf reported another call from Powell a few hours later: "We'll cease offensive operations, but there's been a change. The President will make his announcement at nine o'clock, but we won't actually stop until midnight. That makes it a hundred-hour war" (p. 470). Schwarzkopf's comment: "I had to hand it to them: they really knew how to package an historic event" (p. 470). Not only the beginning but also the ceasing of the war was at least partly influenced by decisions taking aspects of public relations into consideration.

But CNN's success during the Gulf War, with its unbureaucratic, event-focused journalism, does not mean that CNN is the only answer to the world public's need for information where events of international significance are concerned. CNN's limitations were aptly described by Keune (1991). In the first days of November 1989 he viewed CNN and simultaneously listened to the BBC World Service and Deutsche Welle on shortwave radio. On the radio, he heard reports that hundreds of thousands of people were demonstrating in the streets of Leipzig (then part of East Germany) and that there was a real possibility of a military intervention. At the same time this alarming news was on the radio, CNN was running, hour after hour, pictures of a dog from Alabama that could climb a tree. East Germany was only mentioned in passing. The fall of the Berlin Wall could not yet be spectacularly captured in pictures and a medium like CNN, which only wants to capture an event pictures as it is actually taking place, is ill-prepared to provide the analysis and background leading up to an event. CNN does not present the world itself, but an image of the world from the point of view of North American parochialism. (This is not the case, however, with CNN's World Report, where about 150 television stations and other news organizations contribute news items from 120 countries, so the news that is disseminated is produced from many perspectives around the world).

CHAPTER 4

Observations on Image Changes

IMAGE CHANGES AND SELECTIVE PERCEPTION

A famous comment by Lippmann (1922) applies also to the changeability of images: "For the most part we do not first see, and then define, we define first and then see" (p. 81). In other words, from the wealth of events and information available, we select those that conform to the already existing image. That is to say, to begin our perception at the level of the environment is relevant only to the extent that we already possess corresponding perception categories, for, to quote Burke (1935): "A way of seeing is also a way of not seeing -- a focus upon object A involves a neglect of object B"(p. 70). If we have a corresponding picture in our heads, there is no difficulty in processing even presumably contradictory information. Information that clashes with one's own prejudice simply can be ignored.

A field study by Kendall and Wolf (1949) bears this out. They tested the understanding of a cartoon series (Mr. Biggott Cartoons) ridiculing anti-Semitism. The hope that highly prejudiced individuals would identify with Mr. Biggott, then recognize the folly of Mr. Biggott's views, and finally notice how peculiar their own views were, was not met. The more marked the prejudice, the more often the cartoon was misunderstood.

So too can information in which one is not interested be ignored. For example, in September 1947, a six-month propaganda campaign to promote the United Nations was begun in Cincinnati (its slogan was "Peace begins with the United Nations -- the United Nations begin with you"). It was largely unsuccessful because those who paid attention to the message were primarily individuals already interested in and informed about the United Nations. It failed in spite of the fact that the population was bombarded with propaganda material: Meetings and speeches were arranged; pamphlets, leaflets, and posters were distributed; features were run in the newspapers and on the radio. The yield was negligible: Before the campaign 30% of the population had no idea about the general aims of the U.N.; after it 28% still had none. As Star and Hughes (1950) observed, "The conclusion is that the people reached by the campaign were those least in need of it and that the people missed by it were the new audience the plan hoped to gain" (p. 397).

With respect to the impact of the mass media it must be noted that identical factors can be perceived and used completely differently. Every perceiver selects from the great number of phenomena around him or her only a few, depending on life experience, and especially selects those that fit into his or her world view. The frame of reference within which perception takes place is decisive. Thus a worker will likely see a strike very differently than an employer. So too is the frame of references of central importance in the interpretation of "objectively" identical factors. For example, a shoe manufacturer sends two market researchers to central Africa and receives back diametrically opposed interpretations of data: One researcher sees fabulous opportunities to sell because hardly anyone is wearing shoes; the other sees no prospects because no one is wearing shoes.

In this context the so-called "hostile media phenomenon" must also be addressed briefly. Valone, Ross and Lepper (1985) proceeded from the observation that in readers' letters to newspapers and magazines, the same article was often attacked as one-sided, by persons with totally different views from one another. The assumption was that the mass medium concerned was taking a position hostile to one's own. Other also refer to the hostile media: Defeated candidates and retired politicians recall the "unfair treatment" they suffered from the press, spokespersons for various interest groups complain about "conspiracies" by the media to ignore or distort their concerns.

Valone et al. (1985) attempted an empirical examination of the perception of media bias. They collated a videotape of the massacre of civilians in Palestinian refugee camps (Sabra and Chatila), comprised of six excerpts of telecasts by ABC, CBS, and NBC in September 1982, and showed it to 144 students at Stanford University who were either pro-Arab, pro-Israeli, or neutral with regart to the conflict. Both those who had sided with the Israeli position and those who sided with the Palestinian position perceived the news report as contradicting their own opinion. Valone et al. posited two possible explanations: Either the two camps perceived the information differently (selective perception) or they judged identically perceived stimuli differently (selective evaluation). The data presented suggest that both interpretations are valid. Selective perception occurred when the supporters of the contrary positions assessed differently the proportions of pro- or anti-Israeli arguments, whereas selective evaluation took place when the viewers perceived the contents identically but differed in their judgments of fairness and objectivity, depending on their own views. Valone et al. (1985) further found that the more knowledgeable an individual is, the more likely the newscast is to be perceived as directed against one's own viewpoint. However, research into the hostile media phenomenon is still young. In Germany, Donsbach (1991), for example, can find nothing to substantiate this hypothesis.

Individuals are characterized by cognitive selectivity; that is, they tend to select certain objects from the physical and social environment and fit them into their own existing cognitions. And of the selected objects, only certain aspects are perceived, in turn, those that correspond to wishes, emotions, and so forth. Such cognitive selectivity depends on the qualities of the stimulus and on the personality traits of the perceiving individual. It is not possible, therefore, to infer directly and linearly any effect from the dissemination of content by the media because the psychological and social context of the recipients must be taken into account. So the belief held by many people, especially politicians, that the media are all-powerful and only have to shape their output properly to achieve whatever results they seek, is likely misguided. Nevertheless, this belief, that mass media content has a direct effect, appears to be ineradicable. But whereas many thought that the mass media had the power to synchronize or standardise whole societies, even the early empirical findings of mass media effect research disproved this simple stimulus-reaction model. Individual differences in people's personality organization -- for example, different motivation, ability to learn, attentiveness, awareness, and so forth -- were now taken into account.

Donsbach (1991) published an extensive study on the selective perception of West German newspaper readers that clearly confirms the phenomenon of de facto selectivity: In the precommunicative phase recipients choose those media that they assume follow an editorial line as close as possible to their own political persuasions. This implies that contact with information confirming one's own views is more likely than contact with information contradicting them. This holds, of course, only where there is a choice of free media. Donsbach was able to prove that newspaper readers prefer to turn to articles that they expect to confirm their own opinions. But -- and this is very important -- the selection rule applies only when positive information is offered; when negative information is offered, both supporters and opponents of a certain position behave almost the same: They heed it. In other words, the protective shield of selective perception works against information that might result in a positive change of opinion, but not against information that might produce a negative change of opinion. It seems Churchill was right when he said: "To build may have to be the slow and laboring task of years. To destroy can be the thoughtless act of a single day" (Howard, 1986/87).

According to I. L. Janis and M. B. Smith (1965) a country's attempts to improve its image abroad are characterized by a number of structural peculiarities. The most important of these is that, in the view of the recipients, the communicator is a stranger belonging to the outgroup, so messages that put to question generally held views meet with especially strong resistance. Further according to Janis and Smith, "The source of communication is suspect almost by definition. The audience will be quick to attribute propagandistic intent" (p. 191). This is one of the main reasons that image cultivation should be pursued indirectly, that is, so the country generating the propaganda does not become identifiable as the communication source. And typically, the images a country wants to change are undifferentiated black-or-white judgments, based on general consensus rather than individual experience. But if there is wide consensus about a country's image, many people feel no cause to change their position, especially when the country concerned is greatly relevant to one's own nation. It is also difficult for the "communicator from abroad" to reach effective communication channels. Finally, the communication coming in from abroad has to compete with "domestic" messages. In their literature analysis Janis and Smith concluded that "attempts at producing changes in political prejudices and stereotypes generally meet with an extraordinarily high degree of psychological resistance" (p. 195).

Summarizing I. L. Janis and M. B. Smith's (1965) observations, some of the major factors that can produce resistance to countries' attempts at changing images are:

1. The audience is disinterested in the theme; that is, people often ignore information that has no instrumental value for them or is thought to be incredible (so they switch off their radio or TV). The study by Star and Hughes (1950) discussed earlier is an example of how a target group failed to be reached.
2. If people inclined to avoid such information are reached anyway, the message can be modified by selective perception, by misperception, or by selective forgetting so that the effect sought by the communicator does not occur.
3. Even if the message is correctly perceived and interpreted resistance can occur; for example, the credibility of the communication source might be doubted.

Given all this, I certainly do not intent to imply here that mass media propaganda is ineffective, because despite resistance, a propaganda message, if it is perceived as credible, can be quite successful, even if it comes from an incredible communicator (cf. section 4.4). Especially promising in attempts to change images are "side attacks", that is, choosing minor or subsidiary issues that are expected to meet with little resistance. In other words, one tries to change images through the back door, as it were, and slowly to build trust. The findings by Donsbach (1991), that the protective shield of selective perception works asymmetrically, that is, that in contrast to positive information, negative information is not filtered out, suggest important consequences for any attempt at image cultivation: It is much easier to gain a negative image even among supporters of one's own position than to build a positive image among opponents of that position. Building a positive image is always a time-consuming and difficult process, whereas destroying a positive image or creating a negative one can be happened quickly.

But typically in the long run, images of nations once created remain stable. An outstanding recent example of image stability was the image problem caused to Austria by the former secretary-general of the United Nations and Austrian federal president, Kurt Waldheim, labeled "Nazi Kurt" in many American newspapers. Waldheim became the object of an unprecedented international campaign: He was awarded an "Amnesia International" prize during the Montreux film festival in May 1987 (the Swedish satirical sketch won the Golden Rose); he was put on the United States government's "watch-list", which is practically a ban on entering the country[1]; and the Israeli ambassador was withdrawn from Vienna.

---

[1] The U.S. Justice Department's Office of Special Investigation in April 1987 concluded that Kurt Waldheim, while serving as a lieutenant in the German Wehrmacht from 1942 to 1945 "assisted or otherwise participated"(Time, March 28, 1994, p. 29) in a list of Nazi horrors in the Balkans; for example, "the transfer of civilian prisoners to the SS for exploitation as slave labor; the mass deportation of civilians to concentration and death camps; the deportation of Jews from Banja Luka, Yugoslavia, to

The language the media used could not have been more blunt: no matter how often a worm squirmed, it remained a worm. The New York Post called Waldheim an SS butcher and alleged he had also robbed Greek Jews. Its headline read:

"PAPERS SHOW WALDHEIM WAS SS BUTCHER
Nazi-Waldheim robbed Greek Jews -- witness."

According to The New York Times Austria became a pariah nation because of Waldheim, and the Vienna newspaper Die Presse said that the duo Chile and South Africa, with Austria's joining, had become a "Trio infernal" (Der Spiegel, 4, 1988).

In 1987 the American-owned Paris-based International Herald Tribune even went so far as to address the Waldheim affair in a special supplement paid for by the Austrian state-owned industries (December 19/20, 1987). Along with Waldheim, the "Special News Report" also dealt with anti-Semitism in Austria. The report diagnosed an alleged "national neurosis" of the Austrians, caused by their frequent depiction as rustic simpletons -- millions in lederhosen and dirndl dresses. Austria was "more than Mozart and gemütlichkeit" the supplement said, and "soul-searching has become a national neurosis". The stereotypical Austrian as "a manikin in

---

concentration and death camps; the mistreatment and execution of Allied prisoners; and reprisal executions of hostages and other civilians" (Time, March 28, 1994, p. 29). The full contents of the long-withheld report were finally released in March 1994. Washington lawyer David Vladeck, who forced the release of the report, said, "there is an enormous amount of circumstantial evidence. But there is no evidence that shows that Waldheim personally ordered anyone to be executed or personally pulled the trigger" (Time, March 28, 1994, p. 29). The principal author of the Justice department document, Neal Sayers, was cited: "The report makes it clear that he was directly linked. One doesn't have to pull the trigger to be implicated in crimes" (Time, March 28, 1994, p. 29). Waldheim met every accusation with the same argument: He may have been in the wrong place at the wrong time, but he was not the man who did the wrongful deed.

short leather pants and a peaked hat with a feather or a strangely heathen gamsbart" was described as quite valid. That "the Austrians' greatest achievement was to make the world believe that Hitler was a German and Beethoven an Austrian" was described as not wholly undeserved. (The Austrian Adolf Hitler, speaking in Vienna after Austria was joined to Nazi Germany, welcomed his homeland's entering the German Reich; Ludwig van Beethoven was German, born in Bonn.) The supplement argued further: "But creeping quietly out of the history of the Nazi years was not a total success. Too much had to be swept under the carpet and too much did not fit the picture of the Austrians as the 'first victims of Nazi aggression'".

Austria's image was obviously endangered. Vienna's famous white Lippizaner horses, Mozart, waltzes, Sacher cream cake, and so on were no longer the dominant elements of the Austrian image. Instead, Waldheim and Austria's Nazi past were in the foreground. The prestigious Swiss newspaper, Neue Zürcher Zeitung, wrote in 1988: "The former First Lieutenant of the Wehrmacht on a scale which sweeps away all yardsticks of common sense has become a symbol of a despicable epoch, of which he continues to deny that he had ever identified himself with it" (Der Spiegel, No. 4, 1988). Ambassador Wolfgang Schallberg, in 1988 head of the foreign culture section of the Austrian foreign ministry, characterized the "new image" of Austria after the worldwide campaign against Kurt Waldheim in the following way: "The Austrians are horrific Nazis, but they happen to dance well" (Der Spiegel, No. 4, 1988, p. 130). But as was shown earlier (cf. chap. 2, section 2.8), Austria's image has remained stable: Austria is the Mozart country.

RESEARCH FINDINGS AND TRICKS OF THE TRADE

Studies analyzing the effects of persuasive messages are not discussed at length here as has been done extensively elsewhere (e.g., Hovland, 1954; Klapper, 1960; McGuire, 1969; Weiss, 1969).

Instead, only findings important to the theme of this book are cited without detailed sourcing. If one differentiates between communicator variables, effect-relevant aspects of content, and possible discrepancies between communication contents and recipients' attitudes, the main findings can be summarized as follows:

1. The credibility of the communicator is of decisive importance to successful propaganda.

2. If the intention of the communicator is perceived as aimed at persuasion, counterarguments are sought and the credibility of the communicator is doubted.

3. If one distinguishes between one-way and two-way argumentation then the following applies: (a) The use of pro and con arguments (two-way argumentation) is more successful with recipients who are originally of contrary opinion, have a higher level of education, and already know the subject area addressed; and (b) one-sided argumentation is more successful with recipients who originally hold the same opinion, have a lower level of education, and do not yet know the subject area.

4. As to the question of whether "strong" arguments should be brought at the start or the end of a message (primacy vs. recency effect), the research findings are not consistent. For an unknown theme (e.g., building a new image) it seems more advantageous to put the strong argument at the beginning because this can arouse attention. For a well-known theme, on the other hand, it is more advantageous to put the strong argument at the end because it can be remembered longer.

5. Whether it is more advantageous to draw conclusions from a chain of arguments or to leave this for the recipients to do -- which raises the credibility of the communicator -- depends on the complexity of the subject matter as well as the intelligence (respectively, the education and motivation) of

the recipients. There exists the danger that messages not explicitly stated may get "lost".

6. Intensive arousal of fear through propaganda produces hostility toward the communicator and endangers his or her credibility.

7. A message does not strike isolated individuals but people as a part of the group they belong to or wish to belong to, that is, the group they orientate themselves to (reference groups). If the message deviates too strongly from the norms of a recipient group, exactly the opposite of the desired effect may occur. For example, positions attacked may strengthen. This boomerang effect is defined as "adverse effects resulting from emphasis upon certain points with consequent distortion of related ideas" (Hovland, Lumsdaine & Sheffield, 1949/1965, p. 46). Optimal propaganda or image cultivation is possible if one succeeds in disseminating messages containing opinions pointing in the direction desired by the communicator, but not going so far as to incite rejection, that is, messages that are neither accepted nor rejected with regard to a given theme and are somewhat in the middle of the opinion of the recipients.

Propaganda does not mean outright lying, as the Nazi view would suggest. During the Third Reich, the Nazis had cut off the German population from information from abroad, so they were effectively living in a media prison. In such a situation state-controlled media can be very effective. But, propaganda does depend on credibility. According to Lerner (1949) "avoiding detectable lies was one of the cardinal rules guiding psychological warfare operations in World War II" (p. 195). Experienced propagandists avoided using true information if it was possible that recipients might think it was not true. So credibility has nothing to do with "truth" as such, but depends on the cognitive frame of reference of the target group.

There have been many studies about the tricks of the propagandists, usually motivated by the desire to help preserve democracy. Of course, the aim of some researchers may also have been to optimize the manipulation techniques. One of the reasons for founding the "Institute for Propaganda Analysis" in New York in 1938 was to ward off the effects of German radio propaganda transmissions which, according to Zeman (1964) were seen by many as the "biggest and most powerful propaganda machinery in the world" and thus perceived as "the most frightening institution for the spread of political doctrine" (p. 116). A. M. Lee and E. B. Lee (1939) argued: "Once we know that a speaker or writer is using one of these propaganda devices in an attempt to convince us of an idea, we can separate the device from the idea and see what the idea amounts to on its own merits" (p. 24). They analyzed the speeches of Father Charles Edward Coughlin, "the Radio Priest", who in the 1930s had developed an enormous popularity (his weekly Sunday discourse attracted about 40 million listeners). Coughlin, in the beginning of his radio career a Roosevelt supporter later denounced the New Deal as a communist conspiracy and Roosevelt as a dictator and wanted to change the United States into a corporate state very similar to fascist Italy (Brinkley, 1982). The Lees identified the following seven tricks of the trade:

1. Name calling -- giving an idea a bad label -- is used to make us reject and condemn the idea without examining the evidence.

2. Glittering generality -- associating something with a "virtue word" -- is used to make us accept and approve the thing without examining the evidence.

3. Transfer carries the authority, sanction, and prestige of something respected and revered over to something else in order to make the latter acceptable; or it carries authority, sanction, and disapproval to cause us to reject and disapprove something the propagandist would have us reject and disapprove.

4. Testimonial consists of having some respected or hated person say that a given idea or program or product or person is good or bad.

5. Plain folks is the method by which speaker's attempt to convince their audience that they and their ideas are good because they are "of the people", the "plain folks".

6. Card stacking involves the selection and use of facts or falsehoods, illustrations or distractions, and logical or illogical statements in order to give the best or the worst possible case for an idea, program, person, or product.

7. Band wagon has as its theme, "Everybody -- at least all of us -- is doing it"; with it, the propagandist attempts to convince us that all members of a group to which we belong are accepting his or her program and that we must therefore follow our crowd and "jump on the band wagon."

One of the major tasks of propagandistic image policy is the invention or use of propagandistically good slogans. Such slogans can be of an aggressive or inviting nature, or can be religiously, morally, or politico-strategically colored. From Greek antiquity comes this unsourced anecdote: a young ruler asks a philosopher what he should take into account when governing. The wise man answered: "King, clarify the concepts." Plato already recognised the problem. In Phaidros (263) he argues that rhetorics had to address the concepts that we are "unsteady" about and don't have consensus about. We could easily be deceived by such words. "If someone uses the word iron or silver, don't we all think of the same thing? But what about just or good? Doesn't then the one turn this way and the other that way, and are we not disagreed with each other and within ourselves?" That is to say, if thinking can be pushed into so poorly defined and hence extremely ambiguous words it cannot function critically, slithers out of control and finally leaves a state of fearful perplexity.

Words that are widely used, have a vaguely descriptive meaning and carry in them an intense emotional significance are especially suitable for propagandistic manipulation, words like democracy, reform, progress, justice, imperialism, socialism, and so forth. It is relatively easy to shift their descriptive meaning by defining or redefining them, without having to change the negative or positive emotional meanings attached to the word. For instance, although the former Soviet Union did not call itself imperialistic because it tied imperialism to a capitalist order of society, its actual behavior -- for example, the occupation of Hungary, Czechoslovakia, Afghanistan -- said otherwise. Another example is the use of the word socialism in the Nazi ideology. The Italian Fascists tried to justify their rule of terror to the outside world through the image of order achieved: "Trains run on time in Italy" became a famous slogan.[1]

One of the first political leaders to use the power of specific slogans was King Philipp II of Macedonia (b. 382 B.C., d. 336 B.C.), who unified his nation and made it supreme in Greece, laying the foundations for the great expansion accomplished by his son, Alexander the Great. Sturminger (1960) wrote: "Philipp's greatest diplomatic-propagandistic move was espousing the pan-Hellenic idea. When in pursuing his Macedonian great-power plans he set himself up as the executor of this programme this was to be the legitimation of his protectorate over the united Greece" (p. 58). And the French under Napoleon appealed to liberty, equality, and fraternity to pull other nations to their side (for other such image-cultivating slogans, cf. chap. 8, section 8.2).

Moral slogans contain such terms as honor, renown, prestige, and reputation. Otto von Bismarck in 1870, then prime minister of Prussia, transformed a message he had received from the king of Prussia from a surrender to a defiance, the so-called "Ems telegram", to convince the German public that the French had insulted the king and, for the sake of honor, there was no choice but to make war against France. The issue was the "exportation" of a

---

[1] Mussolini used the word fascism, which comes from the Latin fasces (a bundle of rods with protruding ax head carried by classical Roman magistrates as a symbol of office), to try to transfer the image of ancient Roman Empire onto Italy. At the beginning, the fascists did not have a bad image in the United States: A hit by Cole Porter contained the line "You're the top, you're Mussolini".

German prince, Leopold von Hohenzollern-Sigmaringen, to the Spanish throne, to which France objected. King Wilhelm I advised Leopold to drop the matter. Parties in both France and Prussia, interested in war, saw their chances for that war diminish and took action. After Leopold had already taken back his claim, the French ambassador tried to persuade the king, who was taking the waters at Bad Ems, to declare that he would forbid his cousin for all time to try to obtain the Spanish throne, a needless impertinence that the king rejected in a dignified manner. The king then had a dispatch composed about this conversation. Bismarck changed the contents of the dispatch and published the manipulated version. War broke out, costing several hundred thousand people their lives and leading to the founding of the German Reich, which all along had been Bismarck's aim. Soon after the tampering, Bismarck claimed openly that he had caused the war by means of this "Ems telegram", but it is likely that the Bonapartists, who dominated Napoleon III, would have insisted on war in any case.

Examples of foreign-political propagandistic catchphrases are imperialism, anticolonialism, Yellow Peril, pan-Germanism, European balance, splendid isolation, freedom of the seas, mare nostrum, pan-Slavism, warmongers, and self-determination right. Other such labels are Nibelungen-loyalty, strong and unwavering allies, determined and relentless revolutionaries, or reasonable and peace-loving states. Labels such as nordic colossus (Russia) or the sick man of Europe (Turkey) were used worldwide for a long time. And terms like reason of state, natural border, state security, encirclement, communist conspiracy, Jewish-Bolshevist conspiracy, and so forth can also be used to build up an enemy image. During the French Revolution, for instance, the British made use of the fear of the revolutionary ideas infecting people in Britain to agitate against France. Rumors were spread about an allegedly huge conspiracy at work. The government press tried to whip up panic, while at the same time the cabinet was negotiating with France over a possible alliance.

The negative image of Germany for a long time was grounded in the predominance of the notion of European balance (another catchphrase), the principal guideline for political actions. For a hundred years German foreign policy makers had been confronted by the problem of German policy being perceived as directed against the world-political status quo and of Germany as the supreme troublemaker. According to this concept, there could not be a state in Europe in which all Germans lived because such a state would be too powerful for the small Europe. The system of checks and balances, which guaranteed the stability of the whole system, would then no longer work, it was argued. Some propagandistic phrases of contemporary politics are Third World, North and South, rich and poor, backward and highly developed, metropolitan and peripheral. All are difficult to define and often have contradictory connotations. With such concepts as young and mature nations or late-capitalism, even certain historical processes are inferred.

But slogans, like any other concepts, can vary in meaning when compared interculturally. For example, the word mir means peace; however, it does not carry over the full English connotation. Peace in English means both the absence of war and the existence of a condition of tranquility. The condition of tranquility is not included in the concept of mir. The word compromise, as another example, has no equivalent in Russian. After his meeting with the Soviet leader Khrushchev in June 1961 President Kennedy argued in his report to the American people: "The Soviet and ourselves give wholly different meanings to the same words -- 'war', 'peace', 'democracy', and 'popular will'. We have wholly different views of right and wrong, of what is an internal affair and what is aggression, and above all, we have wholly different concepts of where the world is and where it is going" (Krech, Cratchfield & Ballachey, 1962, p. 283).

If a concept has different connotations, flawless communication is difficult. Yet even within a linguistic community, a certain concept can have different connotations. Mead (1974) pointed out, for example, that compromise means different things to Britons and

Americans: "In Britain, the word 'compromise' is a good word, and one may speak approvingly of any arrangement which has been a compromise, including, very often, one in which the other side has gained more than fifty percent of the points at issue . . . Where, in Britain, to compromise means to work out a good solution, in America it usually means to work out a bad one, a solution in which all the points of importance [to both sides] are lost" (p. 146).

It is even questionable whether familiar catchphrases like glasnost and perestroika are properly understood in the West. Colonel Fred E. Walker (1988), Chief of Psychological Operations Divisions Organization of the Joint Chiefs of Staff, argued:

> Gorbachev's reforms under his program of glasnost are being widely touted in the West. Many are being led to believe that this represents a welcome softening of formerly hard Soviet propaganda lines and a true opening of the closed society. In fact, one of the major propaganda efforts to sugarcoat this program seeks to convince people that the term glasnost means openness, where as a more accurate translation would be publicity. The right translation is more than a simple game of semantics; it could shape the debate about what constitutes an effective policy toward Moscow. (p. 47)

During the Cold War, when two clearly identifiable blocks confronted each other, catchphrases such as freedom, democracy, or free world were certainly loaded with different emotions than they are now, when the world is more differentiated. The positive image of the word democracy is used by the political leaders of many countries to create the false impression that their countries are democracies. Dictators like to occupy the word democracy or legitimate it by sham elections. Jerry Komia Domatob (1985) wrote: "African leaders publicly declare that their states are democratic and they proclaim their adherence to the Universal Declaration of Human Rights. Although a majority of these leaders are dictators, they prefer to transfer the positive image of democracy to give the impression that freedom, justice and equality reigns in their states"

(p. 197). But there is absolutely nothing new in that. Goebbels stated to the international press in Geneva on September 29, 1933: "The modern structure of state in Germany is a refined type of democracy in which by mandate of the people there is authoritarian government, without the possibility of parliamentary intervention fudging the will of the nation upwards or even making it fruitless" (Hagemann, 1948, p. 207).

Creating an enemy-image is another propaganda trick of the trade, creating among the population a feeling of being under threat, which in turn arouses a wish for strong leadership, or at least increases the readiness to tolerate authoritarian leadership. The bigger the threat is believed to be from a real or imagined enemy (the Russians, the Americans, the Chinese, etc.) the greater the feeling that strong leaders are needed. Building enemy-images can quite readily serve as a functional equivalent to war, that is, for the projection of internal frustrations outward. Sumner (1906) put it this way: "The relationship of comradeship and peace in the we-group and that of hostility and war towards other-groups are correlative to each other. The exigencies of war with outsiders are what makes peace inside" (p. 12).

Enemy-images have many uses. Authoritarian leaders in particular have a predilection for creating enemy-images. Alleged threats from outside (and/or from within) are put in the foreground. Enemy-images enable the population to be unified while at the same time diverting them from the frustrations they have to suffer while leaders try to realize personal aims. To achieve certain political objectives (e.g., programs such as "Star Wars") enemy-images (the "evil empire", as Ronald Reagan called the Soviet Union) are eminently suitable. Even eliminating an enemy-image can be relevant, particularly in domestic politics. Georgi Arbatov, director of Moscow's Institute for the Study of the United States and Canada, commenting on the effect on the United States of the new Soviet policies under Gorbachev, stated: "We are going to do something terrible to you -- we are going to deprive you of an enemy" (Time, May 23, 1988). Many years earlier Abraham Lincoln put it this way: "The best way to destroy an enemy is to make him a friend" (D'Amore, 1988, p. 23).

One must not forget, however, that the United States was the number-one enemy-image for the Soviet Union. As far as Soviet propagandists after World War II were concerned, the capitalist United States was the whipping boy for all the evil in the world: aggressive, imperialistic, and up to foul play. Politicians were described as "fascist hyenas" and "running dogs of imperialism". American development in and aid to foreign countries were labeled imperialistic tools for colonizing the countries concerned (Barghoorn, 1964, p. 59).

In many developing countries, too (many of which still have to find their national identities and are basically in permanent crisis), there is a great tendency to try to divert attention from internal social and economic problems by creating enemy-images (e.g., foreign imperialists and saboteurs). Attention was drawn to the great danger in this by then-president of Tanzania, Julius Nyerere (1973): "It is perfectly true that many of us in Africa are in danger of getting a phobia about foreign plots and attributing to foreign machinations all the evils we suffer from" (p. 111). Domatob (1985) pointed out that creating enemy-images by vilifying opponents is the done thing in Black Africa where emotionally loaded symbols are pinned on another country or its leader. He cited many examples from the domestic political field, where political opponents might be vilified as murderers, thieves, liars, cheats, or traitors, and leaders of states often relate to each other comparably: "Somalia's Siad Barre and Ethiopia's Mengistu Haile Mariam have horrible names for each other. 'Organiser of Pogroms', 'Son of Hitler', 'Killer' are just a few of their propaganda jibes at each other". Many Black African leaders use such derogatory adjectives as fascist, Stalinist, and Nazi to characterize other African leaders such as Idi Amin of Uganda or Jean Bedel Bokassa of the Central African Republic. Idi Amin denounced Nyerere as "a whore who spreads gonorrhea all over Africa" (Time, July 19, 1976, p. 15). This form of foreign political dispute, however, is also widespread in the European tradition.

But negative images of other nations can also be used for social comparison, for example when developing countries or entire continents like Africa are depicted as poorhouses governed by need, misery, and corruption. If one creates such an image (which may reflect reality, but that is not the point here) then there is a great likelihood of internal peace, of the population being content with its own situation, for contentment does not depend on the "real" quality of life, but on what is chosen as the basic comparative level by which to assess one's own social situation. A poor image of another country allows one to contrast it with one's own situation: One is, after all, better off than they are. For example, the information ministry of Malaysia requested that the country's press publish news that discredits other countries, hoping to divert attention from its own quite frequent human rights violations, an action they called "fair balancing of news flow" (Journalist, issue 10, 1988).

EXAMPLES OF ENEMY-IMAGES

The Red Menace

As mentioned in chapter 2, section 2.3, even privatly held companies either used the image of the Red Menace, if that was adequate for achieving their goals, or actively took part in the fight against communism. The discussion here is not, whether communism was a true menace (I have no doubt it was). Only the aspects of image building are dealt with here. Gilbert (1991) made it clear that, as early as 1919, Churchill believed that of "all the tyrannies in history the Bolshevik tyranny is the worst, the most destructive, the most degrading" (p. 411). Churchill regarded the atrocities committed by the Bolshevists as "incomparably more hideous, on a larger scale, and more numerous than any for which the Kaiser is responsible" (p. 412). On April 9, 1919, Churchill explained his policy to Lloyd George: "Feed Germany, fight

Bolshevism; make Germany fight Bolshevism" (p. 412). When Asquith's daughter in 1919 asked Churchill what his Russian policy was, Churchill replied: "Kill the Bolshie, kiss the Hun" (p. 412). On March 23, 1920 Churchill wrote: "I do not believe that any real harmony is possible between Bolshevism & present civilization" (p. 420). On November 18, 1920 Churchill denounced all evils of communism and characterized the leaders of the revolution as "wicked men", as a "vile group of cosmopolitan fanatics": "The policy I will always advocate is the overthrow and destruction of that criminal regime" (p. 426).

In America, too, after the end of World War I, the image of Bolshevism was used to frighten people. "Professional patriots" (those who tried to exploit patriotic impulses in the States) like the American Defense Society published pamphlets like "Back to Barbarism", an essay on how Reds were rousing "Negroes" to revolution (Hapgood, 1928, p. 205). Hapgood wrote: "The center of attack is of course the communist movement and all friends of Soviet Russia" (p. 13). The founders of the Ku Klux Klan, in "the most disgraceful but albeit successful public relations campaign" (Cutlip, 1994, p. 372) also instrumentalized the mass hysteria about the Red Menace. As Cutlip described it, "The Bolshevik Revolution in Russia had loosed a violent, unthinking Red Scare. Industrialists linked organized labor's efforts to organize unions to this Red Scare" (p. 383). In August 1919 Edgar Hoover was appointed head of the General Intelligence Division and assembled a file of over 200,000 Americans whom he considered to be communists or sympathizers of communism.

In 1934, when Upton Sinclair, the famous muckraker and socialist, was running for governor of California, his Republican opponents put into gear one of the dirtiest campaigns ever waged against a candidate. The campaign to smear Sinclair was managed by PR counselors Clem Whitaker and Leone Baxter who made use of the fear of communism. Hundred of thousands of SincLiar dollars, labeled THE RED CURRENCY and printed in red ink, were circulated through California. The fake bank note contained the motto ENDURE POVERTY IN CALIFORNIA and was "GOOD ONLY IN CALIFORNIA AND RUSSIA -- NOT VERY GOOD ANYWHERE". The note was "signed" by Utopian Sinclair; Governor of California. Cartoons also were used in the campaign. One depicted Hitler, Mussolini, and Stalin playing bridge and Sinclair asking: "May I Make a Fourth". Mitchell (1992) wrote: "All over California, shop owners coaxed customers, employers coerced worker, and newspaper editors courted readers, all in the name of 'keeping California out of the red, and the Reds out of California', as one popular slogan put it" (p. 336). Shortly before election day, leaflets were distributed showing a bearded Russian waving the Soviet flag over the map of California.

Without equating the American senator Joseph McCarthy to the Nazis here, there are, nevertheless, structural similarities. McCarthy claimed that America was under threat from a worldwide conspiracy and communist infiltration and destroyed a great number of political and artistic careers by branding people as dangerous communists. Cardozo (1970) remarked about McCarthy's motives: "Joe McCarthy's initial reasons for seeking out the 'Communists in government' was hardly as patriotic as it sounded. Actually, his own political ambitions prompted his first accusations. 'Communists in government' would make a good campaign issue for the 1952 election" (p. 373). Fortunately the United States of the 1950s was not the Germany of the 1930s, that is, McCarthy was not able to destroy the functioning democracy. However, Cardozo went on to level grave accusations against the American press: "If Joe McCarthy was a political monster, then the press had been his Dr. Frankenstein" (p. 375).

Matthias (1964) maintained that the former United States Secretary of State John Foster Dulles systematically built up the USSR as the enemy-image in the United States after World War II. American public opinion was quite friendly toward the USSR in general; therefore, argued Matthias, that perception had to be changed to a negative one: "Stalin had to be portrayed as a despot under whose government almost 200 million people groaned; as a 'slave holder', as an antipode to the culture and civilisation of the West and hence as an enemy against whom one needed to take defensive precautions in good time lest he should one day have the intention to expand his realm of slavery, to all of Europe and the entire world" (p. 115). However, Dulles' systematic enemy-image building in the case or the Soviet Union was not that simple. The Soviet policy was aggressive and expansive and Stalin was a dictator who cared nothing for human life. The enemy-image was no manipulated fiction but categorized as an existence-threatening reality.

The term Cold War, coined in 1946 by Herbert Bayard Swope, a journalist, became synonymous with the tensions of the post-World War II era. Lippmann popularized the term in a book in 1947. It was also a slogan, used first to characterize what was perceived as a Soviet Union potentially aggressive against the United States, although then still thought to be fundamentally weak. Churchill provided another image for the new age when on May 12, 1945 he telegraphed to Truman: "An iron curtain is drawn down upon their [Russia's] front. We do not know what is going on behind. There seems little doubt that the whole of the region Lübeck-Trieste-Corfu will soon be completely in their hands" (Gilbert, 1991, p. 844). According to Matthias (1964), because there was no American personality attractive enough for the task, Churchill was asked on March 5, 1946 to make an anticommunist speech in Missouri, President Truman's home state, in which the term *Iron Curtain* was used publicly for the first time to denote the Soviet Union's efforts to seal off itself and its Eastern European dependencies from free and open contact with the West and other noncommunist areas: "From Stettin in the Baltic to Trieste in the Adriatic, an Iron Curtain has descended across the Continent" (Gilbert, 1991, p. 866). It was necessary, Churchill said, to protect oneself against two sinister forces, namely war and tyranny. The speech is, at the same time, a telling example of how PR can influence media reporting, for in the media coverage of it the term Iron Curtain cropped up only rarely. The reason for that was quite simple: That passage of the speech was missing from the text handed out to journalists. Only later, when the verbatim transcript of the speech was released, did the appelation Iron Curtain become famous (Sigal, 1973, p. 106). Without such a powerful enemy-image, would the mighty military apparatus of the United States have been possible on that scale? In fact, the Cold War was a relatively riskless business. Yet on the strength of this enemy-image, a whole new United States industry, the arms industry, came into being.

Also worth noting in this context is the so-called domino theory, whereby the potential of a problem in one country evolving into problems in many countries is used to justify action in the first. Drake (1956) argued: "The Chinese communists are embarking on a plan of unparalleled audacity. Their scheme: to turn the Pacific into a communist lake fronting the shores of North and South America. Korea was the site of the first surge. It failed. South Vietnam is the latest . . . Communist conquest of South Vietnam would almost certainly trigger the downfall of neighboring Thailand and Malaysia and yield control of the Strait of Malacca to the Reds, permitting them to seal off trade routes, east, west, and south. It would also put the communists within the easy reach of their next targets of expansion: Indonesia, Australia and Japan" (Reader's Digest in October 1956).

The junta of Greek colonels who seized power in Greece in 1967 found the international publicity surrounding their cause to be extremely unfavourable and potentially disruptive to international recognition. Exploiting the communist enemy-image, "They hired a major New York public relations firm and soon full-page newspaper ads appeared carrying the headline 'Greece Was Saved From Communism', detailing in small print why the takeover was necessary for the stability of Greece and the world" (Kotler & Levy, 1969, p. 11). The Greek colonels also hired the British advertising agency Fraser to help improve their image and deployed cultural events for PR purposes, such as the Greek state-sponsored exhibition about Alexander the Great.

Thomas J. Deegan Co., a most successful New York PR firms whose clients included Time Inc., Coca Cola, and RCA, had a $243,000-per-year contract for 2 years with the Greek junta to do image cultivation (Newsweek, March 18, 1968, p. 70). A company memo makes clear what kind of activities were planned: "The Deegan company would help increase newspaper and magazine coverage of Greece's economy and why it is a good place to invest. An article in Fortune magazine -- the most prestigious business publication in the United States -- on American companies in Greece would be a realistic goal". Management at Fortune denied, however, that a story about Greece was planned or considered, and Deegan was still supporting their client: "We noted their intention to establish a constitution and return to an uncensored Greek press. If they don't follow that, the Deegan company wants no part of the Greek junta".

The junta's PR activities also were revealed by a reporter of the Washington Post, which had previously printed a letter to the editor in which Melina Mercouri, one of the most determined resistance fighters against the junta, had been accused of favoring a "Moscow-type 'democracy' for Greece" (Newsweek, March 18, 1968, p. 70). As it turned out, this letter had been written by the vice-president of a PR company (Burson-Marsteller Associates). Ultimately, however, the most positive PR event that occured for the junta was neither instigated nor staged by them: the marriage between the shipping magnate Aristotle Onassis and Jacqueline Kennedy. This was a no-cost PR campaign for Greece, which the colonels capitalized on by, among other things, releasing 67 political prisoners. When the socialists came to power in Greece in 1981, Prime Minister Papandreou hired the New York PR company, Fenton Communications Inc., for $6,000 a month to persuade Americans that there was nothing wrong with a socialist government (Buie et al., 1983).

In December 1991, when President Bush was confronted with the task of convincing the American public that aid should be given to the dissolving Soviet Union, he chose to "scare the American voter" (Newsweek, December 23, 1991, p. 15) using CIA director Robert Gates and the American ambassador in Moscow, Robert Strauss, to painted the vision of a USSR crumbling away, unable to prevent the proliferation of 27,000 nuclear warheads. Secretary of State James Baker warned in a 1991 address at Princeton University, that a nation in dire financial straits was ripe for a new tyrannical Stalin to seize power: "No one can dismiss the possiblility that darker political forces lurk in the wings". The Bush administration used a carefully prepared and coordinated PR offensive, much like that used to implement the Marshall plan, which in 1947 was approved by Congress because the threat to the United States by the USSR was exaggerated. As foreign minister Dean Acheson remarked at the beginning of the Cold War, sometimes it is necessary to reason in such a way that arguments are "clearer than the truth" (Newsweek, December 23, 1991, p. 15).

Reagan's image of the Soviet Union as the evil empire was unequivocal. On January 29, 1981 he stated: "The only morality they recognize is what will further their cause, meaning they reserve unto themselves the right to commit any crime, to lie, to cheat . . ." (Time, January 2, 1984, p. 6). In a sermonlike address to evangelical Christians in Orlando, Florida, early in 1983, Reagan called the Soviets "the focus of evil in the modern world" and the prime example of "sin and evil" that "we are enjoined by Scripture and the Lord Jesus to oppose . . . with all our might" (Time, January 2, 1984, p. 11). The function of this image of the Soviet Union was clear: to legitimate spending billions of dollars on the Star Wars program. But in the long run Reagan was right when he predicted on June 8, 1982 that, "The march of freedom and democracy . . . will leave Marxism-Leninism on the ash heap of history" (Time, January 2, 1984, p. 12).

The Jewish-Bolshevist Conspiracy

The Nazis created two major enemy-images: Jews and bolshevism. Ultimately, the two were paired to create the supreme enemy responsible for the great world economic crisis: the Jewish-plutocratic-bolshevist conspiracy that would use the Kremlin and Wall Street to destroy the German nation. In 1936 Goebbels gave a speech at the Reich party congress in Nuremberg addressing the theme of "bolshevism in theory and practice." He said, "Bolshevism could have its origin only in the Jewish brain" (p. 3). And in the address to the 1937 Nuremberg party congress Goebbels imputed "a largescale and cunningly executed campaign by international bolshevism against the decent world" (p. 5).

Like the witchhunters of the 16th, 17th, and 18th centuries, who believed there was a worldwide conspiracy of the devil, the National Socialists believed there was a conspiracy of international Jewry. Thus an order to the press by the Reich government on April 29, 1943 stated in part: "Moreover, the Jew must now naturally also be attacked politically in the German press. In every matter it must be stated that the Jews are at fault. The Jews wanted the war! The Jews prepared the war against Germany throughout the world! The Jew is escalating the war! And again and again: the Jew is to blame!" Propaganda minister Goebbels stated: "The Jew is the pussy boil on the body of our national identity. Either he will destroy us, or we put him out of action" (Stephan, 1949, p. 179). In the official language of the day Jews were not humans, but subhumans who had to be cut off the German racial body. The link between the Christian witchhunts, which claimed the lives of millions of innocent victims, and the extermination of the Jews by the Nazis was strengthened when the Reich SS leader, Heinrich Himmler, proposed in all seriousness the convening of a commission to investigate Jewish ritual murders of children -- a crime of which witches have been accused through the ages. Just as the extermination of witches was officially declared a sacred and grave duty for Christians, so was the extermination of the Jews a national task, a grave duty for the Aryan race. The perversity of the Nazi logic is chillingly evident in the speech Himmler made to SS group leaders on October 4, 1943:

I also wish to mention to you here in all frankness a grave matter. It should be brought out in the open among us here for once, but we shall not mention it in public. I am talking about the evacuation of Jews, the eradication of the Jewish race. It is one of those things that are easy to say. Every party member says "The Jewish people will be exterminated -- quite clear, it's in our programme; getting rid of the Jews, we'll do it". And then they all come along, the well-behaved 80 million Germans, and each one's got his decent Jew to show. Sure, all the others are pigs, but this particular one's a decent Jew. Of all those who talk like that, no-one's watched, no-one was able to see it through. Most of you will know what it's like to see a hundred corpses lying together, or 500 lying there or a thousand lying there. To have come through that and in it -- with exceptions of human weakness -- to have remained decent, that has made us hard. That is a never-written and never-to-be-written page of fame in our history.

The objective here is not to again pursue the story of Nazi propaganda (there is a vast body of literature on that), but to show the manipulated change of the enemy-image. On August 23, 1939 Germany and the Soviet Union signed a nonaggression pact in Moscow. The previous day, journalists had received the following order from the Reich press office on how the pact was to be commented on: "The news has acted like a bombshell all over the world. The decision represents a sensational turning point in the relations between the two countries, and it reaches back to the traditional community of German-Russian interests . . . While the democracies talked, we and the Russians have acted." Further, reference was to be made to common economic interests and ideological differences were to be ignored.

As anti-Soviet propaganda was toned down in Germany, so too was the enemy-image of the Nazis softened in the Soviet Union. Leonhard (1955), a German who had lived in the Soviet Union since 1935, described the consequences of the pact on the mass media: "The word fascism no longer appeared in the Soviet press at all. It was as if there had never been any such thing as fascism" (p. 65). Before the German attack on the Soviet Union on June 22, 1941, the Soviet press with increasing frequency blamed Britain and France for the war. The change in enemy-image as influenced by the German-Soviet pact in August 1939 can be seen in changes in May Day slogans, as discussed by Yakobson and Lasswell (1949). In 1938, "Fascism was treated as the worst enemy of international order and of existing friendship among the nations of the world". But in 1940, "The Soviet government was on its guard not to antagonize the Masters of Germany". It was still much the same in 1941, that is, until the German attack on the Soviet Union: "The Soviet government was anxious not to affect adversely, by any hasty or unfriendly word, the established understanding with Berlin".

The anti-Semitic vision of the conspiracy of international Jewry persists. The Polish cardinal Josef Glemp (1989) asserted that the Jews control the world media and wage a campaign against Poland (Die Zeit, June 8, 1989, p. 2). Right-wing Russian politician Vladimir Zhirinovsky believes in a worldwide Zionist conspiracy. He argued that Mossad and the CIA were involved in the dramatic drop of the value of the Russian ruble in October 1994: "It's well known that finance and the press in America -- and also in Western Europe and Russia -- are controlled by Jews" (Zhirinovsky in Time, November 21, 1994).

The Fabulous Orient

Orientalist Said (1979) pointed out that the Orient was almost a European invention, and had been since antiquity a place of romance, exotic beings, haunting memories and landscapes, remarkable experiences. And this constructed Orient helped define Europe (or the West) as its contrasting image, idea, personality, experience. How the image of Arabia was created in Europe is demonstrated by the following episode: In 1877 the Austrian poet Peter Rosegger, who also edited a newspaper, wrote to a friend: "Recently I received an article for my newspaper from an author named Karl May. The article is called "Die Rose von Kahira. Ein Abenteuer in Ägypten" ("The rose of Kahira. An adventure in

Egypt"). The story is written in so skillful and thrilling a manner that I have to congratulate myself. There can be no doubt that this man has lived in the Orient for a long time". In fact, however, Karl May (1842 - 1912), who for nearly a century had greatly influenced the German image of Arabs and Arabia by then had never left Germany. His sources were all from the local lending library.

Another European, whose writings strongly influenced Karl May, however, had gone native: the English adventurer and traveler Sir Richard Francis Burton (1821 - 1890), who had even been to Mekka and Medina, places forbidden to Europeans. In his 1855 book <u>A Personal Narrative of a Pilgrimage to El-Medinah and Mecca</u>, Burton described the "Kayf" of the Arab, the dreaming quietness and idleness (juxtaposed against the European saying "Idle hands are the root of all evil"). The Bedouins of the desert were Burton's noble savages. In fact, when Karl May invented his hero Kara Ben Nemsi, the "Effendi el kebihr", he relied greatly on Burton. Pierre Loti (1850 - 1925) was Karl May's French counterpart. He created in his books a world of the harem that was sultry and decadent and corresponded to the prevailing taste, inspired by Burton. His dreams of the exotic Orient were pure escapism; he wanted to escape the realities of life in France. At the begginning of the 19th century, when Napoleon invaded Egypt, nothing there was familiar to the Europeans. Travellers marvelled at everything they saw. The sheikh, sitting cross-legged by the hour on his divan, appeared to be merely apathetic and dull. Europeans did not realise that the sheiks were anything but apathetic and dull: they didn't realise that they were the men of law and religion in the community and that they were greatly respected for their decision-making.

Paintings too were important image shapers. Eugène Delacroix's (1828) famous picture "The Death of Sardanapal" showed the power of Oriental despotism -- the Assyrian King Sardapanal destroying all his property, including his wives. Of course, the picture was painted before Delacroix had ever been to an Arab country (in 1832 he traveled to North Africa). The famous picture shows naked women being killed by "Arabs". Other famous paintings were "The Slave Market" by Jean-Léon Gerome (1866), which showed a powerless naked woman and Arab slave dealers, and "The White Female Slave" by Jules Jean Antoine Lecomte du Noüy (1888) (again, of course, the girl was naked). The supposed irrational violence of the Arabs was the motif of "Execution Without Verdict Under the Kalif of Granada" by Henri Regnault (1870), which portrays a man beheaded by a horrifying executioner. Oriental law was seen as irrational, European law as rational. Besides naked women, which allowed the sexually frustrated European men to project their own sexual desires on foreigners, Arab horsemen and crusaders at war was a frequent subject.

Movies also projected a certain image of Arabia. Rudolpho Valentino, the Latin lover of Hollywood, appeared in The Sheik in 1921, which was an enormous success. And in 1926 he performed in The Son of the Sheik. The movies even influenced the way people talked and dressed and did their hair. They gave the language new catchphrases ("Come with me to the Casbah"; from the movie Casablanca). The verb to sheik, popular in the 1920s, derived from Valentino's activities in his desert pictures. And Boris Karloff in The Mummy (1932) did his best to shape the image of Egypt. The wartime fashion of women's turbans in the United States and Great Britain was inspired by the oriental extravagances of actress Maria Montez.

So-called classical literature also transports images of Arabs. Shakespeare's "Antony and Cleopatra" (1608) is the tragedy of a rational White man, invincible as commander-in-chief, who weakens in the presence of the exotic queen. Elizabeth Taylor and Richard Burton continued this tradition. Peer Gynt, the famous hero created by the Norwegian author Hendrik Ibsen, lives his last days in a lunatic asylum in Cairo. The beautiful Bedouin woman Anitra robs Peer Gynt and leaves him in the desert. Nathan the Wise by Gotthold Ephraim Lessing deals with the Crusades and the world of Saladin. Then there are The Book of a Thousand and One Nights and the tales of the adventures of Sinbad, the Persian merchant.

Opera also perpetuated this image of the Arabs, for example, Mozart's "Entführung aus dem Serail" (Abduction From the Serail) or Richard Strauss' "Salome", which although Jewish, paints a picture of oriental confusion. Most spectacular was the first performance of Guiseppe Verdi's "Aida" in Cairo, whose images, in fact, in many ways corresponded to reality. The Khedive Ismail was a corrupt, profligate, power-hungry ruler who exploited his people and ruined his country. For the opening of the Suez Canal in 1869, Ismail imported 500 cooks and 1,000 other servants from France and Italy to serve 6,000 guests with the most expensive food and wine. Then in Cairo he built his opera house and commissioned Verdi to write "Aida" for its inauguration.

European historical experience has also contributed the Arab image. Spain up to 1492 fought to expel the Moors. The Turks laid siege on Europe, advancing even as far as Vienna. And on May 25, 1453 the Turks took Constantinople, a Christian bastion for a 1,000 years. The Christian Occident saw itself up against a huge and powerful enemy -- aggressive Muslims threatening Europe. People believed then and still do today in an exotic and dangerous Arabia located in some undefined place and time.

Today the image of Arabia in the Western mass media, especially in entertainment fare, certainly is not positive. Ambassador Amin Hilmy (1975), the Arab League's representative at the U.N. said: "We have been very bad at advertising, at public relations for many years; but we have improved, and we will continue to improve" (Time, June 23, 1975). The ambassador continued: "Today the picture that was painted of us -- as mentally retarded cowards who couldn't handle modern machinery and would not stand and fight -- has been disproved. Now Americans know that's wrong. Instead of our having to plead with them to listen they ask us to tell them more". Shaheen (1981) argued that the Arab has become the latest victim of media stereotyping: "Arabs are shown as oil-rich moguls intent on exploiting the American economy, or as faceless terrorists murdering innocent people" (p. 89). Shaheen cited a Hollywood producer as saying: "The Arabs are the last barbarians".

It should be mentioned here that Israel always has had an interest in perpetuating a bad image of Arab countries -- and sometimes the Arab countries did their best to help Israel. Especially during the government of Gamal Abdel Nasser in Egypt (1954 - 1970) the Arab mass media campaigned to stir up hatred of Israel and build up a sense of mission in the Arab peoples. The creation of this enemy-image was intended at the same time to divert attention from their own domestic failings. Branded as imperialists, Zionists and colonialists, the Israelis adroitly turned the Arab hate propaganda to their own advantage. Koschwitz (1984) commented on this: "Skilfully they planted their rhetorical propagandistic excesses in the international press, thereby alarming Western public opinion and cementing in it a negative image of the Arabs. Hence the Arab propaganda became a precious fountain for gaining the sympathy of a broad international public" (p. 344). The Arabs more or less became prisoners of their own propaganda and were seen primarily as the aggressors against underdog Israel, who had to defend itself against vastly superior numbers.

But the image of the Arabs in the Western media has become improved: Starting with Sadat's visit to Jerusalem, Israel's media image began to worsen compared to that of the Arabs. Many journalists covering that event portrayed Begin as intractable, inflexible, and incapable of peace visions, in stark contrast to Sadat. Indeed, international criticism of Israel reached its first climax during its 1982 intervention in Lebanon. The empathy of most journalists appeared to have shifted to the Arabs. Although there was comprehensive reporting of events in Lebanon, the destruction of one of the world's oldest towns, Hama, in Syria by Syrian troops, who on President Assad's orders acted with incredible brutality against their own people (5,000 - 10,000 people were said to have been massacred) generated little attention in the coverage of the Middle East.

No doubt contributing to criticism of Israel was the reporting of the 1988 uprising in the occupied territories. In fact, in October 1988 the Israeli government withdrew the accreditation of three foreign correspondents -- the bureau chief and one correspondent of Reuters and a correspondent of the Financial Times -- for allegedly breaking the censorship rules. The television coverage of the actions of Israeli soldiers against the rebelling Palestinians, in the view of PLO foreign minister Farouk Kadoumi, had another consequence: Because people around the world could daily follow the uprising on television news, he suggested, the situation had become a lot more positive for the Palestinians: "The world community is now much more willing to accept the idea of a Palestinian state than it was before the Intifada" (Der Spiegel, No. 34, 1988).

In European mass media intellectuals coming from Arabia are promoting an image of Arabic backwardness and missing democracy (here image corresponds to reality). For example the born Syrian, Ali Ahmed Siad (Adonis), argues that in the Arabic world there is no freedom of thought, no possibility to criticize. And Tahar Ben Jelloun, born in Morocco, complains that there is no democracy in Arab countries (Zeitmagazin, No. 15, April 5, 1991). Of course, some people or institutions are interested in perpetuating a negative image of Arabia: They need a scapegoat. Jerusalem's mayor Teddy Kollek said after the stabbing death of a German tourist in Jerusalem's Old City in October 1991: "The cultured world does not understand the type of people who want to solve problems by either blowing up airplanes or by killing tourists. Regrettably, this is in the character of the Arab nation" (Newsweek, October 14, 1991). No doubt an inadaquate description of Arabs, but as already mentioned, there is sometimes no connection between image and reality.

The New Scapegoat: Japan

Between 1639 and 1853 Japan lived in complete isolation. Then, on July 8, 1853 the United States "opened" Japan, resulting in a crash transplantation of technology and a modernized Japan. They became an imperial power, gaining Taiwan in the 1894/1895 war with China and defeating Russia in 1904/1905 in land warfare (Mukden) and in naval warfare (Tsushima). According to the German orientalist Steinbach (1992) even today the victory at Tsushima is important to the image of Japan among Arab intellectuals, who hope to modernize their region in a way similar to Japan's: to be successful in technology and yet preserve old traditions and culture.

Wilkinson (1981) pointed out that the Japanese government had already begun in the early Meiji period to present a modern image of Japan to foreigners. In 1898 the Foreign Ministry began collecting comments about Japan in foreign newspapers. Wilkinson reported that, during the Russo-Japanese War, the Japanese government tried to correct the image of the Yellow Peril: "Newspapers were bribed, editors were offered decorations, journalists were taken on junkets, and friends of Japan were encouraged to express their views; a special press agency to disseminate news about Japan was set up in Germany and roving officials were seconded from their regular duties to go to Europe and America to argue, refute, and propagandize" (p. 265).

As of 1930 Japan had built the third largest navy in the world, yet in the United States the Hearst press was pushing the image of the Yellow Peril (O'Keefe, 1972). According to Wilkinson (1981) in the 1930s Japan made a deliberate effort to justify Japanese actions in China through radio broadcasts, pamphlets, specially commissioned books, goodwill missions overseas, and tours of Japan for foreign visitors. During the period 1931 - 1933, Japan had won control over Manchuria. Then in 1937 Japan invaded China. News reports to the American public told of Japanese massacres (e.g., in Nanking where about 200,000 noncombatants were murdered). President Roosevelt wanted to isolate Japan (in fact, he used the word quarantine) and stigmatized her as one of the "three bandit nations" (Germany and Italy being the other two; Freidel, 1990). Japan's image today is still determined by her aggression. As Peng Jinzhan, Deputy Director of the Institute of Japanese Studies at the Chinese Academy of Social Sciences in Beijing and expert of Japan, said: "We intend to trust them. But it's hard" (Newsweek, September 12, 1988, p. 17). And in 1973, students in Indonesia (members of the National Pride Committee) protested against Japan's cultural imperialism (Anderson, 1980).

In 1932 the Japanese were perceived as intelligent, industrious, progressive, shrewd, sly, quiet, imaginative, alert, suave, neat, treacherous, and aggressive. Then, on December 7, 1941, Japan attacked Pearl Harbor, a deed that President Roosevelt said "will live in infamy". Indeed, 50 years later, both <u>Time</u> and <u>Newsweek</u> published cover stories on the Japanese surprise attack. And the image of Japanese after World War II was that of being sly, treacherous, and extremely nationalistic (Katz & Braly, 1958). This Japanese enemy-image was instrumentalized by the Dutch, who themselves had suffered under German aggression, to justify the waging of a brutal colonial war in Indonesia as a war of liberation (Pollmann, 1991).

The image of Japan is, as already mentioned, closely connected to China's image. In the 1930s the Japanese were the aggressors and the Chinese brave patriots defending themselves. Then, during World War II, the image of Japan became more negative. For instance, they were regarded as insane suicidical fanatics. After World War II their image changed again, to being progressive, peaceful, and friendly. According to Wilkinson (1981), apart from the Tokyo Olympics the most effective piece of public relations "was the decision in the 1960s to present an image of Japan as a northern country both technologically advanced and of great scenic beauty" (p. 266). Japan was not to be confused with a tropical Asian country. In recent years, however, because of their economic success the image of Japan again is negative.

On March 23, 1992, <u>Time</u> columnist Charles Krauthammer summarized American public opinion concerning Japan: "The emerging consensus is that Moscow's successor in infamy is Tokyo, which stands accused of mercilessly shelling the United States with reliable cars" (p. 56). The success of Michael Crichton's (1992) best-seller *Rising Sun* was a strong <u>indicator</u> of Japan's new negative image. A review in <u>Newsweek</u> characterized the book as a caricature, full of anti-Japanese sentiment comparable to anti-Semitic stereotypes; a thriller that defines Japanese national character as bad (Newsweek, May 18, 1992). Like the Jews in the Nazi-movie *Jud Süss*, the Japanese are portrayed as unscrupulous, clever, and mysterious people who care only about their own interests. Intent on impoverishing the rest of mankind, they are a disciplined people who manipulate the mass media, control the banks, and steer corrupt politicians like puppets on a string.

Crichton is not unique. Choate (1990) is thoroughly convinced that Japanese lobbyists are manipulating America's economic and political system. The right of foreign lobbyists to operate legally in the United States leaves the political system open to intervention by Japan. The real work is done behind the scenes by people of substance (the so-called Chrysantemum Club) representing Japan's interests. In Choate's view Chrysantemum Club members put "the relationship" (p. 99) ahead of economic issues. Americans for hire, according to Choate, are responsible for Japan's success in the United States. Massachusetts Institute of Technology (MIT) economist Paul Krugman maintained: "The widespread perception that Japan plays by different rules is basically right. That is not a moral judgement. It's just a statement of facts"(Newsweek, November 25, 1991, p. 46).

In the United States there have been "Buy American" campaigns, aimed especially at reducing the import of Japanese cars. LeBard und Firedman's *The Coming War with Japan* became a best-seller even in Japan and sold about 40,000 copies in the United States. The authors prophecy that there will be a war between Japan and the United States within the next 20 years, contending that the issues are the same as they were in 1941: Japan needs to control access to its mineral supplies in Southeast Asia and the Indian Ocean Basin and to have an export market it can dominate politically. To do this, it must force the United States out of the western Pacific.

That negative stereotypes of Japan are popular is reflected, for example, in an interview with management guru Peter Drucker.

Drucker's assumption is that the *postbusiness society* of the 21st century already exists: "Business is still very important, and greed is as universal as ever; but the values of people are no longer business values, they are professional values. Most people are no longer part of the business society; they are part of the knowledge society" (Time, January 22, 1990). The world be consist of three blocks (Europe, North America, and Asia) competing with each other. The interactions between the three blocks, according to Drucker, should be governed by the norm of reciprocity: "Reciprocity is a two-way street, and that is not the Japanese way of doing business. It is a threat to them. But in some ways Japanese industry is way ahead of the government". And presidential candidate Ross Perot during his election campaign attacked PR firms representing foreign interests, especially Japan's and Germany's (Cutlip, 1994).

The enemy-image of Japan is also perpetuated in advertisements. In The New York Times (September 6, 1990, p. B2) a full-page advertisement was published by Boone, Co., Dallas, Texas, with the following headline: "America, You Lost the Economic War!" The text continued: "That taunt was hurled recently at Boone Pickens and 50 American shareholders in Japan, along with 'Yankee go home!' and 'Remember Pearl Harbor!' . . . They were laughing at us -- because they know corporate Japan has it both ways. They can buy anything they want in America, but keep us out of Japan." Following this are accusations of unfair business practices. Toyota Motor Co. is singled out as the most effective Japanese cartel. Furthermore, Japan is blamed for dumping and for shirking their duties in the foreign policy arena: "The Japanese refuse to play on a level playing field . . . Now Japan is even refusing to fully support America's military effort in the Middle East where Japan gets all of its oil to fuel its economic machine." The ad closes with the appeal: "It's Time to Fight Back!" The Allen-Edmonds Shoe Corporation published an advertisement attacking Japanese import barriers (Onkvisit & Shaw, 1989): "Keep your shoes to yourself. That's the clear message the Japanese government has given Allen-Edmonds and other United States shoe manufacturers. Tough licensing, even tougher tariffs and various other obstacles are making it nearly impossible to do business in Japan" (p. 92).

In an interview with <u>Time</u> Shintaro Ishihara, together with Sony Chairman Akio Morita, author of the book *The Japan That Can Say No*, argued that American shareholders of Japanese enterprises had to adapt to the Japanese rules and had no right to demand American norms to be applied in Japan. In such a case, they asserted,, a clear "No" was the only answer as it was the case with T. Boone Pickins who is called "a man with a disreputable reputation." (<u>Time</u>, November 6, 1989).

How sensitive American public opinion is to Japanese companies' misdeeds was demonstrated by the storm of indignation when, in 1987, it was revealed that a subsidary of Toshiba Machine Co. had illegally sold sensitive military technology to the Soviet Union. According to Manheim (1991) there was an immediate expression of outrage in the United States and strong pressures to exclude Toshiba from the market. The potential cost of a ban was estimated at about $10 billion. Manheim (1994) wrote: "In concert with the Japanese government, Toshiba mounted a campaign to prevent trade sanctions from receiving final congressional approval. In all, the company spent an estimated $20 million on this effort, which was characterized by its Capitol Hill targets as the most massive lobbying effort they ever had experienced" (p. 33). Representative John Bryant (1987) commented: "Toshiba was able to purchase access to those who were writing the legislation. They won, but what they did was very offensive" (<u>Business Week</u>, September 14, 1987, p. 58).

Japan is attacked not only on the economic front but also on the environmental one. Japan was a scapegoat for the Animal Welfare Institute, which advertised in <u>Time</u> (December 11, 1978): "SAVE THE WHALES!" They attacked Japan, the Soviet Union, Norway, and "a handful of other nations" for systematicallly wiping out the highly intelligent great whales, and pointed out that the whaling nations have repeatedly rejected appeals by the United Nations for a 10-year moratorium on commercial whaling: "Japan reportedly used economic blackmail against Panama in June 1978 to force Panama to withdraw its moratorium proposal at the International Whaling Commission (IWC)." They exposed Japan and Norway as circumventing the meager whale conservation measures of the IWC. The Animal Welfare Institute went on to accuse Japan buying illegally caught whale meat and Norway of selling thousands of deadly, grenade-tipped harpoons to non-IWC whalers.

In another advertisement run by the Animal Welfare Institute in Time (April 23, 1990) the motto was the same: "SAVE THE WHALES!" Japan was accused of plundering the last of the whales: "The International Whaling Commission (IWC) has banned all commercial whaling for the last three years. Japan violated the ban. Then, to deflect the growing outcry, the Japanese government declared it was killing the whales for *research*. The IWC's Scientific Committee has repeatedly refused to endorse such fraudulent *science*." They attacked Japan for polluting the environment and ruthlessly exploiting natural resources, then went on to quote former President Ronald Reagan warning Japanese business leaders in a speech: "There's an emotional issue that has the potential to harm Japan greatly -- the issue of the environment. There is growing news coverage of Japan's role in the loss of endangered species, in the practice of drift-net fishing and tropical logging. No country is without blame when it comes to the environment, but Japan will come under increasing pressure, perhaps even the boycott of Japanese products." The readers of the advertisement were asked to write to the Prime Minister of Japan, urging him to comply with the international whaling ban and further, to request that their own government exert pressure on Japan to stop whaling.

In January 1989, Greenpeace started a campaign against Japanese whaling in the Antarctic. For days rubber boats and the Greenpeace ship "Gondwana" hindered the whaling. These actions were supplemented by appeals to boycott Japanese products. Greenpeace asked the readers of their publications to write to the Japanese (and Norwegian) government(s) and to urge friends and relatives to support their cause.

According to Der Spiegel (No. 6, 1993) the Japanese government and fishing industry waged a campaign to promote the consumption of whale meat, emphazising the wholesomeness of the delicacy. They urged that the 9th day of every month should become a day of eating flesh of whale. The campaign was waged to address the drastic drop in sales of whale flesh, caused at least in part by the success of environmentalists' campaigns, especially with younger people. The government, in an appeal to national pride, supposedly maintained that the international ostracim was due to cultural prejudices against Japan.

International pressure has resulted in certain policy change in Japan: The use of huge drag-nets to catch fish has ceased, the ivory trade has stopped, and Japan is willing to cooperate concerning the trade of endangered species. But within Japan there never existed a strong environmentalist movement (Minemata being the exception), so it has always taken international pressure by organizations like Greenpeace or the World Wildlife Fund (WWF) to force Japan to change. The WWF initiated worldwide protests against Japan's destroying the tropical rainforests. As a consequence Japan signed a treaty with Malaysia in fall 1991 to halve imports. Image polishing was the main motive for Japan's offering a large amount of money for environmental protection at the Earth Summit in Rio in June 1992.

The image of Japan, like that of Arab countries, is a construction by Westerners. Oscar Wilde said, "The whole of Japan is a pure invention". Max Weber (1964), in discussing the problem of ideo-typical model construction, pointed out that the logical classification of analytical concepts on the one hand and the empirical arrangement of events on the other, appear to be bound up together such that there is an almost irresistible temptation to do violence to reality in order to prove the real validity of the construct -- which is precisely what the West has done with Japan. Concerning the dominant image of Japan as being a peaceful and harmonious society Befu, (1980) argued: "When reality fits the model, it is regarded as confirmation of the model; when it does not fit the

model it is generally regarded as some curious eclipse or happening
. . . or it is simply ignored" (p. 41). An example of the non
harmonious aspects of Japanese society can even be found in the
field of international PR. According to Der Spiegel (No. 42, 1993),
Japanese railway unionists published in The New York Times a
large advertisement cautioning against riding on the new supertrain
Nozomi, as the test races with about 1,400 passengers could end in
tragedy. In fact, the railway company was asked to cease the
testraces with pasengers. Almost daily there were problems like
bolts breaking, doors sticking, or welding seams bursting. Never
before had Japanese employees publicly compromised their own
company in such a way. Union leader Masao Sato justified the
procedure by warning the people of a big accident. Japanese
newspapers had not been willing to publish such opinions.

Japan, often called Japan, Inc. because of the close cooperation
between government and business is the country most actively
trying to gain influence in the United States. In 1987 they spend
$36.9 million to obtain the services of U.S.-registered PR
consultants (Manheim, 1994). Choate (1990a) characterized
Japanese lobbying activities as "by far [the] best-staffed, best-
organized, and best financed of any nation" (p. 4). According to
Choate, Japan's annual investment in lobbying, politicking, and
propagandizing is about $400 million.

An example of a PR campaign by Japan, Inc. is the one waged in
the United States by the Japan Automobile Manufacturers
Association. The campaign started in 1980 and its aim was to
change the negative public opinion concerning imported cars. A
series of full-page advertisements appeared in leading American
newspapers. Interviews with American economists and leaders of
consumer groups defending the import of cars and supporting free
trade were published. The advertisement's headline was: "In the
Consumer's Interest, Dialogues on the Open Market for
Automobiles." Fear of public opinion, according to Wilcox, Ault,
and Agee (1986) was the main motive for the decision to build

Japanese cars in the United States. In fact, Marubeni, a Japanese firm, emphasized in advertisements the stimulation of the local American economy, then linked the company interests to America's interests explaining: "We exported $3.3 billion to Japan last year" (Onkvisit & Shaw, 1989, p. 146). The advertisement maintained that Marubeni had built some big markets for the United States in Japan in close association with its subsidiary Marubeni American: "And not by chance. Success like this takes more than sales skills it requires deep insight into the realities that create the Japanese marketplaces, and investments to help shape them" (Onkvisit & Shaw, 1989, p. 146).

There is no doubt that Japan is at least partly responsible for her bad image in the United States. Yoshio Sakurauchi, the Speaker of the Lower House of the Diet, characterized American workers as "lazy and illiterate," contending that the "root of America's trade problem lies in the inferior quality of American labour" and that the United States would become a subcontractor of Japan (Time, February 10, 1992). In summer 1988 the United States Congressional Black Caucus, made up of 23 Capitol Hill lawmakers, wrote to Japanese Prime Minister Noboru Takeshita asking him to help end "the negative stereotypic representations of black Americans once and for all" (Time, August 1988, p. 17). The Black legislators were particularly appalled by two recent incidents: a suggestion by Michio Watanabe, a senior strategist in the ruling Liberal Democratic Party, that many Blacks had no qualms about going bankrupt, and news reports that Little Black Sambo dolls and black mannequins with grotesquely large lips were on display in Tokyo stores. Takeshita wrote back expressing sadness that Americans had been offended and promising to try to make his countrymen more sensitive to minority issues.

An important ingredient in Japan's image was (and probably still is) the belief that its future looks quite bright. Some historians (prophets?) maintain that the current of history is with Japan. Time (July 4, 1988) quoted Paul Kennedy, professor of history at Yale: "There's no reason that Japan won't continue to grow . . . Its economic drive is pushing it toward center stage." Clyde Prestowitz, a former Deputy Assistant Secretary of Commerce is also cited: "The American century is over . . . The big development in the latter part of century is the emergence of Japan as a major superpower."

PROPAGANDA AND STABILITY OF IMAGES

Even under extremely difficult conditions, when the public perceive the communicator as incredible and are highly hostile to being influenced, there are cases of mass media propaganda being effective. Dramatic proof of this theory was provided during World War II by a 1942 experiment conducted by F. H. Allport and M. M. Simpson (1946). In April 1942, 30 Syracuse University students listened to Axis broadcast material in 14 half-hour sessions, and recorded their degree of belief or acceptance of what they heard. Twenty-eight programs were presented, consisting of broadcasts from both Berlin and Rome, and involving 14 different speakers. The blatant propaganda themes (attempts to derogate United States war aims, playing up the alleged moral justification for the Nazi war effort) were rejected, but the German broadcasts were surprisingly effective in inducing acceptance of "defeatist" themes conveyed by factual-sounding statements to the effect that the United States was weak and Germany was strong. The category of defeatism was defined as follows: "The attempt is here to make us believe that a United Nations victory is impossible and an Axis victory certain. These theses stress the following points: difficulties of an invasion of Europe, United Nations weaknesses in many lines including shipping losses, the meagerness of United Nations successes, recent Axis victories, and Axis strategical advantage and power" (p. 220). At the time of the study the Axis power had achieved great military successes on three continents, armies and industrial facilities were not fully mobilized in the United States, and the unknown hazards of the projected invasion loomed ominously.

The concern over the unexpected successes of Nazi propaganda caused the researchers not to publish their findings until the end of the war and to make them known only within a small circle. Quite obviously, the allegedly factual material did not create the resistances aroused by statements about political aims and so forth. The findings of this study indicate that even an utterly incredible communicator may by means of allegedly factual statements exert an influence on the image of a country. F. H. Allport and M. M. Simpson (1946) wrote on the success of the propaganda: "It is only the truth, or the reasonable possibility that a statement may be true, which counts. As for their clever 'propaganda' methods the Axis spokesmen might as well have saved their breath" (p. 223). In other words, the usual propagandistic tricks of suggestion, emotionalism, innuendo, dramatics, and deceit remained ineffective. Allport and Simpson named as the most important points: "The thing which does work is truth, provided the truth which is uttered is also plausible from the standpoint of its hearers . . . Defeatism is obviously the appeal which should be used. It is based on the strong possibility of its truth . . . In using the argument of defeatism it must be presented in such a way as not to arouse anger or fear . . . The defeatist Axis theses which were effective upon our listeners had no trace of threat or fear arousal" (p. 224).

Many years later D. D. Smith (1973) carried out another experiment on the effects of foreign propaganda. In it American students (N = 122) listened to broadcasts from Radio Moscow for $2\frac{1}{2}$ months. The starting premise again was the basic assumption that usually individuals have simple and often negative images of other peoples. However, this study did not proceed from the simple assumption that messages contradicting one's own expectations always have negative effects, whereby this negative effect also depends on whether the message comes from a negatively evaluated source or not. The lower the credibility, according to that assumption, the more the recipient emphasizes negative aspects of the message.

Instead, D. D. Smith (1973) proceeded from the concept that the internal yardstick used to evaluate the message is the expectations of the individual about the message (and the communicator) as well the already existing attitudes (pro and con evaluations). It was assumed further that individuals have certain hopes and aims, and of course those can be quite different from expectations. In Smith's example, a person who travels in a country in which there is political tension might expect to be confronted with hostility but might also hope to be received in a friendly manner. In other words, the evaluation of the incoming message or its comparison with the internal yardstick does not happen as a categorical comparison but represents a relative judgment. That is, an individual can respond positively to a negative message from a negative or incredible source if the message is less negative than had actually been expected. In detail, the following hypotheses were examined:

1. A negative message from a low-credibility source will be responded to positively if it is perceived to be less negative than expected.
2. A negative message from a low-credibility source will be responded to negatively if it is perceived to be as negative as expected.
3. A negative message from a low-credibility source will be responded to most negatively if it is perceived to be more negative than expected.

Changes in attitudes were measured in various subject areas concerning international affairs (e.g., assessment of the sincerity of the Soviet Union in international affairs, the legitimacy of the Soviet positions on international problems, the actual efforts toward peace of the Soviet Union, the credibility of information American citizens received from their own government about Vietnam, etc.).

The students who took part in the experiment had never before heard Radio Moscow's broadcasts for North America and in the experiment were exposed to $1^1/_2$ hours of them per week for the $2^1/_2$ months. Image was not perceived in this as a point on a certain scale but as a certain span in the continuum; that is, the concepts of latitude of acceptance/rejection were regarded as adequate to measuring image. After being questioned the experimental group was divided into three categories: those who rated the broadcasts as more positive than expected, those who perceived the broadcasts as conforming to expectations, and those who found the broadcasts worse than expected.

In addition all the test subjects fundamentally considered peace, understanding, and cooperation to be desirable aims (hopes). Furthermore, they all considered the credibility of Radio Moscow to be low and had negative expectations about the broadcasts with respect to quality of content and style of presentation. The broadcasts heard by the subjects were assessed by experts and in a content analysis as "moderately biased, one-sided, dull and boring in presentation and overtly negative to an American audience". The statements on Vietnam were characterized as "very biased, militant and extremely negative".

With respect to Hypothesis 1, the authors found that with the exception of the Vietnam issue the test subjects gained a more positive image of the Soviet Union. This was most clearly evident in responses to the question about the sincerity of the Soviet government in international affairs: 81% of those who thought the broadcasts were better than expected had a more positive impression than before the broadcast. Hypotheses 2 and 3 were also confirmed. Those who found the broadcasts as negative as expected were negatively influenced. Among those who perceived the broadcasts as worse than expected massive boomerang effects occurred, with 72% of the respondents in this category assessing the peace efforts of the Soviet Union as worse than previously thought.

This study shows clearly that reactions to foreign propaganda can vary substantially from subgroup to subgroup. D. D. Smith (1973) concluded: "The international images proved to be highly vulnerable to the broadcast which, for so many respondents, provided a relative refutation of their original expectations" (p. 126). Clearly responsible for the positive effect among the subgroup of those who found the propaganda better than or not as bad as expected was the negative enemy-image prevailing about the Soviet Union. The findings of the study prove what I. L. Janis and M. B. Smith (1965) suspected, namely that in the case of such cemented mutual negative stereotypes as in the East-West conflict "a differentiated and sophisticated image might gradually be substituted if side attacks concentrated on literary, cinematic and medical achievements, leisure time interests and patterns of family life. . . . After the image of a rival nation has become more differentiated in purely political respects, the audience may come to take a somewhat more tolerant view that 'after all, they are not really very different from us'" (p. 213).

With respect to the enemy propaganda of the Nazis, Steinbiss and Eisermann (1988), discussed an almost surrealistic aspect. The Reich Ministry for National Enlightenment and Propaganda used "degenerate" swing and jazz music, banned within the Reich, in foreign propaganda broadcasts to attract the attention of possible listeners. On October 12, 1935, the head of the Reich Radio Corporation, Eugen Hadamovsky, issued the following order: From today "Nigger-Jazz" is banned throughout radio. The propaganda ministry employed the best European swing musicians in the propaganda jazz band, "Charlie And His Orchestra", who not only played the newest hits from the United States and Britain, but also built in propaganda messages. For example, Churchill's request to Roosevelt for support was derided like this: "Frankie, Frankie, The Germans Are Driving Me Nuts/From Narvik Down to Egypt/They Took All My Landing Spots". The Stars and Stripes, the newspaper of the American armed forces, reported at war's end: "We got Goebbels' Band".

Although dramatic events like wars about drastically change a nation's image, normally those images remain stable. As Deutsch and Merritt (1965) put it, "Images and attitudes often persist with little change despite spectacular changes in the external world, or messages about such changes" (p. 147). A good example is the Soviet Union's image in western Europe from 1954 to 1961

(Deutsch & Merritt, 1965). Four countries -- Great Britain, West Germany, Italy, and France -- were examined. People were asked, "What are your feelings about Russia," and the percentage of those who responded very good, good, or fair were note. In October 1954, those percentages were 30% in Great Britain, 24% in France, 30% in Italy, and 18% in Germany with the average level from October 1954 to April 1956 around 35%. After the brutal smashing of the Hungarian popular uprising by the "fraternal" Soviet troops in November 1956 this average fell to 16%. For the individual countries the changes between April 1956 and December 1956 were as follows: Great Britain from 46% to 13%, France from 39% to 18%, Italy from 35% to 20%, West Germany from 21% to 10%.

However, 2 years later those dramatic image losses had been made up again: In October 1958 the image was at the same level as before the Hungarian uprising. Deutsch and Merritt (1965) wrote: "In short, whatever prestige the Soviet Union has lost in Western Europe as a result of its actions in Hungary, it regained it within two years" (p. 149). One of the events that helped repair the image so quickly was the launching of Sputnik in October 1957. Then, in November 1959, 2 weeks after the Soviet Union was able to show for the first time photographs of the reverse side of the moon, the Soviet image was the most positive it had been during the entire period reviewed. Deutsch and Merritt concluded from the data that although images fluctuate within certain limits, they are relatively stable in the long term because people form their own picture of the world on the basis of previous experiences: "If an event should not fit into the expected pattern, momentary doubt and confusion -- even disillusion -- may ensue . . . With time, one or both of two processes might take place: a new event occurs that does fit into the pattern, enabling the perceiver to term the previous nonconforming event an aberration; or such oracles as newspapers or leaders interpret the nonconforming event so that it does fit in the preconceived pattern. In either instance, confidence in the pattern itself will generally return" (p. 151).

One more remark on the effect of the Soviet space program on international public opinion is appropriate here. On the basis of poll data gathered between February 1957 and February 1960, Almond (1963) concluded that the U.S. image suffered long-term damage: "We will have to reckon on the fact that one of the most significant components in the popular support of the American position in international politics -- widespread popular conviction regarding American scientific and technical superiority -- has been lost for the indefinite future and that all the expectations and attitudes that were based on this conviction have also been shaken for the indefinite future" (p. 77).

In connection with the smashing of the Hungarian uprising, examples of extreme distortions of reality by selective perception have also been documented. Cantril (1958) examined the "politics of despair" in France and Italy, contributed greatly to the research on distorted perception. The event meant something completely different to communists and noncommunists. Cantril noted that, "Communist sympathizers were found to have little of the indignation and sorrow that characterized the reactions of noncommunist sympathizers . . . What people believed the Hungarian uprising to be apparently depended on the particular significances they saw. And these significances were determined by the assumptions they brought to the series of happenings that constituted the uprising for them" (p. 185). Indeed, the official version was reported in <u>Pravda</u> as follows:

1. On the afternoon of Tuesday, October 23, 1956, the "honest", socialist, Hungarian working people staged a demonstration against the party mistakes committed by the Rakosi and Gero governments.
2. Fascist, Hitlerite, reactionary, counter-revolutionary hooligans, financed, trained, and equipped by the imperialist, capitalist west, took advantage of the demonstrations to begin a counter-revolution.
3. The honest Hungarian working people under Imre Nagy appealed to Soviet forces stationed in Hungary under the Warsaw Pact for assistance in restoring order.

4. The Nagy government proved to be weak, and it permitted counter-revolutionary influences to penetrate its ranks. It became helpless and fell apart. This is demonstrated by the fact that Nagy denounced the Warsaw Pact.
5. The Hungarian patriots under Janos Kadar broke with the Nagy government and formed the Hungarian revolutionary workers and peasant government. This genuine popular government asked the Soviet command for help in suppressing the counter-revolution.
6. The Hungarian patriots, assisted by Soviet forces, smashed the counter-revolution. (Barghoorn, 1964, p. 233)

Of course, this version had nothing to do with what actually happened but was a lie meant to justify the brutal quelling of the Hungarian uprising. As the journalists of Budapest Radio said on October 30, 1956, "For many years Hungarian radio was no more than a tool of lies and a recipient of orders. It lied day and night. It lied on all frequencies" (Révész, 1974, p. 47).

CHAPTER 5

Short Historical Outline of Image Cultivation by Governments

EARLY EXAMPLES OF IMAGE MANIPULATION

The following short review of early image cultivation by states makes no claim to completeness but is meant merely to underscore that image cultivation did not begin with the age of the mass media. The Bible contains examples showing that the character of a nation, its image, has concerned humanity from the beginning of its history. As reported in Genesis (18: 32) God could not find even 10 innocent people in Sodom for the sake of whom he would not destroy the city. The Apostle Paul, in his letter to Titus, wrote the following about the Cretans: "It was a Cretan himself, one of their own prophets, who spoke the truth when he said, 'Cretans are always liars, wicked beasts, and lazy gluttons'" (Titus 1: 12).

Further examples were gathered by Duijker and Frijda (1960): "Herodotus discusses the characteristic habits of the Scythes, the Phrygians, the Libyans and many others. Vatsayana, in the Kama-Sutra, notices striking differences in the "sexual behaviour of the human female", and one of his classifications is based on region of origin. Tacitus presents, in his famous "Germania", an elaborate description of the attitudes, customs and morals of the Germans. Juvenal speaks rather sarcastically about the "little Greeks" in imperial Rome, and makes it quite clear that he considers them a rather contemptible bunch of spineless good-for-nothings." (p. 1)

152

Paneth (1926) argued that propaganda for entire countries has a long tradition. The fourth book of Moses (Numbers 13) could be regarded as the oldest source; in it we are told that Moses sent 12 spies to get information on the land of Canaan, in which milk and honey were said to flow. They reported that the Canaanites were strong and gigantic, which is why the Israelites consider going back to slavery in Egypt rather than follow Moses to the land promised them by God. Because they doubted, God sent them into the desert for 40 years.

Attempts to influence the image of nations in a plainly propagandistic way can also be found in early human history, although it is difficult to distinguish between attempts to influence one's own population and attempts to manipulate the image abroad. Herodotus (probably born in 484 B.C.), Greek author of the first great narrative history of the ancient world, is described not only as "the father of history writing" but also less sympathetically as "hired press agent for the Athenian state" (Brown, 1963, p. 13), an appropriate characterization because, in contrast to Thucydides who tried to write history objectively, Herodotus allowed his sympathies and antipathies to flow into his writing of history. In his depiction of the Athenians' 333 B.C. war against the Persians, for example, Herodotus manipulated facts and presented plainly biased accounts. When the Persian campaign against Thrace succeeded, Herodotus instead reported that the Persians were unsuccessful in their efforts. He claimed further that the Persians had intended to attack Athens but, with the help of the gods, their fleet had been destroyed on the way by a storm. In actual fact, the Persian fleet was struck by the storm after the successful expedition.

The Greeks were very skillful propagandists during the wars against Persia. Herodotus reported, for instance, that Themistocles had propaganda messages chiseled in stone erected at watering places used by the hostile Ionian fleet. And the Greeks exaggerated the number of Persians who had landed and praised the phalanx tactic invented by them. In a speech about the fallen, Thucydides, an Athenian politician opposed to radical democracy, reported that

Pericles (b. 495 B.C., d. 429 B.C.), who brought ancient Athenian democracy to its height and nearly established Athens as the leading power in Greece, observed that the Spartans, when they had won a small victory, claimed that with a small part of their forces they had vanquished the entire army of Athens; if they lost, they would claim that all the forces of Athens had attacked a small number of Spartans but won only an insignificant victory. (This principle of war reporting is also very common in modern times. During World War I Churchill suppressed bad news until he could offset it with good [Lavine & Wechsler, 1940]. Also during World War I, the official Petrograd Telegraph Agency was instructed by the Government: "All our military and naval success must be published, our losses and unsuccessful operations must not be mentioned or talked about, the number of prisoners taken must always be exaggerated, raids of enemy air forces must never be published" [Lavine & Wechsler, 1940 p. 8].)

Alexander the Great (356 B.C. - 323 B.C.), the king of Macedonia, created what can be described as the first war reporter unit. Reports written to serve his ends were sent to the Macedonian court, reproduced there, and disseminated with propagandistic intent. Callisthenes of Olynthus (c. 360 B.C. - 328 B.C.), appointed to attend Alexander as historian of his Asiatic expedition, spread the claim that the king was the son of Zeus, the supreme god. The sacred oracle of Didyma confirmed the story -- surely under the influence of Alexander's "PR department", which probably made skillful use of the oracle's utterance: It is very difficult to fight the son of so powerful a god!

After Hannibal had crossed the Alps, his message to the Italians was that he was coming not as conqueror but as a friend. His only intention was, he claimed, to help rid them of Roman domination (Whitton & Larson, 1964). Similarly, the French revolutionary troops nearing the Dutch border in 1794 told the population they were coming as fraternal liberators and not as conquerors. Another skillful propagandist was Genghis Khan, who sent out "undercover agents" in advance to spread rumors grossly exaggerating the size and cruelty of his armies.

During the times of the Crusades, communication was predominantly vocal: written communication was nearly the monopoly of the church. But already in those days pseudoevents were staged. Pope Urban II (1035 - 1099) inspired the first crusade (1096 - 1099). In November 1095 the Pope at the synod of Clermont Urban II preached before a great gathering in the decisive sermon that set in motion the first crusade. When the Pope finished his sermon the people shouted *Deus lo volt* (It's God's will). The Pope ordered that the cross as a symbol should be worn. The cry of war was the *Kyrie eleison* (God have mercy). Urban II proclaimed that one could save his soul if he faithfully bore the cross and took the way to the Holy Sepulchre. The eloquent appeals of the Pope were quite successfull. Thousands followed the summons to take up arms. The impetus for the Second Crusade (1147 - 1149), which failed, was primarily the charismatic Bernhard of Clairvaux (1090 - 1153), the "honey-tongued preacher". Pope Eugene III had ordered his followers to heed his former teacher Bernhard, who waged an active campaign for the Crusade. Bernhard not only sent messengers to the places he himself was unable to visit, he also sent propagandistic letters to be read to the faithful.

The Third Crusade (1189 - 1192) was initiated by Pope Gregory VIII's crusading encyclica *Audita tremendi,* issued at Ferrara on October 29, 1187 and circulated in western Europe. Enthusiasm for the Crusade was stirred and emperor Frederick I (Barbarossa) took up the cross at a special court, summoned by the Pope's representative at Mainz in March 1188. In the *Historia de Expeditione Frederici* the (pseudo) event was described:

> On 27 March 1188 a court of Christ was convened at Mainz consisting of princes, bishops, dukes, margraves, counts, noble and the cream of the knights available to fight. Here, and not without the copious tears of many men, the Holy Roman Emperor Frederick I took up the sign of Christ's cross and declared that he was preparing himself for the memorable

journey of Christ with a stout heart, putting himself forward as a
celebrated leader for the faithful members of the crusade and as
their proud standard-bearer (Hallam 1989, p. 169).

Public enthusiasm was generated by other means as well. For
instance, poets created songs of the Crusade and wrote elegiacs
about the fall of Jerusalem in Latin and in other languages.

The Fourth Crusade (1202 - 1204) was initiated by Pope
Innocent III, who repeated in large parts the propaganda of Urban
II and Bernhard of Clairvaux. The failure of the previous two
Crusades was blamed on the sin of mankind. The Pope promised
that all sins would be remissioned after fulfilling the crusading vow.
In the bull *Quia Maior* he appealed to all Christians, the whole of
Christian Europe, ordering monthly processions in all Christian
communities and requiring each diocese to have a "propaganda
office" to distribute papal letters to preachers.

In medieval Europe the propaganda war between the German
emperor Frederick II (1149 - 1250) and the Curia was of major
importance. Frederick II had succeeded in mobilizing almost all
public opinion in the Occident for himself and his cause. Everth
(1930) characterized Frederick II's propaganda as follows: "He
always claimed either that he was being forced to act in a way he
did not like by circumstances beyond his control, or he cited noble
motives, for his intervention in Austria, for example, the complaints
of the widows and orphans it was oppressing, or for his war against
the Lombards and the pope simply the wish for peace and justice"
(p. 74). The propaganda struggle between the emperor and the
papacy assumed major proportions. The emperor attacked the pope
for supporting the Lombardian heretics (which he did for politically
sensible reasons). In a pamphlet entitled "In Exordie", for example,
Pope Gregory IX was characterized as the Antichrist the world was
expecting. In another tract the pope's right to ownership of central
Italian areas was disputed, probably to legitimize ex post facto their
seizure. The emperor's concern about "international public opinion"
is demonstrated in a manifesto of April 20, 1239, which began as

follows: "Lift up your eyes and look all about you, listen all about, you sons of mankind, with your ears! Sit ye down, ye princes, and hear, ye peoples, our cause!"

Within 4 weeks the pope replied with a text that was harsher than even the sharpest utterances of the emperor. The pope wrote:

> There arose from the sea a beast, full of the names of calumny, which with the paws of the bear and the jaws of the lion raged, and in the rest of its body was like a panther; it opens its maw to besmirch the name of God and does not cease to fire similar arrows against the house of the Lord and the saints who dwell in Heaven. With his claws and iron teeth he wants to crush and with his feet to trample everything; to tear down the wall of the Catholic faith it has long built battering rams in secret and is now openly building siege tools; it establishes heathen gambling houses to destroy the soul and rises up against Christ, the redeemer of the human race, whose covenant tablets it has the impunity of extinguishing with the stylus of heretical damnation, as the rumour testifies. Therefore stop ye all to whom the calumnies of this beast directed against us reach to wonder that we, who in all humility are subject to God, become the target of his slanderous arrows, since not even the Lord was spared them. Stop wondering that it draws the dagger of its defamations against us, for it has arisen to extinguish the name of the Lord from the earth. But so that after the truth has been opened to you, you may better resist his lies and make null and void his machinations through the witness of innocence, behold you carefully head, body and tail of this beast, of the socalled emperor Frederick, and if in his words you discover abominations and crimes, arm your innocent hearts against his cunning and with the shield of truth. Take note of how audaciously he besmirched our purity and that of the apostolic chair with letters he sent to all the world, the said Frederick, the artist of falsity, who knows no modesty or shame, who does not blush as he lies (Buchli, 1962, p. 202).

One of the most important propagandists was the famous minnesinger Walther von der Vogelweide (1190 - 1230). Frederick II knew how to polish his image by staging pseudo-events. E.g. at the crowning ceremony at Aachen he took the cross and promised to lead a crusade, therewith provoking pope Innocent III, who himself wanted to be the leader. Also worth mentioning is the Fugger, the famous Augsburg trading firm, a multinational corporation of those days, who were experts in international public relations. They had confidential representatives in different countries, in most cases local persons who were already trusted and respected. The Fuggers did not want to create the impression that foreigners were interfering in local politics and business -- an early example of the third-party approach.

DEVELOPMENTS IN GERMANY AND FRANCE

Gutenberg's invention of the printing press was the point of departure for a new kind of international PR. The first German leader (and as far as I know the first leader of any nation) to manipulate the predecessors of the modern newspaper, the so-called "new newspapers" (newe zeytungen), as an instrument of war was Emperor Maximilian I (1493 - 1519). With biased war reports he tried to influence the mood of the public in his empire, using among other things the new newspapers, which had only recently been published. Maximilian also tried to communicate with the population of the enemy state, for example the commoners of the Republic of Venice. In repeated appeals he tried to incite them to insurrection against the finance aristocracy, and promised them liberation and a share of the city-state's government and the possessions of the rulers.

In 1576, Rudolf II was elected emperor of the Holy Roman Empire of the German Nation by the Reichstag in Regensburg. Rudolf's main opponent was the Turks, whose leader, Sultan Murad III, declared war on the German nation. To mobilize support, Rudolf used the following as instruments of propaganda, aimed mostly at Germman's elite: leaflets, coins, medals, festivities, political acts of symbolic value, art, and architecture (e.g., triumphal arches). In 1593 the Turks attacked and the emperor started his propaganda campaign, including atrocity propaganda. Detailed accounts of Turkish atrocities were published in leaflets and the new newspapers (e.g., disemboweling a pregnant woman and smashing her child against the wall).

In France, Cardinal Richelieu (1585 - 1642), who as leading minister asserted absolutism in France, had a press office geared to fight France's foreign opponents, especially the Habsburgs, through pamphlets. La réputaticn was the political keyword for the cardinal, a PR master. He also established a press department when he went into service for Maria de Medici. Pére Joseph, a Capuchin friar and former Huguenot, became his first minister for "Information and Propaganda". From the beginning of his career, Richelieu used leaflets, sometimes even written by writers for hire to justify his policies and attack his political opponents. The most important instrument of his press policy was the Gazette, a weekly founded by Theophraste Renaudot. In 1635 Richelieu established the Académie Francaise to which the leading literati were appointed. Its main task was to standardize French language and influence long-term public opinion. Richelieu also distributed publications, biased appropriately, in foreign countries. Rome was the center of the world in those days and he who had a good reputation in Rome had a good reputation in the world (i.e., Europe). According to Richelieu the best way for a sovereign to get a good reputation in Rome was to govern decently. France wanted to become the "Arbitre de la Chrestiente" (Arbiter of Christendom), and in order to achieve this aim, even negative information about other countries was disseminated. Without a doubt, Richelieu was a master of PR for France's image and can be regarded as a pioneer in PR for nations as a whole.

Public relations for France reached a high point during the reign of Louis XIV. Louis XIV, the Sun King, reigned for 72 years (1643 - 1715) and was a master of image construction. His personality, life, and body were put on the stage and Louis le Grand was created. To polish the king's image, newspapers were founded, academies were established, castles were built, birthdays and battle victories were celebrated. Numerous of statues of Louis XIV were errected (a statue campaign took place in the 1680s; P. Burke, 1992), and triumphal arches were built in abundance. The palace at Versailles was imitated all over Europe. Every utterance of the king was written down by secretaries. Dozens of painters were kept busy. Among those employed to polish the image of the king were the painter Lebrun, the musician Lully, and the poets Corneille, Racine, and Jean-Baptiste Roquelin (Molière). These extravagant activities, however, ruined France. In 1715 when the king died, France, therefore the richest country of Europe, was on its way to ruin.

Louis XIV also defended France, whose incarnation he believed himself to be ("L'état c'est moi!"), against hostile public opinion in Europe using publicity. P. Burke (1992) examined the parallels between modern publicity agents and the "glory enterprise" of Louis XIV. He analysed "the selling of Ludwig XIV" (p. 4), although the panegyrists of Louis XIV were no Saatchi & Saatchi. According to Burke *gloire* (glory) was a keyword of the time: "Its importance was emphasized in Louis' Mémoires. Mademoiselle de Scudéry received a medal from the Académie Francaise for her essay on the subject" (p. 5). Louis XIV was a master of impression management. As Burke argued he might usefully be viewed as representing himself: He played the part of the king, living the life of a living image.

As P. Burke (1992) pointed out, Louis XIV's image projection was aimed not only at the domestic public: "The foreign public for l'histoire du roi was considered no less important than the domestic one. In 1698, for example, the petite académie was . . . to draw up a list of medals suitable for presentation to foreigners" (p. 158). France had practical reasons for image cultivation in, for example, the Ottoman Empire because both had a common enemy, the Holy Roman Empire of the German Nation. But the main target group of Louis XIV's image policy were the other courts of Europe: "The ambassadors formed a substantial part of the audience for the court festivals, plays, ballets and operas. They were very often presented with gifts, which would enhance the king's name abroad -- medals and tapestries of the events of the reign . . . and jewelled portaits of Louis himself" (p. 162).

Texts glorifying Louis in foreign languages were published. For example, Latin was used to reach the educated people in Europe. And the official defense of the War of Devolution (1667/1668), which was explained as a defense of the rights of Louis XIV's Spanish queen, was immediately translated into Spanish to convince Madrid that there was no reason to intervene. As P. Burke (1992) observed:

> The ground was prepared by pamphlets presenting a favourable image of Louis as a ruler who wanted nothing more than his just rights. Herman Conring, professor of law at the University of Helmstedt, one of the foreign scholars receiving regular gratifications, volunteered to right the king's support. The royal press published an anonymous French treatise on the "the rights of the most Christian queen over varius states of the Spanish Monarchy". The treatise was produced by a team working under the direction of Burzeis (a member of the petite académie) . . . and quickly translated into Latin, Spanish and German (p. 71).

The official justification of the War of Devolution was also translated into German, the language at the court of the Holy Roman Emperor. Praises of the king were translated into Italian, perhaps to impress the pope (P. Burke, 1992).

P. Burke (1992) labeled Louis XIV's image policy "theatre state" and described the life of the king as a grand spectacle. Burke concluded that the main difference between modern image shaping and Louis' image building is technological. Louis was presented by means of print, statues, and medals, whereas 20th-century rulers relied on photography, cinema, radio, and television: "Long before the cinema, the theatre affected perceptions of politics. When the dodge of Genoa arrived at Versailles in 1685, a contemporary observer, who happened to be a playwright, Donneau de Visé, remarked that 'the role which he had to play was not easy'. . . . For his contemporaries as for posterity, the sun-king was a star" (p.

199). Louis used the grandiosity of official architecture and sculpture to dwarf the spectator, to make them conscious of his power. But according to Burke, Louis claimed to derive his power from God not from the people: "He did not need to cultivate any voters. His media were not mass media. He was presented -- indeed, he had to be presented -- as someone special, the Lord's annoited, le Dieudonné. The contrast between seventeenth-century leaders and twentieth-century ones is not a contrast between rhetoric and truth. It is a contrast between two styles of rhetoric" (p. 203).

According to Burke (1992), the foreign reactions to Louis XIV's image-building presentations varied. The Venetian ambassador described the English responses as partial and sometimes obvious. Some courts were shocked by the glorification of Louis, yet other imitated it, especially Philip V of Spain and Karl XI of Sweden. Austria's Leopold I (ruling from 1658 to 1705) modeled Schönbrunn on the palace at Versailles. As Burke (1992) pointed out, however, there also existed a negative image of Louis XIV. Paintings, engravings, poems, prose texts, and so on -- usually created by his enemies, many of them foreigners (British, Dutch, German) -- were used to attack the Sun King. Louis was the usurper, denounced as "The French Attila", "The French Nero", or "The French Macchiavelli". Pamphlets described Louis as cowardly, vainglorious, and unjust. The king's official title of "The Most Christian King" was changed to "The Most Christian Turk" or "the most Christian needs to become Christian". The title of a German pamphlet concentrating on Louis' "enormous vanity" was "Eigenlob stinckt gern" (self-praise stinks). The exact number of pamphlets attacking Louis is impossible to determine; Burke alone identified 75.

The idea of nationalism had become a political force in Europe at the start of the 19th century. It was assumed that a law of nature separated humanity into nations that differed according to certain objectively definable characteristics (e.g., language) and that the only legal form of government was based on a national state order. With that, propaganda had to change, too. Napoleon was the first to perceive this. He engaged in a veritable propaganda battle with the rest of Europe, a battle of big words. Against Britain, which was waging a caricature campaign against Napoleon, the battle was fought in the press. Napoleon, however, mainly reached only the French and those who lived in French territories. The English, on the other hand, were far-reaching in their ridiculing of "Little Bonny", whom they characterized as a malicious monster or greedy dwarf trying to swallow the world, the devil's companion or the devil's favorite, or the Corsican Bloodhound fighting with the English Bulldog.

Napoleon understood the power of public opinion: "Government is nothing unless supported by public opinion". But he also knew about the importance of manipulation: "The truth is half so important as what people think to be true". With the French Revolution the French had become accustomed to the idea of "volonté general" (sovereignty of the people) which was regarded as the basis of French policy. So Napoleon, who in 1804 became Emperor of France, did not simply crowned himself but held a plebiscit beforehand. But Napoleon was convinced that his task was to steer public opinion, not discuss it, and so he invested a large amount of time and energy influencing public opinion in France and abroad. He used not only the press, but also manifestos and bulletins. And in the tradition of French kings, he instrumentalized artists for his glorification: Pictures and statues apotheosized him; the china manufacturers of Sévres produced only pieces that idolized him. Napoleon created an image of himself as a superman (Holtman, 1950), a genius of moral excellence, but not aloof from the common people. Napoleon was a propagandist of incredible genius. He had no standard procedure but adapted his tactics to the circumstances (Sturminger, 1938).[1] To complement his press policy ("I shall never allow the papers to say or do anything contrary to my interest"; Holtman ,1950, p. 44), Napoleon instigated whispering

---

[1] Holtman (1950) contended just the opposite: "Perhaps the greatest weakness of Napoleonic propaganda was its failure to adapt its messages and mediums to those whom it was designed to influence" (p. 245).

campaigns, especially when he had the impression that press articles would appear to be too official, that is, incredible. He also spread rumors about his political plans to gauge public opinion. Exaggerated reports were circulated so that when plans were realized they appeared more tolerable (Kircheisen, 1912).

Napoleon also knew that paradoxical communication was an effective way of deceiving the English (cf. chap. 8, section 8.1). Before embarking on his military campaign in Egypt, he published his war plans in his official newspaper *Le Moniteur Universel*, with the idea that the British would consider such publication an attempt to deceive them and would dismiss the plans as false, when in fact they were true. Napoleon's clever tactic was successful (Everth, 1931). And as Napoleon wrote to his brother Joseph on February 24, 1814, one has to create the impression in his enemies that one's own forces are of enormous strength compared to the enemy's. Napoleon was convinced that nothing is more contrary to military rules than to make known the strength of one's own army.

Napoleon's propaganda also aimed at winning allies and creating public support for his policy in occupied countries. The biggest campaign of this kind was waged in Spain (Holtman, 1950). Press guidelines were issued in occupied areas. In the kingdom of Saxony, for example, the guideline prescribed that anything "that might be objectionable to the French imperial court must be avoided with the greatest care" (Sturminger, 1960, p. 205). In 1803 he forced the *Hamburgische unpartheyische Correspondent*, a newspaper appearing in the then independent German Hanseatic town Hamburg, to publish a false and defamatory article against the English government, no easy task, as in Germany at that time there were many who hated the French. For example, Friedrich Ludwig Jahn (1778 - 1852), the founder of the German gymnastics movement who had called for a crusade against the French, publicly asserted that anyone who let his daughter learn French, the fashionable language of the German aristocracy and upper middle class at the time, was automatically leading her into prostitution.

Napoleon also communicated selectively with foreign countries. In 1796 he directed a manifesto to the Tiroleans to give up "the hopeless cause of their emperor" (Everth, 1931, p. 440). In 1800 addressed the population of the Cisalpine Republic, a French satellite state he had set up 3 years earlier in northern Italy. He promised the country, now occupied by the enemy, freedom, equality, order, and freedom of religion. In 1809 Napoleon addressed a manifesto to the Hungarians in which he called on them to give themselves a king: "Your union with Austria was your disaster. You have national customs, a national language, you profess pride in an illustrious and ancient origin, so become a nation again! Give yourselves a king chosen by you, who rules only through you, who lives in your midst, who is surrounded only by your fellow citizens and your soldiers" (Everth, 1931, p. 441). And a speech to the Egyptian population during his campaign there, he described himself as their friend: "Kadis, sheiks, immans, tell the people that we are the friends of the true Moslems. Did we not depose the Pope who said that war should be made on the Moslems? Did we not destroy the Knights of Malta because these senseless men believed that God wanted them to make war on the Moslems? Thrice blissful those who will be with us!" (Sturminger, 1960, p. 195).

Napoleon's main enemy was England which he attacked in newspaper articles, parts of which he wrote himself. An evaluation of the effect of these articles is nearly impossible but there is no doubt the English elite were aware of them. Napoleon wanted Europeans to fed the enemy-image of "perfidious Albion" (an expression coined during the French Revolution because England turned away from France after the execution of Louis XVI) and to awake suspicion against England among her allies. As Napoleon wrote to Fouché in a letter dated June 1, 1805, the press was to disparage England. Newspapers were urged to attack England, her fashions, customs, literature, and constitution and to call attention to her brutality and unscrupulousness. Napoleon disseminated the information that England helped Indians kill White people in North

America. According to Napoleonic propaganda, England ignored maritime law, disregarded international law, and recognized only the law of force. As described by Holtman (1950), "the French propagandist loved to make the havoc thorough-going and wanton" (p. 8). Nelson's attack on Copenhagen and the massacres there were cited as examples of British "uprightness". The British were described as selfish and mercenary, deceitful and corrupt, not worthy of being called civilized. England was accused of bringing poisoned bales of cotton to the French coast to weaken France by epidemic disease. Atrocity propaganda was used also by Napoleon (e.g., stories about rapes and massacres), especially after the allies had entered French territory in 1814: "The allies had mistreated women, slaughtered or driven off all the farm animals, pillaged, and burned. They had cut off fingers to get gold rings and torn off ears to get earrings" (Holtman, 1950, p. 9).

Austria and Prussia, two rival German-speaking states, fought each other in the press between 1848 and 1871. The Austrian envoy in Berlin, Prokesch-Osten, recognizing the importance to modern politics of skillfully guided publicity, provided articles to opposition newspapers. This case is so well documented because Prokesch-Osten never destroyed the drafts of his work. In fact, he forgot about them and they languished in his desk until it was sold along with the writings, which was how they came into possession of the Prussian government (Bauer, 1930). Subsequently, the Prussian and Austrian governments accused each other of bribing the press.

Prussia tried to steer the press inconspicuously, long a French practice. Governments set up special sections in their ministries to ensure contact with the press, usually appointing experienced journalists and making them civil servants. Their job was to use their personal experiences and contacts to carry out the government's instructions. The purpose of the Prussian Pressbüro, established around 1850, was to quietly channel ministerial views into the independent newspapers. Prussian governmental leaders -- especially Bismarck -- were quite aware that the credibility of the press was of decisive importance. What was debated in the official paper was not trusted precisely because it was published by the government. So the chancellor manipulated and bribed the press to publish at home and abroad reports reflecting official views. Indeed, under Bismarck, the foreign office established a press policy that selectively used the press as a means to foreign political ends but, in the tradition of secret diplomacy, these efforts were camouflaged. Parallel to most foreign policy actions, press measures were taken; diplomacy and the press moved so closely together for Bismarck that they were treated as two rails leading to the same destination. And he had no problems doing this financially, as he had a secret fund at his disposal. Though officially designated for other purposes, the fund also financed implementation of the foreign press policy. In 1869, for example, more money was spent influencing the French press than anywhere else.

One of the most famous examples of inconsistent media foreign policy, dating back to the time of the German empire, was the interview Kaiser Wilhelm II gave Colonel Stewart Wortley for Britain's <u>Daily Telegraph</u>. The interview produced a storm of indignation and a wave of hostility toward Germany in Britain. Not only had the Kaiser undermined German foreign policy and made it incredible, but he had indisputably breached good taste. Wortley wrote:

> As I have said, his Majesty honoured me with a long conversation and spoke with impulsive and unusual frankness. "You English", he said, "are mad, mad as March hares. What has come over you that you are so completely given over to suspicions quite unworthy of a great nation? What more can I do than I have done? . . . Have I ever been false to my word? Falsehood and prevarication are alien to my nature. My actions ought to speak for themselves, but you listen not to them, but to those who misinterpret and distort them. That is a personal insult which I feel and resent. To be for ever with jealous, mistrustful eyes, taxes my patience severely. I have said time after time that I am a friend of England, and your press -- or, at least, a considerable section of it -- bids the people of England

refuse my proffered hand, and insinuates that the other holds a dagger."

In the course of the conversation Wilhelm claimed further that he had sent the British a plan for the campaign against the Boers after he had received from his "revered grandmother", Queen Victoria, a letter "written in sorrow and affliction and bearing manifest traces of the anxieties which were preying upon her mind and health". The Kaiser thought it "a matter of curious coincidence . . . that the plan which I formulated ran very much on the same lines as that which was actually adopted by Lord Roberts, and carried by him into successful operation". The Kaiser also put forth his views on German navy policy:

> But, you will say, what of the German navy? Surely that is a menace to England! Against whom but England are my squadrons being prepared? . . . My answer is clear. Germany is a young and growing empire. She has a world-wide commerce, which is rapidly expanding, and to which the legitimate ambition of patriotic Germans refuses to assign any bounds. Germany must have a powerful fleet to protect that commerce, and her manifold interests in even the most distant seas. She expects those interests to go on growing, and she must be able to champion them manfully in any quarter of the globe . . .

A response appeared on November 4, 1908 in the satirical magazine <u>Punch</u>, titled "The Great Misunderstood. Open letter to H.I.M. The German Kaiser" from which were taken the following passages on the Boer War:

> I think it was awfully sweet of you making that war-map for Lord Roberts. If you had only been told about it earlier. But, you see, we got your Kruger telegram (which we didn't care for) fixed in our minds, and we never heard about the map until the other day; and I'm afraid we shall always remember the telegram best. On the other hand, your own people were very pleased with the telegram, and now they're quite cross about the map. And I expect they'll remember the map best. Anyhow, it

> makes it very difficult for posterity to discover which side you
> were really on, and I'm very glad that I shall not be asked to
> have anything to do with delivering "the serenely impartial
> verdict of history" . . . I trust you will take this letter in the
> genial spirit in which it is composed. I'm sure your heart is in
> the right place. It's simply your head that causes me anxiety.

Joined to this "letter" was an extended version of certain passages in the famous interview that <u>Punch</u> had received from "Our Special Eavesdropper at Potsdam": "You English are mad, mad, mad, mad -- mad as March hatters. You seem to have forgotten all I have done for you and am still doing. Ask your Admiralty who was it who designed the First 'Dreadnought' and sent them the plan. Pigeon holed somewhere in Whitehall that plan awaits calmly the verdict of an impartial posterity. Your War Minister will tell you who it was who gave him the idea of the Territorial Army. Was that the work of a secret enemy? You make it very difficult for me . . ."

THE BIRTH OF PROFESSIONAL IMAGE CULTIVATION: THE FIGHT FOR AMERICA'S NEUTRALITY DURING WORLD WAR I

British Activities

At the end of the 19th century Great Britain, because of her imperial telegraph cable communications strategy, had an enormous advantage in the field of international communication. Referring to Germany, a report to the Cabinet dated December 11, 1911 concluded that "it would be possible to isolate Germany from practically the whole world outside Europe . . ." (Kennedy, 1971, p. 744). Indeed, in World War I the first British act of war was to cut Germany's overseas cables on August 5, cutting Germany off from the world's most important neutral country, America, at the very moment when American public opinion on the so-called *Kriegsschuldfrage* (question of responsibility for the outbreak of war) was being formed. McAdoo (1931), Secretary of the Treasury and Wilson's son-in-law, reported that, because of cable control: "Nearly everything in the newspapers which came from Europe during the war was censored and colored in the Allied interest" (p. 322). According to Grattan (1929/1969) "honest, unbiased news simply disappeared out of the American papers along about the middle of August, 1914" (p. 44). In fact, the British Defense of Realm Act (DORA, 1914) made it an offense to publish information "of such a nature as is calculated to be or might be directly or indirectly useful to the enemy" (Sanders & Taylor, 1982, p. 9). H. C. Peterson (1939) observed: "Newspapers in America during the years of neutrality represented the endpoint of the British propaganda campaign" (p. 159). A content analysis of news items that appeared in <u>The New York Times</u> and in Chicago's daily press between the outbreak of World War I and America's entry into the war, demonstrates that American newspaper readers in fact almost exclusively depended on war information that either came from or was at least controlled by the Entente powers (Foster, 1935, 1937). News about such important events as the German invasion of Belgium or the sinking of the *Lusitania* came without exception from Germany's enemies. Foster (1935) wrote: "During the first year of the war, 70 per cent of the front-page war news was of Entente origin, and the proportion received directly from Germany did not exceed 4 per cent" (p. 468).

At the beginning of the war the British government was concerned about German propaganda activities in the United States (Sanders, 1975; Squires, 1935). In September Charles F. G. Masterman, a member of the Cabinet, became head of the British propaganda organization, known as "Wellington House". The activities of Wellington House were kept secret, even from Parliament (Sanders, 1975; Squires, 1935). In fact, secrecy was the main characteristic of British propaganda, resulting in credibility because no connections to official sources could be located. As Nicholson (1931), an assistant to Masterman, pointed out, "It was an obvious advantage to conceal as far as possible the existence and the sources of propaganda . . ." (p. 594).

Wellington House was concerned with the production, translation, and distribution of books, pamphlets, government publications, speeches, and so forth. They also assisted with the placing of articles and interviews designed to influence the opinion in the world's newspapers and magazines, especially in America. Furthermore, they helped to provide information and facilities to London correspondents of neutral papers, and managed personal correspondence with influential people abroad as well as arrangements for the interchange of visits and personal tours to neutral and Allied countries (Nicholson, 1931). Wellington House never used official channels of communication, preferring instead personal contacts (Peterson, 1939; Squires, 1935) or organizations that were credible per se. Oxford University, for example, published 87 *Oxford Pamphlets*, whose authors were able "to give a patriotic bias to the apparent objective presentation of material" (Squires, 1935, p. 17). Masterman's propaganda aim was not simply to present a one-sided point of view, but to let the recipients draw their own conclusions from the facts presented in the publications (Sanders, 1975).

The subtlety with which personal contacts were handled is evidenced by the organization of the visit to the United States by James Barrie, the famous creator of Peter Pan, and the popular adventure writer A. E. W. Mason. Roosevelt received a letter from Sir Edward Grey, dated September 10, 1914, which he replied on October 3, 1914 as follows: "My dear Grey -- I have just received your letter and immediately asked Barrie and Mason to lunch with me. I have just written an article for the *Outlook*, and a series of articles for various daily papers upon the war, in which, while I did my best not to be offensive to Germany I emphatically backed the position that England, and specifically you, have taken" (Grattan, 1929/1969, 52). It was public relations carried out masterfully.

To a degree that had no historical precedent, British intellectuals took part in the great propaganda effort to stigmatize Germany as the only one responsible for the outbreak of the war.[1] British authors soon created a propaganda myth that prevailed until the end of war: "The Allies, particularly Britain, had no responsibility of starting the war, which was a product of German militarism and lust for conquest" (Buitenhuis, 1987, p. XVI). Masterman was primarily responsibile for this Gleichschaltung (bringing into line) of intellectuals. He invited many of England's major writers to take part in a secret meeting on September 2, 1914 (Buitenhuis, 1987). Most attended, among them G. K. Chesterton, Sir Arthur Conan Doyle, John Galsworthy, Sir Gilbert Parker, George Trevelyan, and Herbert George Wells. No minutes exist, however, documenting this Wellington House meeting. The British authors announced their support of the war in a so-called *Author's Manifesto,* which appeared in The New York Times on September 18, 1914 and was reprinted on a full page in the Sunday Supplement of The New York Times on October 18, with the authors' signatures. The headlines read: "Famous British Authors Defend England's War. Fifty-Three of the Best-Known Writers of the Empire Sign a Vigorous Document Saying That Great Britain Could Not Have Refused to Join the War Without Dishonor."

Throughout the war, Wellington House used writers to sustain the illusion of present glory and coming victory. S. K. Ratcliffe (1917) concluded that never before had so many literary craftsmen

---

[1] In Germany, too, intellectuals were willingly cooperating with the government, treating the horrors of war in rather euphemistic terms and pointing out the superiority of German culture. The "Declaration of the 93" was a document signed at first by 93 personalities of academic and cultural life: "We as representatives of German science and art protest herewith before the entire world of culture against the lies and defamations with which the enemies of Germany strive to dirty the pure intentions of Germany in the difficult battle for existence which has been forced upon it" (Doerries, 1989, p. 48). Link (1960) reported that the declaration was distributed throughout the United States: "Have faith in us! Believe, that we shall carry on this war to the end as a civilized nation, to whom the legacy of a Goethe, a Beethoven, and a Kant, is just as sacred as its own hearths and homes. For this we pledge you our names and our honour" (p. 34).

been drawn into public service, for example, as censors, pamphleteers, employees of the press bureau and the propaganda agencies. Apart from George Bernhard Shaw and the Cambridge group, the literati "ha[d] nearly all undergone a spiritual conversation" (Buitenhuis, 1987, p. 6). H. G. Wells, one of the great literary figures of the 20th century, worked for the British propaganda machine. He hated Germany and felt obligated to warn the world of "Frankenstein Germany", inhabited by people of intellectual inferiority. He also coined the famous phrase "The War that will end War". Wells distinguished between the German people and Prussian militarism: "We fight not to destroy a nation, but a nest of evil ideas" (Smith, 1986, p. 219). Wells also remarked: "Not Germany for Germans would we destroy, but that double-headed crow, Kaiserism *cum* Kruppism, is the blackest omen mankind has ever seen" (Smith, 1986, p. 219).

In contrast to the Germans, who did not allow neutral correspondents to visit the front[1], the Britons handled journalists perfectly. American correspondents, accompanied by diplomatic officers, were driven to the front: "They were then wined and dined at the headquarters chateau and quietly briefed about the British case" (Knightley, 1975, p. 121). The British were extraordinarily successful in this foreign press-influencing effort. Indeed, Frederick Palmer, who represented all three major American news agencies, was the only non-British journalist in the original group accredited to the British Expeditionary Force in France (Palmer, 1934).

The Neutral Press Committee was established on September 11, 1914 (Sanders & Taylor, 1982) and directed by the journalist H. G.

---

[1] Sven Hedin was the exception. The famous Swedish explorer published his experiences in <u>Nach Osten!</u> (1916). German military was strictly opposed to conducted tours to the front. According to Matthias Erzberger (1920), who was in charge of the German foreign propaganda, the military's ideal of masculinity was responsible for not being allowed to appeal to the sympathy of the neutral nations in propaganda and to point out that due to the British blockade Germany was starving. The motto of the military was *"Uns kann keiner!"*

Mair, former assistant editor of the Daily Chronicle. Its task was to influence journalists from Allied and neutral countries. Sanders and Taylor argued that, by appealing to opinionmakers rather than to the opinion itself, the Neutral Press Committee worked effectively. Perhaps the best description of the British work with the press can be found in Beaverbrook (1925): "Better than any pumped-in propaganda abroad was this method of making the leaders of the Imperial, neutral or allied press themselves the propagandists when they returned home" (p. 12). Friendly relations with the press were cultivated intensively in London. There was a meeting every week with American correspondents including regular access to high-ranking people in politics whose names alone guaranteed the event worth reporting. Against this background Peterson's (1939) assertion is understandable: "The censorship bureau in Great Britain must be considered a determining factor in controlling American opinion, because the news it passed was the version the American press released" (p. 14).

Wellington House had a special America section headed by the novelist Sir Gilbert Parker,[1] "who gave his entire time voluntarily" (Masterman, 1939/1968, p. 274). Parker spent the first months of the war analyzing American newspapers and working out a plan to influence them. With the help of *Who's Who* he compiled a mailing list of Americans likely to be able to sway public opinion.[2] The

---

[1] Sir Gilbert (1918), Canadian-born and a former MP, had good personal contacts and a respected reputation in the United States: "I was fortunate in having a wide acquaintance in the United States and in knowing that a great many people had read my books and were not prejudiced against me. . . . Practically since the day war broke out between England and the Central Powers I became responsible for American publicity" (p. 522).

[2] Ford (1919) maintained that Parker had a mailing list of about 50,000 or 60,000 names of individuals who were most likely to be active in the formation of public opinion (cf. also Peterson, 1939). According to Sanders and P. M. Taylor (1982) by 1917 the list had increased to 170,000 addresses, eventually containing 260,000 entries. Parker resigned on grounds of ill health in February 1917. His successor was Professor William Macneile Dixon from Glasgow University. Dixon described in a letter how he carried

fundamental principle of Britain's propaganda in the United States was to establish and instrumentalize personal contacts. Arthur Willert, Washington correspondent of <u>The Times</u>, had warned Britain to use open propaganda techniques, because the Americans "would dislike any machinery for the manipulation of their public opinion" (Sanders & Taylor, 1982, p. 168). British interests would be served best by sympathetic Americans.

Even years after the war, prominent Britons were still being quoted as saying that before America came into the war there had been no British propaganda in the United States (Squires, 1935). The activities were so secret[1] that in the letters of the British ambassador, written between August 1914 and April 1917, the name Gilbert Parker is not mentioned once (Squires, 1935), although in practical terms he had been assigned the task of influencing American public opinion when war broke out. Viereck (1930) reported that Parker had said to him about 10 years after the

---

on the propaganda work of Parker: "My method was very simple. I had a list of all principal newspapers published in the States, a list of all Doctors, a list of all the ministers and engineers and so forth. Any book or pamphlet which I thought would be of interest to Doctors I sent to Doctors, and so on. If any were of general interest, I sent them to the newspapers and perhaps to some of the others" (Squires, 1935, p. 57).

[1] It is doubtful whether British propaganda activities took place in such absolute secrecy that no American noticed it, as Knightley (1975) maintained. Josephus Daniels (1944), Secretary of the Navy in Wilson's Cabinet, recalled: "Hardly had the reverberations of the first guns in Belgium died away the propaganda for Uncle Sam to fight with the Allies began" (p. 565). McAdoo (1931) remarked on Germany's propaganda: "I'm morally convinced that the Allies were doing the same thing, but we had no documentary proof" (p. 330). McAdoo commented in his memoirs that British propaganda, "disguised as news and opinions, was undoubtly a violation of American neutrality, but what could be done about it?" (p. 322). At least some American journalists must have been aware of the fact that there were propaganda efforts. A commentary in *The New York Times* (September 9, 1914) was published with the headline: "The Press Agents' War". The author argued: "The present European war . . . deserves to be distinguished as *first press agents* war" (p. 8).

end of the war: "Every penny of our expense was paid by the British Government except for the contributions which I received from Americans" (p. 129). When questioned whether he would describe his activities in his memoirs Parker said: "I shall say nothing except what I have already written in my article on propaganda. I have no right to reveal the innermost secrets of the British Government" (p. 129). Viereck continued: "Allied propagandists covered their tracks very well. They destroyed every compromising document wherever possible"[2] (p. 139). The German propaganda on the other hand was exposed in various ways. U.S. Secretary of State Robert Lansing (1935), reported that the improper activities of German and Austrian officials and agents were then a matter "of constant investigations by the United States Secret Service, the special agents of the Department of Justice, and the inspectors of the Post Office Department, who were also aided by the police in many of our cities" (p. 67).

Although Parker's activities are not well documented, there are several accounts of his operations (Millis, 1935; Peterson, 1939; Silber, 1932; Squires, 1935), revealing that American correspondents willingly received articles written by patriotic "intellectuals". The Oxford Pamphlets were successfully disseminated in the United States. They went to opinion makers such as journalists, publicists, government officials, and so on. Parker maintained credibility in two ways. First the publications of Wellington House were sent off by Parker himself, a personal letter enclosed, in order to create the image of an English patriot performing his duty spontaneously (one such letter is reprinted in Peterson, 1939, p. 52). Second Parker also tried to make it appear that pro-Allied propaganda emanated largely from the spontaneous overflow of generous emotions by Americans themselves on behalf

---

[2] Viereck (1930) quoted Colonel Norman G. Thwaites, who was working for the British Secret Service in the United States: "We kept our affairs pretty well to ourselves. So little was known about English organization that when America declared war, even the Chief of Police in New York could not give the name of more than one" (p. 35).

of the Allied cause, which soon became identified with the cause of civilization itself.

In an article published in *Harper's Monthly Magazine* in 1918, Parker gave an account of his activities in America. For example, he supplied 360 newspapers in the smaller states with an English newspaper, which gave a weekly review and commentary of the affairs of the war. Furthermore he advised and stimulated many people to write articles and established associations by personal correspondences with influential and eminent people of every profession in the United States. Parker wrote: "Besides an immense private correspondence with individuals, we had our documents and literature sent to a great number of public libraries, Y.M.C.A. societies, universities, colleges, historical societies, clubs, and newspapers" (p. 522).

Parker (1918) issued a weekly or biweekly report to the British Cabinet on the state of opinion in America (*American Press Résumé*; Peterson, 1939). Furthermore, he was in "constant touch with the permanent correspondents of American newspapers in England. I also frequently arranged for important public men in England to act for us by interviews in American newspapers" (p. 521). Parker held the view that the United States entered the war "because they believed that the German policy is a betrayal of civilization" (p. 521). He continued his argument: "Everyone knows that the Prussian military organization had thrown overboard all rules of war which centuries of civilization had produced and imposed . . ." (p. 522).

One clever move by Parker was to arrange for the translation, printing, and U.S. distribution of the works of extreme German nationalists, militarists, and exponents of *Machtpolitik* like von Treitschke, Nietzsche, and von Bernhardi (Link, 1960; Peterson, 1939). The aim was to explain to America the motivating forces of the terrible character of Imperial Germany -- militarism, ruthlessness that knew no restraints, exaltation of the state, and worship of power and might -- and the consequences should a nation thus obsessed triumph.[1]

The British were not only in the business of intellectual and sophisticated propaganda but of atrocity propaganda, too. Wells was not alone in his fight. He was assisted by Kipling, who not only warned "The Hun is at the gate"[2] but also said: "This is not war. It is against wild beasts that we fight. There is no arrangement possible with wild beasts." Stories of Germans cutting off the hands of children, boiling corpses to make soap, crucifying prisoners of war, and using priests as clappers in cathedral bells were widely believed among both Allies and neutrals. Atrocity propaganda was part of the strategy of the British propagandists to make a more or less "normal" war appear to be a fight between the forces of good and evil. British propaganda aimed at convincing America that the British, or even better, the Allied cause was America's cause, too.[3]

---

[1] The New York Times on August 9, 1914 gave the whole front page of its Sunday Magazine to an article on the "remarkable prophetic book" of General Friedrich von Bernhardi, Germany and the Next War, which had "foretold Germany's war plans". This chauvinistic book "was reprinted by the million to flood the United States as well as the Allied and other neutral countries." Millis (1935) wrote: "Bernhardi, moreover, served but to point to a whole vast field lying ready for exploitation. Nietzsche, Treitschke and the invaluable literature of the Pan-German League were instantly laid under contribution and the stupified Germans discovered themselves convicted before world opinion on the evidence of a few writers whom the vast majority of Germans had never read or never even heard of. (p. 77). Houston (1926) commented on Bernhardi: "The lessons of history confirm the view that wars which have been deliberately provoked by far-seeing statesmen have had the happiest results" (p. 289).

[2] According to Roetter (1974) "the only protest against calling the Germans 'Huns' came from a group of English scholars who argued that identifying the Germans with the Huns was an insult to the Mongols living in Central Asia" (p. 46).

[3] According to Lasswell (1927) the widespread reports about horrors allegedly perpetrated by the Germans, in particular about massacres of Belgian children, produced a marked change in the image of Germans in the United States and Great Britain. However, in the long term the spreading of the horror stories had negative effects in Britain. After the war the British

So as not to produce a boomerang effect in the United States, where a strong German minority lived the Allied propaganda tried to produce a split image of Germany, consisting on the one hand of Prussian militarism and on the other hand emphasizing Germany's culture (e.g., Goethe, Kant, Beethoven, etc.).[1] President Wilson (1918) reinforced this split image. In his address to Congress on April 2, 1917, he said: "We have no quarrel with the German people. We have no feeling toward them but one of sympathy and friendship" (p. 42). And in his speech of June 14, 1917, he remarked: "The war was begun by the military masters of Germany, who proved to be also the masters of Austria-Hungary. These men have never regarded nations as peoples, men, women, and children of like blood and frame as themselves, for whom governments existed and in whom governments had their life. They have regarded them merely as serviceable organizations which they could, by force or intrigue, bend or corrupt to their own purpose" (p. 53).

---

population learned that their own propaganda had been lying to them (cf. Ponsonby, 1928) and from then on it was regarded as incredible. So when in World War II the Germans did perpetrate unspeakable atrocities, nobody believed reports about them because it was assumed their own propaganda was spreading lies again. The Nazis themselves used the British atrocity propaganda in order to deny that they were torturing Jews in concentration camps. Wanderscheck (1940) wrote: "Der Bryce-Bericht entspricht etwa dem englischen Weißbuch von 1939 über die Mißhandlung der Juden in deutschen Konzentrationslagern" (The Bryce Report is more or less an equivalent to the 1939 English White Book on the mistreatment of Jews in German concentration camps; p. 31).

[1] Abbott (1915) discussed this problem and asked the question "this great war and business machine, is this the Germany which so many of us have so long known and loved? Is this the land of *Freundlichkeit* and *Gemütlichkeit*, of quaint costume and custom, of friendly hearts and simple ways, of Christmas trees and toys, Rhine wine, Bavarian beer, of art, music, letters, science, philosophy, universities?" (p. 678). The answer was simple and self-evident: "We face, in the field of politics, not Germany but Prussia, a Prussia which, however is seeking to disguise itself in the robe of German culture, still remains what it has always been, no thinker, nor musician, nor poet, but a conqueror . . ." (p. 678).

German Propaganda in the United States

German propagandists in the United States were not as stupid or naive as some authors argue. The German Embassy in Washington was quite aware of the importance of propaganda in the United States, but presenting the German position was a difficult task, communication with Germany was not easy, and no coordination was done in Berlin. The main actors for Germany (the German Propaganda Cabinet) were ambassador Count von Bernstorff, the German-American journalist George S. Viereck, Dr. Bernhard Dernburg, who officially represented the German Red Cross and who was in charge of the German Press Bureau and Information Service, and Dr. Heinrich Albert of the Department of the Interior.

Also active in German propaganda was psychologist Professor Hugo Münsterberg of Harvard, who tried to influence American public opinion and to win sympathy for the German side. For example, Undersecretary Arthur Zimmermann instructed Ambassador Bernstorff on December 27, 1914 to ask Münsterberg to answer Roosevelt on the Belgian question (Link, 1960). On August 5, 1914, in an article entitled "Fair Play" published in the Boston Herald, he defended Germany against the accusation of sole responsibility for the outbreak of war. Münsterberg sent the article to Roosevelt and, in an accompanying letter (dated August 5, 1914; cf. Roosevelt Papers), asked him not to join the "rush against Germany". Münsterberg also had some meetings with Roosevelt whom he regarded as a friend of Germany. In September 1914 Münsterberg published The War and America; a second book The Peace and America followed in 1915. Münsterberg also wrote to President Wilson on November 7, 1914, complaining that America was favoring the Allies at Germany's expense. The professor not only referred to possible effects on the vote of German, Swedish, Irish, and Jewish groups, but also threatened a "regular systematic campaign . . . to take care that the Democratic party becomes tabooed as the one which has made America practically an ally of England" (Baker, 1968, p. 222). Baker (1968) commented: "It was so often the misfortune of the German sympathizers to have been impolitic or offensive in their methods" (p. 223). The philosopher Professor Eugen Kühnemann also engaged in publicity work, traveling around the United States and making speeches to German-American groups. Another German propagandist was the Celticist Kuno Meyer, who had been sent by the Foreign Office to the United States propagandize in Irish circles (Doerries, 1989).

The first step taken to advance the German cause was the establishment of the German Information Bureau. The Germans, like the British, preferred to use interpersonal channels of communication to distribute their point of view. According to Wilke (1993) the German Embassy had a list of 60,000 names, mostly passengers of the *Hamburg-Amerika-Linie*. They also had lists of members of Congress, leading members of the administration, public libraries, colleges, clubs, and so forth. Ambassador Bernstorff recommended using libraries, especially the Library of the Congress, which he regarded as excellent places for circulating German propaganda material. The German Press Bureau and Information Service could rely on help from the German-American Alliance -- which was well established in St. Louis, Chicago, Cincinatti, and Milwaukee -- to distribute its bulletins. The Lutherian Church, with over 6,000 congregations in the United States with parishioners numbering some 3,000,000 helped, too (Erzberger, 1920; Roetter, 1974). Germany, after having tried in vain to buy the New York Sun and the Washington Post, bought the New York Evening Mail (for $1.5 million) with sole the purpose of reaching a large metropolitan audience (Doerries, 1989).

The Germans, also like the English, made use of the third-party approach and tried to influence public opinion through the publication of books written by Americans. Millis (1935) reported that the authors Frank Harris and Edwin J. Clapp were on Dr. Albert's payroll. When Dr. Albert heard of Clapp's lectures on British interference with American trade, he urged him to expand his ideas into a book and paid some $20,000 in all to cover costs of preparation, publication, and advertising.

According to Lansing (1935) "publicity agents were sent out by the German Government to aid the propagandists in their endeavour to influence American public opinion" (p. 75), but Lansing does not specify who the publicity agents were. May (1959) maintained that German agents organized publicity for an arms embargo as a step to hasten peace. In December 1914 the services of William Bayard Hale, a leading American journalist[1] and former advisor of President Wilson, were secured. According to Viereck (1930) Dernburg had engaged Hale to wage a publicity campaign. Grattan (1929/1969) elaborated: "He was put in immediate charge of the news sheet, and was detailed to prepare pamphlets and other matter for the general public. His salary was to be $15,000 a year and he apparently continued in active service for almost precisely a year, although his contract did not expire until the middle of 1918" (p. 87). Among other things, Hale negotiated with the League of American Women for Strict Neutrality, who claimed to have gathered 200,000 signatures for a petition to Congress (Millis, 1935).

Two cases of misfortune hampered the German propaganda machine. On July 24, 1915, Dr. Albert "lost" his briefcase, which was stuffed with documents relating to the German propaganda activities, in an elevated train. The daily <u>New York World</u> obtained these papers and started a series of articles on German intrigues and

---

[1] Hearst was not informed about his correspondent's second job (Doerries, 1989). How close the connections between Wilson and Hale was documented by Josephus Daniels (1944), Secretary of the Navy in Wilson's cabinet. He pointed out that early in the campaign that put Wilson in the White House, the Democratic Party circulated a number of copies of William Bayard Hale's *Woodrow Wilson: The Story of His Life*: "It was the *vade mecum* of all Democratic speakers. It was the best story of Wilson before he became President, that had been written" (p. 76). In 1913 Wilson sent "his personal friend and biographer" (p. 181) Hale to Mexico to make a firsthand study and report on the situation over there; Hale was entrusted with an important and confidential mission in the critical days of Watchful Waiting (Daniels, 1944).

conspiracies (Tansill, 1939).[1] Lansing (1935) speculated on the motivation to publish the papers: "The purpose of publishing this interesting correspondence of Doctor Albert was to counteract, in a measure, the political effect of the slanderous articles on the government and its officials, which were constantly appearing in the newspapers and periodicals receiving subsidies from Germany" (p. 77).

The second mishap occurred on August 30, 1915, when James Archibald, an American citizen and journalist, was searched by the British at Falmouth (D. W. Martin, 1959). Archibald was a dispatch bearer for Dr. Dumba, the Austro-Hungarian ambassador.[2] This time he was also carrying papers written by Captain von Papen (Franz von Papen was Chancellor of the Reich from June 1932 till November 1932), whose responsibility in the German Embassy was to purchase munitions and raw materials. The British, who had been tipped off by the Czech Intelligence Service, informed the Americans. The American Foreign Office demanded that Dr. Dumba be recalled and informed the German Embassy that von Papen was no longer welcome in the United States. The Dumba-Archibald affair was the finishing stroke for Austro-German propaganda in the United States.

---

[1] According to Peterson (1939) these disclosures resulted from the theft of the Albert portfolio by Frank Burke, an American Secret Service operator. The most reliable source of this event is McAdoo (1931). The Secretary of the Treasury supervised the U.S. Secret Service, which was organized for the purpose of running down counterfeiters. Witcover (1989) suggested that the United States did not want to acknowledge that a government agent had seized the private papers of a fully accredited diplomat, so the documents were slipped to the *New York World.*

[2] According to Roetter (1974), Austro-Hungary played no significant part in the struggle for American public opinion. Masaryk (1927/1969) told another story. He pointed out that Austria and the Magyars made quite intensive efforts in propaganda and one of their tactics was to create the impression that Austro-Hungaria was the victim of Germany, having been compelled into the war by her. D. W. Martin (1959) gave a detailed analysis of the propaganda activities of Austro-Hungary in the United States.

Count von Bernstorff had excellent relations with the press. According to Link (1960), he "by assiduous effort won the confidence of the newspapermen and constantly fed them information, most of it actually quite accurate, that portrayed German actions and policies in a favorable light" (p. 352). Heckscher (1991) portrayed Bernstorff as "a genial character, liked by the Washington press corps whom he greeted individually as he walked the streets or drove himself about the city in his big Packard, providing a source of news when almost everyone else in Washington was close-mouthed. Wilson felt he could talk man-to-man with Bernstorff. Just prior to dispatching the first *Lusitania* note he received the ambassador in what the latter reported to Berlin as *an extraordinarily friendly exchange of views*" (p. 374). Bernstorff, the "master in the art of public relations" according to Kevin J. O'Keefe (1972, p. 193), had a working agreement with New Yorker journalists to quote him as a source only when he had given permission. Bernstorff (1920) himself wrote that a few weeks after his arrival in New York he ceased his propaganda work because it would have endangered his relationship with the Administration. But he admitted continuing his close contacts with journalists whom he fed confidential information.

Regardless of these apparently good relations with the press, Germany's main problem was that she had to work against a culture shaped mostly by British heritage. According to Roetter (1974), the Germans "imagined that their purpose perhaps might best be served by setting on the discontented section of society -- Protestant against Catholic, worker against employer, Jew against gentile, Negroe against White" (p. 55f). In their efforts to keep the United States out of the war, the Germans tried to instrumentalize the peace movements and even set some foot on themselves (Grattan, 1929/1969; Millis, 1935). The pacifists were carrying on a vigorous campaign against the idea of the United States in any way participating in the war (Lansing, 1935). Bernstorff telegraphed Berlin on November 1, 1916: "Since the *Lusitania* case we have strictly confined ourselves to such propaganda as cannot hurt us if it becomes known. The sole exception is perhaps the Peace propaganda which has cost the largest amount, but which also has been the most successful."

Two events drastically changed public opinion and the opinion of decision makers: the sinking of the *Lusitania* and the execution of Edith Cavell on October 12, 1915. Edith Cavell was a nurse who had helped Allied soldiers escape from prison camps. According to Walworth (1965) "her martyrdom impressed American hearts once more with the frightfulness of Prussian militarism" (p. 28).

After the British blockade of the North Sea on February 4, 1915, Germany announced her countermeasure, the submarine blockade of Britain. On May 1, the day the Cunard liner *Lusitania* sailed with 1,257 passengers from New York to Liverpool, an advertisement composed by the German embassy's "PR department" was published in seven New York dailies in close proximity to the notice of the *Lusitania*'s sailing. The advertisement reminded travelers that British ships sailing in the war zone do so at their own risk (reprinted in Bernstorff, 1920; Link, 1954). On May 7, the liner was sunk by a submarine.

The press reaction was moderate; only a minority demanded the United States enter the war. Secretary of State William Jennings Bryan was of the opinion that "England has been using our citizens to protect her munitions" (Borchard & Lage, 1949, p. 144).[1] But after the *Lusitania* incident German propaganda broke down. Bernstorff (1920) cabled Chancellor von Bethmann-Hollweg on May 17, 1915: "Our best plan is frankly to acknowldege that our propaganda in this country has, as the result of the *Lusitania* incident, completely collapsed" (p. 25). The *Lusitania* affair transformed former President Roosevelt into an all-out

---

[1] Bryan (1925) wrote to Wilson: "Germany has a right to prevent contraband from going to the Allies, and a ship carrying contraband should not rely upon passengers to protect her from attack - it would be like putting women and children in front of an army" (p. 399).

interventionist.[1]   Roosevelt   prepared   an   editorial   for   the
Metropolitan magazine called "Murder on the High Sea" and later
explained: "I never wished to take part in the European war until the
sinking of the *Lusitania*" (Miller, 1992, p. 546).

Wilson's decision to declare war surely was not determined solely
by British propaganda. Two additional German actions were
decisive in America's decision: the declaration of unrestricted
submarine warfare against all ships, neutral or belligerent, in the war
zone; and the Zimmermann Telegram, in which the German Foreign
Secretary, Dr. Alfred Zimmermann, on January 1917 informed the
German Ambassador in Mexico City that in the event of war with
the United States he was to negotiate for a German-Mexican
alliance, holding out to the Mexicans the bait of regaining Texas,
New Mexico, and Arizona.

The Creel Committee

President Woodrow Wilson recognized public opinion as a major
force in the war, and on April 14, 1917 established the Committee
on Public Information (CPI) headed by the journalist George Creel
to conduct propaganda abroad and in the United States. The task
was the "whole business of mobilizing the mind of the world"
(Creel, 1920, p. XIII). That is, America should be represented not
merely as a strong man fully armed, but as a strong man fully armed
and believing in the cause for which he is fighting, that is fighting for
ideas and ideals. According to Creel (1920), the CPI's charter was
to carry "to every corner of the civilized globe the full message of
America's idealism, unselfishness, and indomitable purpose" (p. 4).

---

[1] Roosevelt commented on the advertising placed beside the Cunard Line
announcement of the sailing of the Lusitania: "Had he been president when
the Germans placed such a notice in the papers . . . he would have
immediately summoned the German ambassador, given him his passport . .
. and hustled him under guard on board the *Lusitania*" (Miller, 1992, p.
544).

The CPI was able to build on experience gained in the commercial sector. Creel (1920) described the fight for the minds of men, for the "conquest of their convictions" (p. 4): "In all things, from first to last, without halt or change, it was a plain publicity proposition, a vast enterprise in salesmanship, the world's greatest adventure in advertising" (p. 4). He avoided describing the activity as propaganda "for that word, in German hands, had come to be associated with deceit and corruption" (p. 4).

The propaganda output was aimed predominantly at the home audience in the United States. And in some places the propaganda successfully whipped up mass hysteria, as illustrated by Fosdick (1932). He recalled attending a meeting in New England, held under the auspices of a Christian church: "A speaker demanded that the Kaiser, when captured, be boiled in oil, and the entire audience stood on chairs to scream its hysterical approval. This was the mood we were in. This was the kind of madness that had seized us. It was a holy crusade, a war to end war" (p. 322). Goldman (1948), who characterized America's entry into the war as "brilliant publicity for publicity" (p. 12), reported "thousands were cheering proposals to change the name of German measles to *Liberty measles* and sauerkraut to *Liberty cabbage*" (p. 12).

Creel (1920) contended that one of his most effective ideas was to bring to the United States, periodically, delegations of foreign newspaper men so they might "see with their own eyes, hear with their own ears" (p. 227), and on their return be able to report fully on America's morale and effort. According to Creel, "these trips were of incalculable value in our foreign educational work" (p. 227). Mexico was selected for the initial experiment, the Swiss came next, then Italian journalists, and finally a fourth group from Scandinavia.

The start-up of the propaganda effort in foreign countries was difficult because, according to Creel (1920), "America controlled no cables, manipulated no press association, operated no propaganda machinery of any kind. We were, and always had been, dependent upon foreign press agencies for intercourse with the world" (p.

238). When America's world news service was created, the cables were foreign owned, the rates were prohibitive, and the cables themselves were overburdened. The CPI did not engage in atrocity propaganda, but instead attacked the military masters of Germany who had begun the war. Creel (1941) reported a conversation with Wilson shortly after America entered the war: "And there were the neutral nations to be fired with enthusiasm for a new and nobler world order. And the Central Powers too, for he did not believe, and could not bring himself to believe, that the peoples of Germany and Austria-Hungary were infatuated with the Kaiser's dream of world-wide dominion. Surely I could find ways and means of getting our war aims and peace terms into the enemy countries. Above all, he stressed the importance of intensive campaigns in England, France, Italy and Russia" (p. 27).

One CPI staff member was E. L. Bernays (1965), one of whose concerns was public opinion in Italy: "I started a service of colored postcards, showing our war preparations for overseas distribution, to bolster our allies when they thought the 'Yankees' were too slow in coming. We dispatched thousands of postcards to the Italian front soldiers to send back home and improve Italian morale" (p. 155). After the defeat of the Entente at the Piave River in August 1918, an American cargo ship was named *Piave* to suggest, for image reasons, an unbroken will to fight. Prominent Italian-Americans like Enrico Caruso signed declarations supporting the American policy and expressing their confidence in American help for Italy.

Resume -- The Birth of Professional Image Cultivation

At the outbreak of the war in 1914, America was clearly unwilling to participate. But the British "paper bullets" (a term coined by George Creel), gradually changed the climate of public opinion. It cannot be quantitatively ascertained what influence this one-sided information had on the later decision to declare war on the German Reich, but it certainly influenced public opinion and perhaps even the Congress. Any interpretation stressing propaganda as a major cause of the entrance into the war must illustrate first how that propaganda reached the White House, that is, Wilson and/or his advisors. To say the propaganda effect is evidenced by the influence of public opinion on the White House decision does not prove anything; it must be proven how much public opinion was influenced by propaganda and how this in turn influenced the Congress.

Propaganda during the First World War was public relations in the modern meaning of the word. Before E. L. Bernays (1965) ever started his "one-man campaign for public relations" (p. 289), British, German, and American propagandists waged PR campaigns. Nor must one forget the PR activities of the nations striving for their independence like Poland and Czechoslovakia. Reading Masaryk's (1927/1969) _The Making of a State: Memoirs and Observations, 1914 - 1918_ is like reading a guide to efficient international public relations, but the history of PR does need to be rewritten.

The campaigns discussed in section 5.3 were carried out in a way that contradicted the dominant paradigm in science. The initial approaches to the theoretical comprehension of mass communication were closely intertwined with doctrines of mass psychology and proceeded from the assumption that an omnipotent medium can influence the defenseless, isolated recipients at will; atrocity campaigns were based on this stimulus-response model of mass communication. Many of the PR campaigns waged during World War I forestalled results of later empirical studies of mass media effects research (e.g., the two-step flow of communication). Before scientific refutation of the simple stimulus-reaction model took place, the PR practitioners knew by intuition what to do. The propagandists of World War I even practiced symmetrical PR in the sense of Grunig (1989) (cf. the exchange of letters between Roosevelt and Grey). Furthermore, different PR tactics were employed according to the respective target group. Masterman's propaganda aim, for example, was not simply to present a one-sided point of view, but to let the recipients draw their own conclusions from the facts presented in the publications.[1] Leaving the public to make up their own minds appears to produce higher communicator credibility without being linked directly to a change of attitude.

---

[1] Whether it is more effective to draw explicit conclusions from a chain of arguments or let the addressees make up their own minds - which can be quite effect boosting in itself - depends on the complexity of the issues discussed and the intelligence, education, and motivation of the people addressed. Messages with no explicit conclusions can be lost on less intelligent and less motivated people. There are, however, adequate indications that the proportion of recipients who are caused to change their minds by a message without explicit conclusion rises with time (McGuire, 1969).

CHAPTER 6

Selected Cases of International Public Relations

IVY LEE AND PR FOR NAZI GERMANY

One of the first consultants to political PR for Nazi Germany was Carl Byoir. Basically, from the beginning, the firm of Carl Byoir & Associates took every client it could get. In 1933 Byoir opened business relations with the German Tourist Information Office, to which the connections with Nazi Germany were obvious. According to Ross (1959), the business relationship lasted 18 months. Byoir was paid 6,000 dollars a month. Ironically, Byoir was a Jew. In this context, Ross quoted Byoir's old boss, Gerry Swinehart: "Byoir always said that at the time he took the contract he did not know what Hitler was planning to do with the Jews" -- which would suggest that Byoir was the rare press agent who did not read the newspapers -- "but you can be sure that the criticism hurt him personally -- as a man inside" (p. 114). The firm of Carl Byoir & Associates was still being accused in 1976 by The New York Times of "a lingering stigma of having handled the German tourism account 40 years ago during the Hitler era" (Bender, 1976).

Even Ivy Lee, one of the most influential PR counsels in the United States, was harshly attacked in 1934 because of his connections to Nazi Germany when it was revealed that for $25,000 Lee was working for the German Dye Trust (I.G. Farben). Testifying before a committee of the House of Representatives, he made the point that he had no formal relationship with the Nazi government, but conceded that the advice he offered his client was ultimately intended to guide the German government in its public relations in the United States. Among other things, he made suggestions for German statements on disarmament: "Germany does not want armament in itself. It is willing to destroy every weapon of war if other nations will do the same. If other nations, however, continue to refuse to disarm, the German government is left with no choice except to demand an equality of armament. The German people are unwilling to believe that any people will deny them this right today" (Hiebert, 1966, p. 289). Lee also proposed that Joachim von Ribbentrop, the special commissioner for disarmament, should visit the United States to explain Germany's position to President Roosevelt and also to enlighten the Foreign Policy Association and the Council on Foreign Relations on the issue. Lee testified that he had disseminated no German propaganda in the United States, that he only acted as adviser, and that his advice included the repeated suggestion that "they could never in the world get the American people reconciled to their treatment of the Jews and that Nazi propaganda in the United States was a mistake" (Hiebert, 1966, p. 290).

Regarding Lee's handling of the negative image of Hitler's storm troops, Hiebert (1966) reported: "Lee advised that the government issue a frank statement on this subject, including in the information that the storm troops number about 2,500,000 men, were 'between the ages of 18 and 60, physically well-trained and disciplined, but not armed, not prepared for war, and organized only for the purpose of preventing for all time the return of the Communist peril" (p. 289). This was an unimaginable masterpiece of ethics and moral elasticity because at the same time Lee worked for the recognition of the Soviet Union. When the United States recognized the Soviet Union in 1933, the communists in power (the "Communist peril" the storm troops were fighting) gave part of the the credit to Lee. Hiebert wrote: "Upon notification of American recognition, one of the first things done by Maxim Litvinov, Soviet Foreign Minister, was to send a cable to Ivy Lee expressing appreciation for the part he had played in paving the way for a closer Russian-American relationship" (p. 283).

It should not be assumed, however, that all PR firms would work for an client unscrupulous. For instance, shortly after the Nazi seizure of power in 1933, a representative of Adolf Hitler approached Bernays to recruit him as a PR agent for the Third Reich. Bernays remarked about this: "He wanted me to do some work for the German railroad or one of the concerns he was in charge of. I turned him down. I also turned down Somoza -- and Franco, too, even though the United States accepted Franco" (J. Blyskal & M. Blyskal, 1985, p. 85).

NAZI PROPAGANDA TO FOREIGN NATIONS

Germany's National Socialists were believers in a crude mass psychology with respect to propaganda. Like Freud in his 1921/1961 study Group Psychology and the Analysis of the Ego, the Nazis equated the relationship between leader and followers to that between hypnotist and subject -- the mass of two. It was Freud's theory that the conscience formed in the course of socialization is relinquished by the mass and assigned to the leader. In his 1895 study, Psychologie des foules, LeBon (1896) similarly saw a conscious personality decline when individuals became a mass. Regression to a state of abnormal, atavistic suggestibility allowed a mass soul to emerge. The mass was a single being governed by the law of spiritual unity of the mass, whose members acted mechanically, without their own will coming into it.

Adolf Hitler (1937/1962) took up this idea writing in Mein Kampf:

> The psyche of the great masses is not receptive to anything that is half-hearted and weak. Like the woman, whose psychic state is determined less by grounds of abstract reason than by an indefinable emotional longing for a force which will complement her nature, and who, consequently, would rather

> bow to a strong man than dominate a weakling, likewise the masses love a commander more than a petitioner and feel inwardly more satisfied by a doctrine, tolerating no other beside itself, than by the granting of liberalistic freedom with which, as a rule, they can do little, and are prone to feel that they have been abandoned. (p. 42)

On propaganda Hitler wrote:

> The receptivity of the great masses is very limited, their intelligence is small, but their power of forgetting is enormous. In consequence of these facts, all effective propaganda must be limited to a very few points and must harp on these in slogans until the last member of the public understands what you want him to understand by your slogan. As soon as you sacrifice this slogan and try to be many-sided, the effect will piddle away, for the crowd can neither digest nor retain the material offered. In this way the result is weakened and in the end entirely cancelled out. (p. 180)

So for Nazi propagandists the rules were: (a) It had to be primitive and oriented such that it could be absorbed by the least educated, and (b) propaganda is the art of incessant repetition.

Goebbels, the minister for propaganda in the Third Reich, took the view that "as a mass, the Volk is of female sex and demands a firm, secure hand" (Stephan, 1949, p. 66). Lying is part of the technique of propaganda. As Goebbels said, "I am for the old basic rule: once you have started to lie, stick to it. What we have said once is true and stays true. There must, after all, be something firm and of enduring value. A propagandist has no other choice. I know myself in this and I have no scruples" (Stephan, 1949, p. 69). In Zeman's (1964) assessment Nazi foreign propaganda was practically no different from domestic propaganda, except that breaking the enemy's morale was the ultimate objective of foreign propaganda. According to Zeman, Hitler supposedly said: "The place of artillery preparation for frontal attack by the infantry in trench warfare will in future be taken by revolutionary propaganda, to break down the

enemy psychologically before the armies begin to function at all . . .
How to achieve the moral breakdown of the enemy before the war
has started -- that is the problem that interests me" (p. 77).

Two examples of Nazi foreign propaganda are discussed here:
the "radio war" with Austria nd the influence of the 1936 Olympic
Games on Nazi image cultivation (Pohle, 1955). The Nazis' first all-
out propaganda attack was in summer 1933, shortly after the
Austrian chancellor Engelbert Dollfuss banned the Austrian National
Socialist Party, which was agitating for "Heimkehr ins Reich"
("return home to the Reich"). There followed what became known
as the "German-Austrian radio war" in 1933/1934, which was
characterized by aggressively destructive propaganda. The "war"
began with an announcement on Munich radio, audible throughout
Austria, that in the future Germany intended to pay more attention
to the situation in Austria and to report to Germans, on both sides
of the border, about the brutal fight being waged in Austria by a
small group of separatists against everything German. Earlier, on
March 18, 1933, in the run-up to the "war", the Bavarian justice
minister, Hans Frank, had warned the Austrian government on
Munich radio "in the friendliest way" not to do anything that might
cause the National Socialists in the Reich interfere in Austria on
behalf of the security and freedom of the German "Volksgenossen"
("members of the German people") in Austria. Austria, of course,
protested this, causing Hitler to remark to the Austrian ambassador
in Berlin that he "couldn't run after every talker".

Originally Chancellor Dollfuss had intended to attack the Nazi
radio propaganda in a speech at the January 1934 session of the
League of Nations, thereby appealing to world public opinion. But
he changed his plans and instead went to Hungary on a state visit.
German radio continued to call for the "overthrow of the Dollfuss
government" and reported on conditions in Austria in the bleakest
terms -- the population suffering shortages, worsened by a boycott
of German tourists, persecution of the National Socialists and
Socialists, and so forth. In Austria there was keen interest in all of
this. For one thing, the Munich transmissions could be received

clearly nearly everywhere in the country, and for another Austrian radio geared its political program to rebutting the German accusations and reports. It also reported the world's reactions to the German radio aggression. A feeling grew in the Austrian population that they were at the center of world interest, which in turn increased the popularity of the transmissions from Munich.

On July 25, 1934, Dollfuss was shot dead by the Austrian SS, who at the same time forced their way into the headquarters of Austrian radio and at pistol point made the announcer read the following statement on the air: "The Dollfuss government has resigned. Dr. Rintelen has taken over the business of government". But the Austrian coup that the Nazis had hoped for never materialized for various reasons. One was resistance by Mussolini, who had been Hitler's principal foreign ally and now marshaled troops at the Austrian border. Also, the German government distanced itself from the events in Vienna and Theo Habicht, "the person responsible for the Austria-propaganda" had to resign. German radio held back with comments on events in Austria until just before she was annexed by the German Reich in 1938.

The 1936 Olympic Games in Berlin offered the Nazis a chance to burnish the image of the German state, although ironically Berlin's hosting the games was due not to the Nazis, but to the Weimar Republic they had replaced. Before the foreign visitors arrived in Berlin there was a big "cleanup" which Zeman (1964) described as a "Potemkin village operation" (p. 109). The signs saying "Jews not wanted" disappeared; the aggressive Nazi newspaper Stürmer was no longer sold on the street. On the use of radio Pohle (1955) wrote: "The relaying of reports about the Olympic Games from Berlin to almost all radio countries of the world must indubitably rank as one of the great radio achievements in world broadcasting" (p. 416). Indeed, the "Olympia Organizer" of the Reich Broadcasting Company expressed German radio's greater role as follows: "With the first ever relaying of the Olympic Games German radio has been charged with a task of greatest cultural and state-political importance" (p. 416).

German radio passed its first major test by successfully relaying the winter Olympics from Garmisch-Partenkirchen in February 1936, with 300 reports and commentaries being relayed to 19 countries in the space of 10 days. As part of its preparations for the Olympic summer games, the German shortwave radio station ran special 3-month language courses for Englishspeaking listeners overseas to give them enough knowledge of German to travel to and stay in Germany and to understand the Olympic competitions. There were reports in various languages to make traveling in Germany easy and enjoyable. In Berlin, people offering accommodations were taught English, Italian, French, and Swedish. In addition to its normal budget, the radio was allocated 2 million Reichsmarks for the international relays. Pohle (1955) reported:

> 450 radio employees -- technicians, announcers, musicians, administration personnel -- were ordered to Berlin from all over the Reich. 300 microphones, 220 amplifiers, 20 outside broadcast vans created the technical prerequisites for the main operating panel, the socalled "centre for 40 countries" to handle simultaneously reports in many languages going to 20 European, and by shortwave, to 10 non-European countries from Berlin. Thus in the 16 days of the Olympic Games 2,500 reports in 28 languages went abroad, in addition to the 500 German reports. (p. 417)

From the German government's point of view the broadcast of the games were a total success. The technical input had paid off, exemplified by the telegrams of thanks sent by 67 foreign radio reporters to the Reich Minister for Popular Enlightenment and Propaganda (Goebbels) after the games: "We depart from Berlin full of admiration for the great achievements of German radio in both the technical and organisational fields". The director of NBC commented in a broadcast in the United States that the work done by the Reich's broadcasting system was unique in radio history, the first time an Olympics had been reported by radio. Goebbels himself rejected the occasional accusation in the foreign press that the Olympics was being misused for Nazi propaganda: "I can assure you that it is not so. If it were the case I would most probably know about it. However, Germany is at pains to show itself to its guests in the best possible light. We want them to see Germany the way it is, and not to put Potemkian villages up for them" (Hagemann, 1948, p. 209).

EDWARD L. BERNAYS: GAINING GOODWILL FOR INDIA

Bernays (1965) reported in his memoirs on image cultivation PR activities carried out by India in the United States from October 1951 to May 1952. The Indians had long been aware that Americans thought of clichés such as man-eating tigers, child brides, sacred cows, untouchables, wolf-children, snake charmers, and exotic religious sects in connection with India. Also, because India had remained neutral during the 1951 U.N. campaign in Korea it had a very negative image, apparently by virtue of the sentiment if you're not for me, you're against me. As Bernays observed, "India had become the scapegoat for the frustrations of millions of Americans for the Korean mess" (p. 714). But the Indians themselves wanted to be regarded by Americans as a young democratic state.

Bernays landed the contract with India primarily because of the mediation of India's U.S. ambassador, Pandit Nehru, a sister of President Nehru. Mrs. Nehru was sure she could get the Indian parliament to approve an annual fee of $35,000 for the PR campaign as well as a onetime payment of $175,000 for "out-of-pocket expenses for comprehensive information activities". Bernays claimed that he obtained information about India from such government sources as the State Department and the CIA so as not to acquire the reputation of doing PR for an opponent of the United States. The government agencies cooperated, believing Bernays work for India was in the national interest because India could become a bulwark of democracy in Asia.

Among other things, Bernays (1965) sent to India a list of questions for Nehru to be prepared to answer when he was interviewed or asked to give statements aimed at the American market, including the following: (a) What is Nehru's real attitude toward the United States? (b) What are areas of agreement in the policies of the United States and India? (c) What is India's real policy toward Russia? (d) What would India do if Russia became an aggressor against her? (e) What is India's role in preserving democracy in Asia? (f) What is India's attitude toward American investments?

Bernays (1965) suggested to Mrs. Nehru that he compose a statement explaining India's policy toward the United States: "I wrote the statement, emphasizing the mutuality of interest of India and the United States. The statement was cabled to New Delhi, where it appeared in the newspapers. Several days later Robert Trumbull cabled it to The New York Times, which played it up under a New Delhi dateline. The State Department and the public regarded the statement as a significant indication of the new Indian policy, which was drawing the nations closer together, and commented on it in an official statement" (p. 719).

On October 25, 1951, Mrs. Nehru informed Bernays that she had to leave America. Bernays' contract did not begin until November 6. The new Indian ambassador, Beney Rayan Sen -- whom Bernays (1965) described as a stiff, boring man -- arrived on November 26. Bernays arranged a dinner with journalists interested in India and a meeting with American journalists specializing in Indian affairs. According to Bernays, Sen proved a boring guest who did not make a good impression. Apparently, the ambassador's only success was an address to the "English-Speaking Union", probably because Bernays (whose memoirs contain not a hint of self-criticism) had prestructured the speech, to emphasize, among other things, that India welcomed American capital, evoking positive comment in the press.

Generally, the relationship developed quite unfavorably. According to Bernays (1965), Sen's annual report contained much wrong information and many distortions, as well as attacks against the United States. Bernays wrote that the official "castigated most of the American press and radio, making them scapegoats for his [Sen's] own ineptitude" (p. 723). Bernays also reported about difficulties in asserting his own views. For instance, if his recommendation which deviated from Sen's, Bernays alleged he was accused by Sen of being bribed by Pakistan.

Despite this Bernays (1965) started a "frontal attack" on American opinion leaders:

> [. . .] the communications leaders who were editorial heads of newspapers, columnists, writers known for their interests in women's affairs, education, business and finance, labor and social welfare, agriculture and farming, science and technology, arts and letters, special features, house organs, writers and lecturers, government officials, foundations, fraternal orders and so on. A carefully prepared letter offered material geared to the particular interest of each group. By January 35,000 letters had gone out, and we received thousands of requests for material about India, which we prepared in stories for publication, fact sheets, forum outlines and similar data, facts and points of view we felt were important for the American people to have. (p. 724)

In addition, the ambassador traveled throughout the United States giving speeches prepared by Bernays to selected audiences. Different press materials were prepared for each town. In Bernays' (1965) assessment this kind of PR was successful. In February 1952 Nehru made a speech about India's relations with the United States and its stand on communism in which -- and we have only Bernays' word on this -- he again kept to the guidelines set by Bernays. The speech was received positively by the American media. And finally, on March 13, 1952 India had the chance, and did so successfully, to present itself in a half-hour television program.

Bernays and India broke off relations when in May 1957 Ambassador Sen tried to find out why The New York Times did not side with India in the Kashmir dispute. The Indian embassy tried to pressure the paper with threats -- an unwise tatic in so far as image cultivation is concerned as it certainly aroused resistance from the journalists effected. The New York Times editor in charge of India, Herbert Matthews, told Bernays (1965) that the Indian consul-general, Arthur Lall, had visited him and "threatened war" (p. 727) on the paper unless it changed its stance. Matthews himself characterized Lall's visit as "an attempt at undue moral pressure and intimidation" (p. 727).

Bernays dissolved his contract with India and sent his letter of notice to the Ambassador Sen on May 26. In the letter, he pointed out that the Indian officials were not prepared to listen to his counsel on questions of public opinion. Moreover, the Indians wrongly believed that their judgment on questions of American public opinion was the only possible and right one. They had no understanding of the freedom and independence of the American press. Further, according to Bernays, the Indians had an arrogant tendency to do things their own way ignoring reality. In his memoirs, however, Bernays showed a tendency to attribute PR successes to himself and the failures to others.

THE TACTIC OF WITHDRAWAL: PUBLIC RELATIONS IN THE UNITED STATES FOR DEVELOPING COUNTRIES

Many developing countries work hard to cultivate their images abroad. Manheim and Albritton (1984) studied the influence of the activities of PR agencies on the images of nations. The authors proceeded from the premise that according to Justice Department data 25 nation-states entered into PR contracts in the United States from 1974 to 1978. They examined in particular The New York Times coverage of six of those countries: the Republic of Korea, The Philippines, Yugoslavia, Argentina, Indonesia, and Rhodesia. Coverage of Mexico, although it had no contract with any agency, was also monitored. The New York Times was chosen because it is the newspaper most widely read by the American elite, is most frequently quoted by political decision makers, is known from previous research to have a strong agenda-setting effect on public opinion, and provides more foreign coverage than comparable American daily newspapers.

A 2-year period of coverage was monitored in each country's case, starting in the month following the contract signing. (In the case of Mexico, which in December 1975 expressly declined to contract for such services, the period was January 1975 through December 1976.) In addition to the number of reports (visibility) the study also listed positive or negative references (valence). Negative references included any mention of decline, weakness, poverty, liability, lack of progress, instability, or unreliability. Positive references included mentioning progress, advances, resources, assets, strength, continuity, stability, reliability, or dependability.

The major service the PR firms offered was to improve the respective governments' access to American journalists. In addition, they wrote press releases, did direct mailings, and sent out newsletters and brochures. In some cases, embassy personnel were trained how to speak about sensitive issues such as terrorism or human rights. Field trips for the press, visits with editors, and lunches with business groups were organized. But no precise linkage between PR activities and what was reported could be traced in the context of the study. Manheim and Albritton (1984) observed: "We can do little more than guess at the specifics of what suggestions were made, which were accepted, and how they were implemented . . . [The] precise nature [of the intervention] is . . . something like a black box" (p. 647).

Nevertheless, some of the emphases of the PR activities can be illustrated. They included such events as visits by heads of state, invitations to the president or vice-president of the United States to make state visits, the release of political prisoners, trips for American journalists organized by the respective governments, establishment of information offices, cosmetic redistribution of power within a country, scheduling of elections, and so on. All the countries had negative images at the start of the study. Using the percentage of negative reports as the yardstick Argentina's image was the worst and Yugoslavia's the best: 75% of the reports on Argentina were negative, whereas only 23.7% of those on Yugoslavia were negative. However, using the absolute number of articles, Rhodesia had to be categorized as particularly negative. One of the main effects of the PR activity was that, with the exception of Indonesia, the visibility -- that is, the amount of coverage -- was reduced. This corresponds to research findings of research on the effects of mass communications whereby the image of a country that makes negative headlines and also has a negative image in public opinion cannot be changed by the sudden appearance of positive reporting because this would be perceived as incredible. Withdrawal from public attention makes people forget, providing an opportunity to build slowly a positive new image.

In an experiment using a promotional film about Japan, Wolfsfeld (1983) was able to prove that positive image change can be achieved if there is relatively little knowledge about a country and there are no prevailing opinions about it, that is, if the country is a "nonsalient object". The experiment showed clearly that middle-knowledge subjects exhibit the largest amount of attitude change when the political object involved is a distant one. No comparable effect can be ascertained if the object is salient. Where the images of nations are concerned the mass media very often achieve the strongest effect on people who are least informed and have only little interest in a country, and therefore perceive it as unimportant. In other words, the degree of involvement of the respective target group is key to the tactics of image cultivation. Where involvement is low, a slow, gradual approach is appropriate. Where involvement is high -- as for instance has been in the case of South Africa -- attitudes are generally so stable anyway that image change is practically impossible.

Withdrawal is further supported by the fact that good news and bad news do not have the same effect. Whereas bad news always has a negative effect on the image, good news very often does not seem to make any better impression than neutral news (Galician & Vestre, 1987). Too much positive reporting in any case would probably only reduce credibility. At first glance, the withdrawal tactic appears to clash with the complaint that developing countries receive too little attention in the media of industrial countries, however, a planned reduction in coverage for a certain period ensures better control of the quality and amount of coverage.

Manheim and Albritton (1984) concluded: "There exists a clear temporal correspondence between the signing of a public relations contract by a given nation and shifts in the image of that nation as portrayed in The New York Times" (p. 655). They argued that it is not surprising that states try to influence their images; what is surprising is how successful they are at it. For instance, with regard to Korea and Argentina, about which relatively much had been reported and that mostly negative, fewer articles began appearing and reports became more positive. In the cases of the Philippines and Yugoslavia, which were not very visible at the time they signed their contracts, their presence was reduced further, but the valence -- that is, the relationship between the number of negative and positive articles -- did not change. For Indonesia, the least visible of all the countries, the PR activities did change the valence; the proportion of positive articles increased. In the case of Mexico, which was used for comparison, instead of a falling or static presence there was a strong drop in positive articles: The changes were running exactly opposite the desired direction.

A special case was the coverage of Rhodesia (now Zimbabwe), with both visibility and valence depending on the fighting between the Smith regime and the guerrillas. Albritton and Manheim (1983) showed how the PR contract brought about a marked reduction in the reporting of violence. In the year before the contract was signed, The New York Times reporting was characterized to a large degree by government-announced casualty counts, conveyed the overarching image of an extremely violent society. Immediately after the contract was signed the government-controlled reports about acts of violence stopped. Although the reporting still reflected the violent events in this country the overall news was less violent than before.

The ability to influence reporting by PR naturally varies with the kind of reporting. Research shows that "objective" reporting of violent events, regardless of which side perpetrates them should be difficult to manage. Editorials and other news commentary, as well as statements by international leaders, should be more susceptible to influence. Articles based on government reports and bulletins are easiest to control.

THE BIG RIP-OFF: IMAGE CULTIVATION BY GENERAL CHIANG KAI-SHEK

Although difficult to quantify, it appears that Time magazine, particularly its founder Henry Robinson Luce, decisively influenced the change in China's image in the United States (Halberstam, 1979). T. H. White (1978), long-time China correspondent for Time, characterized Luce's perception of China as follows: "Luce felt, rightly or wrongly, by his morality, that he must take his stand: support Chiang, or else godless Communism would take over. The lesser facts of events must be suppressed for what he considered the great truth; and his magazines [Time, Life, and Fortune] were his instruments" (p. 207). According to Halberstam (1979), Communism represented what Luce hated most: "his feeling took him beyond journalism to the edge of crusade" (p. 76). Swanberg (1972) argued that Chiang Kai-shek was "the most important man in Luce's life -- his pride, joy, worry and disaster" (p. 2).

First it is important to note that, for a long time, there was practically no publicly available information about Chiang Kai-shek's rise to power (Seagrave, 1985). The way Chiang clung to power does not correspond to Western democratic notions about political action. Having said that, however, only the matter of image cultivation is addressed here. According to Seagrave (1985), the Chiang regime was known to have spent hundreds of millions of dollars each year in the 1940s, 1950s, and 1960s to guarantee its image in America and, thus, the continuation of the regime. At the same time the regime suppressed negative reporting. Indeed, a critical biography of Chiang Kai-shek, written by one of his former wives, was bought by the Taiwan authorities for what is believed to have been more than $1 million and then apparently destroyed. Important to understanding Chiang Kai-shek's PR is the following: 3 weeks after his merciless massacre of workers and the Chinese communists in Shanghai in 1927, he asked for May-ling Soong's hand in marriage. She would become his best propaganda instrument, inspiring two generations of Americans and, in Seagrave's (1985) estimation, influencing the decisions of top American politicians for a period of more than 30 years. Luce, who spent his youth in China as the son of a missionary, had a very close personal relationship with Chiang Kai-shek and Mrs. Chiang. Chiang appeared on the title page of Time for the first time in April 1927. In the first issue of 1938 he and his wife were pictured on the cover as man and woman of the year. This made May-ling Soong Chiang even more widely known internationally.

On May 16, 1933, a message from T. V. Soong, Chiang's finance minister, to the American public was broadcast on radio from London and quoted extensively the next day, in The New York Times. T. V. Soong was courting America (Seagrave, 1985) and many Americans responded positively to him. He said, for instance, "Do you realize that over half the Cabinet of our government are graduates of your colleges? I have the honor of being an alumnus of Harvard. In my immediate family, one of my sisters, Mrs. Chiang Kai-shek, went to Wellesley. Two sisters, Mrs. Sun Yat-sen and Mrs. H. H. Kung, whose husband was Minister of Commerce and Labor, attended Wesleyan College in Macon, Ga." (p. 315). Also in 1933 Luce devoted the June issue of Fortune T. V. Soong. Luce described him as a supertycoon; indeed, for a time Soong was the richest man in the world.

Soong had an influential lobby in the United States who backed Chiang's anticommunist cause, including such journalists as Edgar Ansel Mowrer and Joseph Alsop (Alsop was related to both President Roosevelt and Roosevelt's close adviser, Thomas G.

Corcoran, nicknamed "Tommy the Cork"). Seagrave went further (1985) explaining Roosevelt's reasons for helping Chiang:

> Because of his family's old ties to the Shanghai opium trade, which his relatives never tired of resurrecting as evidence of their worldliness and sagacity, the President seemed to think he had a comprehension of China transcending the need for facts, experience, and details. Like many other Americans who imagined themselves to be old China hands, not least among them Henry Luce, FDR [Roosevelt] had a highly colored and idealized image of the Orient. Knowing this through their diplomatic representatives in Washington, both T.V. Soong and H.H. Kung had taken advantage of their government posts in Nanking over the years to write letters to Roosevelt, cultivating him, sending him gifts of tea that -- with shrewd calculation -- were not sufficiently ostentatious to be turned down as a bribe. (p. 366)

Because of this, Soong became a recognized personality in the White House. On December 2, 1940 Roosevelt applied to Congress for a $100 million loan to China, which was approved. According to Seagrave (1985, p. 403), Roosevelt imagined himself as having a serious grasp of the Chinese mentality, but the core of the China lobby -- the senators, the generals, and the captains of industry -- knew very little about Asia. Their image of China was full of nostalgia and melancholy. And to them Madame Chiang played the role of the tragic heroine in real life.

Wendell Willkie, who had lost the 1940 election to Roosevelt, made a goodwill tour to China in 1942. According to Seagrave (1985), Willkie was electrified by May-ling and dazzled by the Generalissimo. Willkie suggested that Madame Chiang make a tour of America and rushed back to share his insights on China with his fellow Americans on radio and in newspapers. Seagrave printed a letter from K. C. Li, a multimillionaire in the Chinese rubber business who lived in New York, to T. V. Soong describing how Americans responded to Willkie's reports:

His visit to China has made a deep impression on the American people. His report, impressive for its sincerity and deep conviction, was widely heard. Indeed, no private citizen has ever commanded so huge an audience as when Mr. Willkie broadcast his report to the American people over all stations on the evening of October 26, 1942. The *New York Herald-Tribune* expressed national sentiment when it said the following morning: "It is a noble gospel that Mr. Willkie preaches, both with respect to American duty in the world and with respect to American duty at home." . . . Some of Mr. Willkie's pro-China sentiments have inspired objections. Mr. Willkie referred to the reservoir of goodwill to the American people that is leaking because of holes punched in it by American "bungling" . . . The reaction . . . has been unmistakable. . . . Mr. Walter Lippmann, in his widely read column on "Mr. Willkie in Asia", warned: "The Chinese people are the last people on earth who have the right to question our good faith, and what we did in refusing to sell out China in the darkest hour is more important that all the words that can be pronounced on the subject of war aims or liberty and justice." . . . The reaction indicates that, even when differences need to be submerged for the sake of unity, American opinion is sensitive about any question of her loyalty or aid to China. . . . Certainly we should clear up our position, and do all we can to clarify the American mind, and reach an understanding with public spokesmen as to the real cause of America's entry into the war. . . . It seems a job well worth assigning to the China propagandists and China propaganda organizations in this country. (p. 378)

In February 1943 May-ling did indeed visit the United States staying in the White House as Roosevelt's guest. On March 1, 1943 Newsweek reported on May-ling's address to Congress in which she stressed the traditional friendship between China and America. May-ling also held a conference in the Oval Office of the White House, with 172 Washington correspondents, and it was comprehensively reported. Time's March 1, 1943 issue pictured May-ling on the cover. Henry Luce campaigned to raise donations for China, for instance, sending Time subscribers a personal letter. This brought in about $250,000. At the end of 1942, $17 million had been raised and was donated by nationwide America to the United China Relief organization. Unfortunately, the money was of little use for relief, because the currency had to be exchanged at the official rate of $1 U.S. = 20 Chinese dollars, which could not compete with the prevailing black market rate of 3,250 Chinese dollars to the $1 U.S.. Ultimately, the only one to benefit were the currency exchange institutions, that is, Chiang Kai-shek's regime.

Luce had organized the rest of May-ling's PR tour well. In New York, she was welcomed by among others, John D. Rockefeller. She attended exclusive private banquets with top politicians (including the future presidential candidate, Thomas E. Dewey, then governor of New York) and leading businesspeople. On March 2, 1943 May-ling (whom Wendell Willkie called "an avenging angel . . . a soldier unafraid to fight for justice") was guest of honor at a mass rally in Madison Square Garden. She also visited New York's Chinatown. In all, Madame Chiang spent 6 weeks traveling through the United States. May-ling's visit was a huge success. According to the press, she took America by storm. Seagrave (1985) described the high point of the PR trip, an even staged in the Hollywood Bowl in Los Angeles on March 31, 1943:

> The Committee to receive Madame Chiang included Mary Pickford, Rita Hayworth, Marlene Dietrich, Ingrid Bergman, Ginger Rogers, and Shirley Temple. She was escorted by the governor and the mayor, and introduced by Spencer Tracy and Henry Fonda. 'The Madame Chiang Kai-shek March' (composed for the occasion by Herbert Stothart) was played by the Los Angeles Philharmonic Orchestra; and a symphonic narrative about China was delivered soberly by Walter Huston and Edward G. Robinson. It was all 'Arranged and Supervised by David O. Selznick', better remembered for 'Gone With the Wind'. (p. 389)

Chiang experienced a serious setback when Thomas Dewey lost the 1948 presidential election to Harry S. Truman, whom the Chinese considered stingy toward them. Truman characterized the activities of the China lobby as follows: "They had a great many Congressmen and Senators lined up to do pretty much what they were told, and they had billions of dollars to spend. . . . I'm not saying that they bought anybody, but there was a lot of money floating around, and a lot of people in Washington were following . . . the China Lobby" (Seagrave, 1985, p. 432). The China lobby was indeed powerful, described by Seagrave as follows: "Employed by Chiang's government were a great many people -- Chinese, Europeans and Americans -- involved exclusively in image protection, public relations, and propaganda. One of their jobs was to keep scandals out of the papers" (p. 420).

While the 1948 election campaign was still in full swing, Congress, however, approved more than $1 billion for Chiang to fight the "Red Menace". Chiang signaled immediately that this was not enough and instructed May-ling to ask for $3 billion. At the end of November 1948 May-ling again was sent to Washington on a PR mission. But she met with only modest success this time. Truman, who had just won the election, remarked: "She came to the United States for some more handouts. I wouldn't let her stay in the White House like Roosevelt did. I don't think she liked it very much, but I didn't care one way or the other what she liked and what she didn't like" (Seagrave, 1985, p. 433). Later visits to the United States by May-ling -- for example, from August 1952 to March 1953 and in April 1954 or in 1965 -- were more or less unsuccessful.

The Chiang government's influence on American foreign policy was significant. Seagrave (1985) provided the following overall assessment:

> Chiang's government used existing American corporations headed by men who shared its viewpoint; it hired advertising agencies; it created dummy corporations as blinds for propaganda; it set up a "propaganda ministry" of its own in the United States; it cultivated influential, sympathetic Americans who set up bipartisan, "non-profit" committees that served as pressure groups. Few activities were directed personally by the Soongs. That was no longer necessary. The Chinese technocrats who guided daily operations were a new generation of Soong protégés slickly groomed on Soong techniques. The New York

public-relations firm Allied Syndicates, Inc., counted among its major clients the Bank of China . . . Another public-relations firm, Hamilton Wright, worked for six years as a registered agent for Nationalist China, writing and distributing stories, news articles, photographs, and movies to create a favorable image of Chiang Kai-shek and his regime. One clause of the Wright organization's contract with the Nationalist government guaranteed that: "In 75 per cent of the releases, neither the editor of the newspaper -- nor the newspaper reader -- HAS ANY KNOWLEDGE WHERE THE MATERIAL ORIGINATED." The Herald Tribune Service, for one, owned by Henry Luce's Republican friend Jock Whitney, fed this spurious material to unsuspecting American newspapers for years without ever identifying the source. T.V.'s wartime Universal Trading Corporation was listed in 1949 as a foreign agent working for the Chinese government, with assets of nearly $22 million. The Chinese News Service based in Taiwan established branches in Washington, New York, Chicago, and San Francisco, and distributed millions of copies of a journal called "This Week in Free China". It also circulated news stories and feature articles, thinly-disguised propaganda, to fill the columns of American papers. Taiwan's Central News Agency, which went to great lengths to emulate the Associated Press, spent $654 million United States in only three years, 1946 - 49, producing articles on Chiang's anti-Communist struggle, and on lavishly entertaining American editors and correspondents in the United States and the Far East -- more than $200 million each year. Small wonder that a large segment of the American public believed that Chiang was the essence of virtue and his cause a just one. Similar amounts were spent during the Korean War and the periodic crises over the defense of the Formosa Strait. Guesses at the grand total spent by Taiwan to stupefy Americans ran as high as $1 billion each year." (emphasis in the original; p. 443)

The PR campaign of Chiang Kai-shek is one of those rare known examples of a dictatorship able to preserve a positive image through long-term cultivation, though due, in part, to a unique constellation of historic and personal circumstances.

MULDERGATE: APARTHEID AND IMAGE POLICY OF
SOUTH AFRICA

Wilhelmus Gerhardus Meyer (1968), then information counselor of the South African embassy in Washington, summed up the general prejudices about South Africa as follows: "At every possible occasion South Africa has been presented to the world as practising a policy of oppression contrary to all accepted moral standards and religious concepts; no less than a threat to world peace" (p. 100). Meyer argued that, in fact, the often predicted racial explosion had not yet occurred in South Africa. On the contrary, he maintained, development had been peaceful, successful, and benefied the population as a whole, Whites, Blacks, and people of mixed race. He went on to say, "The ultimate goal is the creation of equal black states in which each of these nations will be in a position to manage its own affairs and be the equal in every respect to the whites in the country" (p. 102).

In the 1980s Bernardus G. Fourie, then South Africa's U.S. ambassador, had a running battle with the American news media because, in his view, they portrayed the South African government as an "inflexible, racist regime that eventually will be overthrown by violent revolution" (Buie et al., 1983). For example, Fourie attacked Newsweek columnist Meg Greenfield over an article about the "fundamental monstrosity" of the apartheid system. And in a letter to Newsweek the ambassador referred to "reforms enacted by the South African Government" and claimed that the government's objective was "peaceful and progressive change".

Given South Africa's many image problems, it is hardly surprising that its authorities resorted to image-polishing activities. South Africa wanted to be perceived as a nation belonging to and being accepted by the world community, and used advertisements to achieve this goal. Burgess (1977) gave many examples of advertisements published in 1974 and 1975 in newspapers in the United States, Great Britain, and Austria: "Could an organisation like NATO have a base in Simonstown, South Africa?"; "Could the next Olympics be in Pretoria, South Africa?"; "Could the Headquarters of the UN Economic Commission for Africa be in Johannesburg, South Africa?" The South African-based Trust Bank of Africa paid for a series of advertisements placed in foreign newspapers in which three African leaders made statements: Chief Gatsha Buthelezi, Chief Executive Councelor of the Kwa Zulu; Chief Lucas Mangope, Chief Minister of Bophuthatswana; and Mrs. Lucy Mvubelo, secretary of the National Union of Clothing Workers in South Africa. The advertisements appeared in New Zealand, Australia, United States, and Great Britain. In one of them, for instance, Mrs. Mvubelo said the following: "I have often expressed my differences with the white government of Pretoria in no uncertain terms. But the mere idea of total economic sanctions from abroad to assist us, makes me shudder. We, the black people, will be the first to suffer" (Burgess, 1977, 27).

Some of the South Africa PR activities could be considered unusual, to say the least. What follows here is based largely on a (1983) book by Eschel Rhoodie, a former South African secretary of information, about South Africa's secret information policy activities. In 1978 details of this secret campaign became known in South Africa as the "Muldergate Scandal". Rhoodie's immediate superior, Minister of Information Connie Mulder, had to resign. Rhoodie fled to Europe, was extradited by France to South Africa, and charged there with fraud. An independent commission of inquiry under Mr. Justice Rudolph Erasmus, appointed by then State President John Vorster, was established. Rhoodie was sentenced to six years' in prison but appealed successfully and the sentence was overturned. Details of the propaganda campaign became public knowledge, partly because Rhoodie indulged in some eccentric behavior, sometimes while traveling on official business. Regarding the consequences of the revelation of the secret PR activities, Rhoodie wrote: "In the international community South Africa became a laughing stock as the government went through its convulsions of political nudism. Influential people who had worked for many years to cover South Africa's difficult case abroad ran for cover, never to emerge again" (p. 8).

In his very subjective book, Rhoodie (1983), of course, denied all accusations against him. Indeed, the book opens as follows: "*The Real Information Scandal* is about propaganda warfare, political deceit, treachery, cowardice, courage and love, about callous and malicious journalism, the abuse of government power and administrative terrorism. It is a story of ruthless, selfish individuals . . . of foreign policy disasters and international intrigue, of blind faith and idealism" (p. 1). Clearly Rhoodie's book is no seriously researched scientific work. Yet most of the relevant passages about the scandal discussed here rely heavily on the book. In spite of the danger of merely presenting a reproduction of Rhoodie's views, and because it is such an important case, I feel obliged to use them for the sake of thoroughness. In no way does this imply an endorsement of Rhoodie's claims and, wherever possible, other sources have been used for verification.

The starting premise for the secret propaganda activities was the following definition of the situation by South African politicians: "The world-wide psychological and propaganda onslaught against South Africa reached its peak at the beginning of the seventies, and the government of Mr. John Vorster began to fear, for the first time, that isolation, political and economical isolation was going to be forced on the country". The New York Times, the Washington Post, The Guardian (Britain), The Observer (Britain), and Der Spiegel (Germany), among others, were accused of "journalistic racism" concentrating on one-sided, negative reporting of South Africa. Rhoodie (1983) cited as one complaint that "the slaughter of 220,000 human beings in Burundi in 1972 received infinitely less publicity in The New York Times than the 70 odd killed at Sharpville" (p. 32).

Vorster decided "to launch a secretly financed information offensive, a propaganda war, to help South Africa break out of the grip of growing isolation, and to reach and influence policy-makers and decision-takers" (Rhoodie, 1983, p. 26). A meeting was convened in February 1974, attended by, among others, Vorster, head of South Africa's Bureau of State Security (BOSS) General Hendrik van den Bergh, Information Minister Cornelius Mulder, and Secretary of Information Eschel Rhoodie himself, to discuss what should be done to fight back against the country's growing international isolation (Rhoodie, 1983). Rhoodie argued for a PR offensive. He told the Rand Daily Mail in an interview that he had said to Vorster: "I want you to approve not an information asset but a propaganda war in which no rules or regulations would count" (Rothmyer, 1980, p. 455).

Between 160 and 180 secret projects, costing some 75 million rand, were implemented by 1978. Rhoodie, who had done PR for the government before, was in charge of the covert activities. According to him, the Department of Information spent some 2.5 million rand between 1965 and 1975 to bring public opinion formers from all over the world to South Africa, an investment that paid off. He wrote: "Almost all of them were left rather bewildered at the contrast between what they saw and what they read in the hostile English morning press" (p. 315). The most important targets of the new secret activities were the United States and Western Europe. But they also needed Israel as an ally, which it became. In a letter to Rhoodie, Shimon Peres, then Israel's defence minister, wrote: "It is to a very large extent due to your perspicacity, foresight and political imagination that a vitally important cooperation between our two countries has been initiated. This cooperation is based not only on common interests and on the determination to resist equally our enemies, but also on the unshakable foundations of our common hatred of injustice and our refusal to submit to it" (p. 117).

The South African government's propaganda activities in the United States covered a broad spectrum, including such things as hospitality for members of congress, attempts to buy American newspapers, sponsoring scientific conferences and even invitations to important American businesspeople to play golf in South Africa. The aim was to achieve a positive image among American opinion leaders. For example, John McGoff, the owner of the Panax newspaper chain in Michigan who, according to Stone (1979), had investments in South Africa, in 1974 offered $25 million to buy The Washington Star newspaper, which was in financial trouble. Of that $25 million, $10 million came from Rhoodie's secret coffers (cf. Stone, 1979). Although the attempt to buy the paper failed in the end, probably because the rest of the money could not be raised, the intention was to counter the influence of the Washington Post and The New York Times on the South African image (Rhoodie, 1983). The money was used instead to buy controlling stock in the *Sacramento Union*, described by Rhoodie as "the biggest and most important newspaper in the capital of California" (p. 379). Shares were also bought in other newspapers. In 1975 McGoff again used South African money ($1.35 million) to buy a half-interest in United Press International Television News (UPITN), the second largest news-film producer and distributor in the world, which had clients in more than 110 countries. Rhoodie observed: "Because McGoff managed to get his vice President, Clarence Rhodes, into the Chairman's position in London, it gave South Africa virtually unlimited access to all of the international outlets of this television news distributing agency" (p. 391). An interview with John Vorster was arranged and, according to Rhoodie, was screened in more than 90 countries. Other programs were broadcast via UPITN, for example, covering the Transkei and Bophuthatswana's independence. According to Rothmyer (1980) there are no indications, however, that UPITN (or indeed any of McGoff's other share acquisitions) in any way became a South African propaganda instrument. UPI president Roderick Beaton called any suggestion that McGoff influenced news coverage "pure baloney and libelous" (Rothmyer, 1980).

In 1974 McGoff helped to bring about a meeting between information minister Mulder and President Ford. And in 1978, "he urged business leaders at a conference in Houston to give money to help defeat Senator Dick Clark of Iowa, chairman of the Senate Subcommittee on African Affairs, whom McGoff described as having a penchant for the destruction of South Africa" (Rothmyer,

1980). According to Rothmyer, Rhoodie said that election campaigns were supported from the secret fund: "In addition, the South African press reported that $3.9 million was channeled into the Ford presidential campaign in 1976" (Rothmyer, 1980).

In 1974 and 1976, respectively, Rhoodie hired two PR firms, lobbyist de Kieffer and Sydney S. Baron & Associates, which were, according to Rothmyer (1980), paid a total of at least $3 million out of Rhoodie's secret fund. Sydney S. Baron & Associates (see Rhoodie, 1983, for a complete discussion on the role of Sydney Baron, who had also done PR for Trujillo's Dominican Republic, the Japanese electrical industry, and Taiwan; cf. Stone, 1979) not only carried out the usual PR activities of providing background information and issuing press releases about South Africa, but also organized two large "investment seminars" attended by more than 300 top American businesspeople. Each conference cost 60,000 rand. William Simon, minister of finance during the Ford administration, was paid $10,000 to deliver a speech at the first seminar in which he encouraged investment in South Africa. Also for a fee of $10,000, then ex-President Ford came to the second conference in Houston where he, too, emphasized the advantages of investing in South Africa.

Influential South Africans were also recruited for the secret activities. For example, Sydney Baron and others brokered a meeting between Dr. Christian Barnard of heart transplant fame and George Meany, the American labor leader. Meany was so impressed by Barnard that a planned boycott of South African ships by American unions did not take place. According to Rhoodie (1983), "After a long meeting Barnard convinced Meany that instead of a boycott he should send a fact finding team to South Africa. Meany agreed" (p. 189). (Union officials for their part insisted that the meeting brought no change in union policy.) Barnard campaigned generally for a more tolerant attitude toward South Africa, arguing that the problems there were very complex and hard for outsiders to understand. He received $25,000 from the secret fund to help finance his international trips. But, as he told the <u>Sunday Times</u> of

Johannesburg, "I never did this for the Government but for South Africa" (Rothmye, 1980, p. 458).

According to Rhoodie (1983), "one of the best kept secrets of the Baron organisation was the role they played in assisting us to break out of our sports isolation" (p. 171). He elaborated:

> The Committee of Fairness in Sports was set up by us in South Africa and financed entirely in secret. The committee was extremely active in countries such as the USA, Britain and Australia, with whom South Africa had maintained close sporting ties over the years, and which were threatened by the actions of the UN and the anti-apartheid movement. . . . Apart from visits to various countries, including Britain, Japan, the USA and Australia, the Committee took out large advertisements in several newspapers all over the world. . . . These advertisements challenged the governments of the world to drop their political discrimination against South African sportsmen of all colours. The committee also published brochures in German, French and English. All in all the project cost more than R520 000. (p. 171)

By and large, however, South Africa remained isolated in international sports. Particular use was made of golf to influence American investors. Gary Player, a South African and one of the best known golfers in the world in his time, was worked into Rhoodie's plans. Between 1975 and 1978 Player was asked to write letters to the top managers of major firms in the United States, such as MacDonnel Douglas, Bank of America, and Union Carbide. The letters went to chairmen, presidents, chief executives, and managing directors of companies whose combined gross assets were equal to that of all South Africa. Player invited these captains of industry to play golf with him for a week in South Africa. All the expenses incurred within South Africa were paid from Rhoodie's secret fund, as were Player's losses from missing professional golf tournaments. The attraction of being able to play golf in South Africa with one of the world's best golfers was apparently huge; even the Prime Minister joined in a game from time to time. In Rhoodie's (1983) estimation, a personal invitation from Gary Player was worth at least 10 invitations from the foreign minister. On at least three occasions Player invited groups of 10 - 15 top-level United States businessmen to South Africa for 2 weeks. According to Rothmyer (1980), he told reporters: "I am a professional player and I am proud of having been able to be of assistance" (p. 458). And according to Rhoodie, he said, "I am prepared to do something like this for any party as long as it is to the advantage of the country" (p. 187).

Overall, the golf diplomacy was a total success: All of the companies represented retained their interest in South Africa. Rhoodie (1983) reproduced from many of the attendees letters in his book. Following are excerpts from four of them:

> You, as well as Gary Player, are to be complimented for the initiative and imagination required to develop a trip such as this which I believe will result in inestimable value to the Republic of South Africa.

> I am sure you know that the object of the visit was achieved beyond the wildest hopes of those of us who are already persuaded and that South Africa has acquired a platoon of new ambassadors in the United States.

> I think that we collectively expressed our sentiments when we said that, at the very least, South Africa had acquired fifteen new ambassadors. Incidentally, for your information, I have already started making arrangements to meet with the South African desk of our State Department so that I can tell them of my personal observations.

> In addition to the pleasure of playing golf with you and many others, I certainly appreciate the opportunity of meeting your Prime Minister, members of his cabinet, and many other influential business and government men. The trip and these contacts provided a deeper understanding of the South African scene and left me with the impression that highly qualified South Africans are doing everything possible to resolve a complex situation.

Invitations to leading American politicians to visit South Africa were also part of the PR activities. According to Rothmyer (1980), "Meldrim Thomson, while still Governor of New Hampshire, visited South Africa in 1978 . . . Thomson came back to report effusively that Soweto, the black township outside Johannesburg, is *just wonderful* as a place to live and that Vorster was *a statesman of great courage*" (p. 457). Rhoodie's projects also included the following activities: "$15 million (by South African Government estimate) to underwrite a subtly slanted news magazine, TO THE POINT, which was distributed free to 30,000 persons in England and the United States; $1 million to underwrite ads attacking U.N. Ambassador Andrew Young and others, which were signed by the 'Club of Ten', a secret British based organisation, and appeared in a number of papers, including The New York Times and the Washington Post" (Rothmyer, 1980, p. 458). Further, a news agency was launched in Nairobi to supply European TV stations with films. And, according to Rhoodie (1983), a German photographer set up a photo agency that supplied pictures and articles to 70 European media.

In February 1976 the "Club of Ten" sponsored a series of advertisements in British newspapers, pointing out the importance of South Africa for the West in the Cold War: "The Free World stands today in greater danger than at any time since the darkest days of World War Two" (Burgess, 1977, p. 56). In particular, the developments in Angola were emphasized: "In some quarters of the West it was argued that having Russia take over Angola would be preferable to being caught on the same side as racist South Africa. In the First and Second World Wars the free world heard no such arguments when South Africa (infinitely more racist than today) fought and died on our side" (Burgess, 1977, p. 56). Another "Club of Ten" advertisement showed a photo with the following explanation: "Photographed in Angola; firepower the Russians have put into the hands of Cuban-led pro-Marxist forces . . . automatic weapons from behind the Iron Curtain carried by MPLA soldiers" (Burgess, 1977, p. 56).

In Europe the secret information program was concentrated on Holland, West Germany, France, and Great Britain (Rhoodie, 1983). There were ambitious plans for this region. For example, a second 5-year plan beginning in 1980 included acquiring for European media (Rhoodie, 1983): "This programme would involve attempts to take over several prominent newspapers and magazines in the Western world, including The Observer in England" (p. 218). To this end, Production Editoriale, a Swiss company, was purchased in 1975 to serve as camouflage. Rhoodie's attempt to buy into the periodical L'Expresse (he used this spelling of its name throughout his book) through Jean-Jacques Servan-Schreiber failed, however, because, according to Rhoodie, Servan-Schreiber wanted to receive the money outside France and Rhoodie doubted that the money then could be covertly channeled to France and used for the intended purpose. But the South Africans did succeed in bringing the conservative intellectual magazine Le Monde Nouvelle under their control (Rhoodie, 1983). Moereover, books friendly to South Africa were published with South African financial backing. Rhoodie reported on one success without naming names: "An extremely successful operation . . . is the film company set up in a European country, and which contracted with film producers in various other states to produce high quality films promoting inter alia the strategic importance of South Africa. In my time this one group completed six films at a cost of R407,000 and which were shown on the most important television networks of Europe, the United States and Australasia" (p. 25).

It is impossible to list here all the activities Rhoodie claimed the South Africans carried out without greatly expanding this book. Hence only a few more references are made here on secret operations he claimed were carried out in West Germany. I reiterate that source of the details is almost exclusively Rhoodie (1983). However, on July 24, 1989 an article appeared in Der Spiegel, that confirmed some of Rhoodie's revelations. Rhoodie claimed that a very influential West German journalist until 1978 received from South Africa, through a Hamburg firm he owned (PRO-

International), 1.42 million rand to cultivate South Africa's image. The journalist, who had access to virtually all German newspapers, was responsible for more than 600 press reports a year about South Africa. He also, according to Rhoodie, succeeded in influencing television and radio in South Africa's favor. Further, he had taken about 15 media people to South Africa every year. Rhoodie rated his performance on behalf of South Africa as excellent. Behrens also apparently successfully lobbied for investments in South Africa.

According to Rhoodie (1983), Gerd Hennenhofer, a "former editor-in-chief" of Der Spiegel, also worked for South Africa and was particularly successful. Because the journal was anti-South Africa, nobody suspected him of representing South African interests. Hennenhofer was said to have worked on target groups and in particular organized tours to South Africa by top West German politicians, for example, a speaker of the West German parliament and members of the Bundestag (the House of Assembly). According to Rhoodie, through Hennenhofer an organization was set up that made it possible to bring up to 15 top politicians and newspaper editors from Germany to South Africa every year. On July 24, 1989, Der Spiegel reported that in the 1970s Hennenhofer took West German politicians to South Africa at South African expense. More than 60 members of the Bundestag supposedly accepted invitations to South Africa in 1977. They included later federal ministers, the present European Community Commissioner, Martin Bangemann, and a chief spokesman of the Bonn government. According to Rhoodie, Hennenhofer received more than half a million rand from the secret fund, which was a good investment because under Hennenhofer's auspices the highest-ranking German politicians visited South Africa. Hennenhofer made a PR contract with South Africa on February 27, 1980 of the contractual objectives. One was to influence church officials to support South Africa. The fee for this was 1.2 million deutschmarks per year. Hennenhofer apparently succeeded in bringing 133 leading church personalities to South Africa, and met with some success, judging by the church leader's statements to the magazine. A high official of the South African information ministry rated Hennenhofer's firm as the most effective by far among the four agencies working for the South African government, the other three being American (Der Spiegel, July 24, 1989).

Because of the "Muldergate Affair" South Africa changed its propaganda strategy in the United States. They no longer used covert manipulation, but quite openly attempted to persuade opinion leaders and gain their understanding of South Africa's complex problems (Jowett & O'Donnell, 1986). Venues such as Rotary Clubs or even religious TV programs were used as PR forums. The propagandists' main argument was that American values and methods could not be imposed on South Africa because it had a different demographic and racial composition than the United States. It emphasized, of course, that changes were in process, but that they could not turn into visible successes overnight. The propagandists emphasized especially that South Africa was the West's best friend in Africa, the last anticommunist bastion on the Black Continent. Withdrawal of investments, it was argued, would only hurt those who most needed help, the Black population. At the same time it would endanger a smooth-running and efficient economy, which in turn might threaten access to South Africa's precious metals on which "the free world" depended so vitally.

South African enterprises were also running advertisements to polish the country's international image. In a full-page advertisement in Der Spiegel (No. 32, August 8, 1988) the Anglo American Corporation published extracts from its chairman's annual report, also referred to topical political and social problems (e.g., press censorship, apartheid) seeking empathy for a reform policy. The advertisement, in part quite critical of the government in Pretoria, argued that reforms could not be implemented without economic growth. It criticized South African military actions against other countries, the curbing of political activities, and attacks on press freedom because this was so greatly increasing antipathy abroad that many were distancing themselves from the desirable process of change.

Anglo American was not alone. In 1987 Shell South Africa started publishing advertisements in South African newspapers, for example, Business Day, Weekly Mail, and South. The advertisements included statements like: "Working to make a difference now"; "Shell is fully commited to the concept of freedom for all in an equal society."; "Shell supports a free press."; "Everyone has the right to freedom of thought, conscience and belief, and the right to express these beliefs."; "Shell supports freedom of association." In 1989, the advertisements became more aggressive. An advertisement in Weekly Mail (May 26 to June 1) said: "Let the people speak! Shell urges the government to: 1. End the state of emergency 2. Release and unban all politcal leaders 3. Lift restrictions on democratic organisations 4. Allow and encourage freedom of expression." An advertisement in South (May 11 to May 17) expressed the following: "How many must die before we find peace? We mourn the death of David Webster and the deaths of all those who have died in the cause of peace and freedom." Also in South (October 12 to October 19) was this message from Shell: "We look forward to the release of all political prisoners, the unbanning of political organisations and the freeing of the democratic process." Shell also welcomed the release of political prisoners. The release of Nelson Mandela prompted the following full-page advertisement in Business Day on February 12, 1990: "Welcome back Nelson Mandela! The stars will shine brighter tonight . . . Tomorrow, a brilliant future beckons." In 1989 Shell Oil International even published a brochure called "Shell and South Africa," which included arguments to end apartheid. Shell actively supported the goal of political participation for all South Africans.

South Africa's propaganda in West Germany was outlined in an article in Der Spiegel (No. 22, 1988). The magazine reported that the South African embassy in Bonn, like other embassies do for their countries, conducted propaganda for South Africa by press releases, invitations, and letters. However, the policy of apartheid had become an almost unsellable product in West Germany, especially because of the many human rights violations by South Africans. This was not always so, however, because of strong West German economic interests in South Africa. Official Bonn policy has been to reject economic sanctions against South Africa, arguing that sanctions would in any case only hurt the Blacks.

Tourism was also used indirectly as an image cultivation tool. Anyone in Germany who cut out a South African Airways coupon from magazines and sent it in with a request for further information received a letter from the embassy setting out the official version of the political situation in South Africa. With the help of a PR agency, the embassy worked on the image simply by glossing over details. There were also societies, such as the German-South African Society (which Rhoodie [1983] claimed was also supported within the secret information project) or the Society for International Study Travels, that worked on the image from the German side. In 1988 there was a veritable boom in tourism to South Africa, with about 1 million visitors. Tourism appeared to have recovered since a dramatic decline in 1984 due to the Black revolt. It is possible that in this context, South Africa gained from its strict press censorship and the state of PR emergency because negative reporting about the country obviously declined.

If the general public is the target group, then such image-polishing efforts as those just discussed are small scale compared to such global activities against South Africa as the rock concert given by top stars of the international pop scene in London's Wembley Stadium on June 11, 1988 to mark the 70th birthday of Nelson Mandela. The hit song "Free Nelson Mandela" by then had spread the message of the South African resistance worldwide. According to press reports the concert was televised in 60 countries and seen by 750 million people. In West Germany, for example, several stations ran it for 10 hours; they showed a film beforehand explaining Mandela's life and the difficult situation in South Africa, featuring, among others, Mandela's wife Winnie and other representatives of the South African resistance.

On November 2, 1985 the South African government banned reporting by "photographic and sound recordings" of the racial unrest. The declared aim of the ban was to deprive the protesters of the international stage and thereby reduce the scale of politically motivated violence. According to Lacob (1986), as a consequence of the government ban, television and other reports showing the violent confrontations between young Blacks on the one side and police and troops on the other side practically stopped. Lacob also gained the impression that the flow of dramatic photographs streaming into the print media shrank to a trickle.

Singer and Ludwig (1987) examined the effects in the United States of the ban on media reporting and on American public opinion about South Africa. They looked at the coverage of The New York Times and the evening television newscasts of the three big networks from May 1985 to February 1986. The opinion data were collected in August and October 1985 and in March 1986. The authors observed: "Ironically, some journalists said that interest in the South Africa story had been waning in the weeks before the ban, and that the imposition of press restrictions stimulated a renewal of attention" (p. 331). They could not trace the decline in coverage in January and February back to press restrictions. None of the three indicators used -- total coverage, prominence and protest-related stories -- showed any dramatic drop in coverage in October and November. Nor did the press restrictions have any overall effect on public opinion in the United States.

CHAPTER 7

International Image Cultivation
During Cold War Times

IMAGE CULTIVATION BY THE UNITED STATES

The image of the United States is hard to define. Sorensen (1968) characterized it as: "Part fact and part mirage, part expectation and part disillusionment. It is a picture magnified by the modern mass media, blurred by the fantasies of Hollywood, distorted by the falsifications of our adversaries, and complicated by the sheer size of America's population, wealth, power, and problems" (p. 2). Gallup (1970) reported that the image America had abroad in 1970 was a more or less contradictory mixture of approval and rejection, of like and dislike. Among the negative characteristics attributed were "intolerant", "violent", and "imperialistic" and among the positive ones "friendly", "generous", "practical", and "hardworking"; also mentioned were "economic cooperation, foreign aid, and Peace Corps" (p. 14). Gallup (1970) identified three major factors in 1969 as responsible for the continual worsening of the American image in the 1960s: the Vietnam War, race relations in the United States, and crime and lawlessness. Two other events also impacted greatly on the image abroad at that time: the moon landing on July 18, 1969 and the invasion of Czechoslovakia by Soviet forces which, similarly to the attack on Hungary, caused a short-term tremendous loss of image for the Soviet Union, leading Gallup in turn to assume that the Soviet Union's loss would become America's gain.

Foreign image cultivation for the United States, as an open society, is a lot more difficult than in societies with a policy of information control. As a rule there will be conflicting information coming out of the United States on any given subject, a veritable cacophony of views. This was pointed out by Bernays in a hearing: "In an open society and free flow of news here and abroad, foreign relationships start with our domestic conduct. Leadership must remind our citizens that actions deviating from our national ideals often adversely affect our international relations" (Bernays & Hershey, 1970, p. 126). Image cultivation -- public relations however -- is conducted in the United States by a number of institutions with a number of objectives. For example, there is PR for free enterprise, that is for the capitalist economic order. The International Executive Service Corps (IESC) has the task of promoting the private enterprise system in less industrialized countries. IESC asks retired U.S. executives to go to foreign countries and apply their particular expertise in counseling a local company (cf. Center, 1975, Case 18). Time even devoted its March 27, 1989 cover story to America's image; the cover's subhead read: "Brash and secure America is often heedless about the world. So what does the world think?" The report was a response to the claim by then Vice-President Dan Quayle: "We are the envy of the world. The United States". The American image is varicolored and almost indefinable. For some the "Yankees" are "the enemy of humanity" ("We fight against the Yankee, enemy of humanity" -- a line from the Sandinista national anthem); for others the United States is the dreamland.

International image cultivation has become a fixed part of United States foreign policy, with effective public diplomacy requiring careful planning. The 1980 Report of the United States Advisory Commission stated: "Public diplomacy is as important to the national interests as military preparedness". The money spent on image cultivation, the report continued, was by no means wasted, but on the contrary, indispensably important to national security. Under President Reagan, U.S. image cultivation took on a new media diplomatic quality. A presidential directive ("PD 75") written in August 1983 declared that the aims of American policy were to be made as transparent as possible among Western and Eastern European populations. Previously, in the fall of 1981, Reagan had presented a new European arms control proposal to an audience of 200 journalists and a battery of television cameras that carried his speech live to Europe and other parts of the world. It was the first time in history that a U.S. president made a live telecast from Washington that was timed for foreign broadcast systems rather than the United States networks.

For both his foreign policy image and the home audience, Reagan trusted his media advisers to create the right setting for him. For instance, it was decided that Reagan would visit the Berlin Wall at Checkpoint Charlie and not at the Brandenburg Gate. The reason was simple: At Checkpoint Charlie East Berlin appeared uglier than at the Brandenburg Gate, making the difference between the two systems of society easier for the TV cameras to capture. And when Reagan attended the ceremonies marking the 40th anniversary of the Allied landing in Normandy, his appearance was timed so that it would be seen live on morning TV programs in America. Reagan's 1984 visit to the demilitarized zone of Korea was also a media spectacle. The president was dressed in an Army parka and flak jacket and placed behind sandbags (piled only as high as 4 inches above his belly button, so that a good photo could be shot; the Secret Service, fearing snipers, had wanted the sandbags virtually up to his neck) and made his appearance at the most exposed American bunker, Guardpost Collier. Cameras were placed behind Reagan looking over his shoulder as he raised binoculars toward North Korea, enemy country. The message was clear: Ronald Reagan, the determined fighter at the front. Just like on stage, the President's image workers placed red tape on the ground, showing Reagan precisely where to stand for the memorable shot. Bill Henkel, one of Reagan's image advisers, commented: "This was it, the commander in chief on the front line against Communism. It was Ronald

Reagan's statement on American strength and resolve" (Smith, 1988, p. 461).

Reagan's image team also played a decisive part in setting the stage for the 1985 summit meeting between Reagan and Gorbachev. They selected an elegant, telegenic old chateau that had a walkway leading to a pool house. The house had a big fireplace, facilitating the image of friendly, man-to-man talks by the fire. Before the "fireside summit" began, the marketing strategy had been laid down. According to Smith (1988) the news blackout imposed during the summit was the image makers' delight, because the media then gave greater value to little scraps about how the two leaders got along. Symbolic details -- for example, Reagan and Gorbachev going together into the fireside room -- without great informative value became media events. Even the short postsummit stop in Brussels -- ostensibly to brief NATO leaders -- actually had a different purpose: to delay Reagan's homecoming so as to synchronize it with the evening news shows. Smith described the media spectacle as follows: "The live coverage, arranged by Deaver and Henkel, created a magnetic effect: helicopters ferrying the president from his encounter with the Kremlin boss on the final leg home to report to Congress and the nation. It was a production to inspire envy in Hollywood and to project an aura of success, however modest the reality" (p. 44).

Image Cultivation by the USIA

The USIA (United States Information Agency), part of the State Department, was established in its present form at the height of the Cold War in 1953. The charter of the USIA is explained in a statement by director Charles Winick to the Senate Foreign Relations Committee: "The money we seek is security for all Americans, for our national security. Not to buy military weapons -- but to provide the United States with another kind of protection and peace; the kind that is won when the people of one nation freely communicate their values and aspirations to the people of other nations, refute disinformation and other manipulative measures calculated to destabilize free world unity -- all through public diplomacy" (Alexandre, 1987, p. 31). Compared with the propaganda activities of the Soviet Union, those of the USIA -- unlike the CIA or the National Security Agency (NSA) -- are almost public. In 1954, Bogart even conducted an empirical study of the USIA, entitled "The United States Information Agency's Operating Assumptions in the Cold War", which was based on interviews with staff and was later published in 1976.

Among the activities of the USIA are operation of the Voice of America (radio), the production and distribution of films, TV programs, magazines in English and other languages, and operation of libraries. According to Wick (1987), the USIA operates 159 libraries and reading rooms in 100 countries. Other programs involve the distribution of books to target groups and book translation. The USIA also sponsors lecture and seminar programs, English-teaching programs, educational exchange programs, and so on. Part of the educational exchange program is the International Visitor Program (IV) under whose auspices 1,500 - 2,000 important foreigners are invited to study every year. Former IV grantees include Anwar el-Sadat, Valérie Giscard d'Estaing, Helmut Schmidt, Margaret Thatcher, and Indira Gandhi. Also part of the educational exchange program is the Fulbright Program of academic exchanges. There is also an American Participation Program under which an average of 500 Americans a year are sent abroad to explain the policies of the United States and how American democracy and society work. Cultural presentations include performing and nonperforming artists, and there are exhibits and American Studies programs. Among activities backed by the USIA are the East-West Center at the University of Hawaii as well as American Schools abroad and youth exchange programs. Just how broadly defined the USIA brief is was demonstrated when it was asked to distribute worldwide the tape recordings of the shooting down of the South Korean airliner (KAL 007) in 1983 (cf. section

7.2.3). Its job is also to prevent the appearance of articles in the press that portray the United States negatively.

The cultural activities of the State Department are laid down in the Fulbright-Hays Act of 1961, whose preamble sets out these goals: "To increase mutual understanding between the people of the United States and other countries . . . by demonstrating the educational and cultural interests . . . of the United States and other nations". Sorensen (1968) gave the following example of the Department's broad perception of image cultivation: "When an American Nobel laureate physics addresses an assembly of Latin American physicists, the speech may be pure science. But his appearance also tells something about education in the United States and about cultural values, and that is good propaganda" (p. 73).

The list of image cultivation activities is almost endless. When the American astronauts landed on the moon it was the Voice of America that spread the famous words by Neil Armstrong: "That's one small step for a man, one giant leap for mankind." When students in developing countries use facilities of the American Center, they are using an institution whose purpose is to serve the United States' public diplomacy. Sorensen (1968) even gave an example of differentiated deployment of culture: "If Tennessee Williams' play or Martha Graham's modern dance troop are understood and appreciated as art in one country but not in another, they should go to the first but not to the second" (p. 73).

Among the long-term strategies of American image enhancement is the deployment of the Peace Corps. Exchange programs whereby foreign youngsters live in American families for a period should also be included here. Under President Reagan special importance was attached to spreading the "American message". For instance, National Security Council Directive 130 asserted that "strategically targeted information and communications assistance to other countries" represented an integral component of American policy. According to David and Aufderheide (1985), the most successful USIA activity, "the real blockbusters of the USIA productions" (p.

23), are interactive press conferences in which Washington is linked by satellite with foreign news media. These follow no fixed schedule, the authors noted, but are being mounted with increasing frequency.

According to Bernays (1970), in 1970 the USIA still had "no fundamental operating assumptions, no defined objectives" (p. 8). Bernays identified seven areas in which the USIA operates: "1. Promoting the flow of ideas about the United States in the world. 2. Presenting United States policies programs to the world. 3. Reporting current United States foreign policy. 4. Furthering goodwill and public understanding between the United States and other peoples. 5. Providing counsel on public relations to the United States Government on foreign policy. 6. Advancing United States education and the arts and sciences of the United States to the world. 7. Countering propaganda inimical to the United States, wherever and whenever it appears" (p. 8).

In 1950 President Harry S. Truman launched a "Campaign of Truth". In an address to the American Society of Newspaper Editors he said: "Everywhere that the propaganda of Communist totalitarianism is spread, we must meet it and overcome it with honest information about freedom and democracy . . . We pool our efforts with those of them other free peoples in a sustained, intensified program to promote the cause of freedom against the propaganda of slavery. We must make ourselves heard around the world in a great campaign of truth" (Martin, 1982, p. 48). However, in the McCarthy era America's foreign propaganda suffered a serious loss of credibility. Sorensen (1968) remarked: "Particularly damaging was the highly publicized expedition of McCarthy's two young aides, Cohn and Schine. Arrogant carbon copies of their boss, they insulted both foreigners and Americans as they toured United StatesI.S. offices and libraries in Europe . . . looking for evidences of Communism, subversion, and sexual deviation. Astonished Europeans watched, laughed -- and wept for America" (p. 35).

President Kennedy defined the mission of USIA on January 25, 1963, just after taking office: "The mission of the United States Information Agency is to help achieve United States foreign policy objectives by (a) influencing public attitudes in other nations, and (b) advising the President, his representatives abroad, and the various departments and agencies of the implications of foreign opinion for present and contemplated United States policies, programs, and official statements" (Bernays & Hershey, 1970, p. 24). The task of USIA staffs abroad makes them responsible "for the conduct of overt public information, public relations, and cultural activities" aimed "to inform or influence foreign public opinion" (Bernays & Hershey, 1970, p. 8). Similarly Carter saw the task of the USIA as conveying to other countries "the best possible understanding of our policies and intentions, and sufficient information about American society culture to comprehend why we have chosen certain policies over others". The USIA also was restricted to white propaganda; that is, it was ordered that "the agency will undertake no activities which are covert, manipulative, or propagandistic" (Hansen, 1984, p. 7).

Edward R. Murrow, a former head of America's propaganda program, declared the following action maxim of the USIA still valid today: "To be persuasive we must be believable; to be believable we must be credible; to be credible we must be truthful. It is as simple as that" (Sorensen, 1968, p. 4). The widespread belief among American propagandists was that at worst they were involved with white propaganda, which was why the USIA attempt to counter Soviet propaganda, begun in 1981, was called "Project Truth" (Alexandre, 1987, p. 33). However we are very obviously dealing with an ethnocentric perception of truth that defines truth from the perspective of the U.S. interests. Alexandre summarized some of the "Alerts" sent to American embassies under "Project Truth: Soviet Propaganda Alerts". Alert No. 2 (November 1981), for example, described as a propaganda lie the assertion of the Soviets that the United States was planning to invade Grenada. The assertion that the CIA was involved in Third World countries (No.

7, May 1982) or that the United States used chemical and biological warfare in Vietnam (No. 6, April 1982) were also characterized as propaganda lies.

Among the practitioners, however, there does appear to be an awareness, although not very pronounced, that they are not altogether "objective" proponents of truth. Thus Sorensen (1968), for example, expounded on the meaning of the term propaganda and the work of American propaganda: "When I joined United States Government's foreign information program in 1951, I had the typical liberal's suspicion of the word. I did not consider my colleagues and myself to be 'propagandists'. We were disseminating only 'information' designed to 'tell America's story to the world', and our hope was that if others could come to know us better they would learn to appreciate, respect, and sometimes even love us. I was wrong; it is not that simple. . . . We had to be advocates, persuaders -- propagandists" (p. X). In other words, trying to separate propaganda from public diplomacy is at best a semantic exercise. Sorensen maintained, however, that there was neither lying nor news manipulation. Similar remarks by USIA counselor Stan Burnett are on record: "We are advocates. We are supposed to create a public climate for United States policy" (Time, September 9, 1985).

President Eisenhower was absolutely clear about the instrumental character of American propaganda when he addressed the USIA in a speech in November 1953: "We are now conducting a Cold War. The Cold War must have some objective, otherwise it would be senseless. It is conducted in the belief that if there is no war, if two systems of government are allowed to live side by side, that ours, because of its greater appeal to men everywhere, to mankind, in the long run will win out. That it will defeat all forms of dictatorial government because of its greater appeal to the human soul, the human heart, the human mind" (Bogart, 1976, p. XIV). Much the same sentiments were expressed in September 1985 by Wick: "The only war the United States has fought in the past four years has been the propaganda war" (Time, September 9, 1985). One of the

USIA's main target groups in this propaganda war was the youth of Western Europe, whom Wick perceived as dangerously neutralist: "They don't have the indissoluble link with their blood brothers fighting totalitarianism" (Time, September 9, 1985). A 1983 report said: "We've got to close the memory gaps between older Europeans -- whose images of America were shaped by the CARE packages, Marshall Plan aid and the Berlin airlift -- and their children, who have been influenced by Vietnam and Watergate" (Alexandre, 1987, p. 39).

The great importance credibility had and continues to have to American image cultivation was demonstrated by the case of the Voice of America (VOA). The VOA's efforts to be as credible as possible, frequently prompted criticism that it was not doing enough propaganda. Thus Adelman (1981), then head of the United States Arms Control and Disarmament Agency, thought the VOA "could allocate slightly less time to Western economic woes, crimes and racial unrest -- not because these put America in an unfavorable light but simply because the Soviet press already gives them sufficient if not inordinate play" (p. 921). Solzhenitsyn (1980) attacked the VOA: "It is clear that the directors of the Voice of America are constantly trying not to arouse the anger of the Soviet leadership. In their zeal to serve detente, they remove everything from their programs which might irritate the communists in power" (p. 823). He went so far as to claim that the VOA "dances to the tune called by the communist regime or indeed becomes indistinguishable from a Moscow radio station" (p. 823), an attack strongly reminiscent of McCarthy: "One of McCarthy's allegations was that 'Communist Influence' had led the Voice to eliminate its Hebrew-language broadcasts to Israel" (Sorensen, 1968, p. 31).

The importance of the Voice of America to United States image cultivation is underscored in a statement by L. F. Kaemba (1968), then information attache at the embassy of the Republic of Zambia in Washington: "For example, I have to work at times with the Voice of America. I may find it necessary to broadcast to Zambia and explain something that has taken place at the United Nations, perhaps in reference to the Zambia economic mission or within the Security Council. I pick up a phone and call someone with whom I have previously made contact at VOA and say, 'At such and such a time can you let me broadcast to Zambia?'" (p. 39).

The VOA played a decisive part in the "radio war" between the United States and the USSR, which began in 1947 when the VOA first broadcasted via shortwave to the Soviet Union to counter the anti-American propaganda. In the early 1980s the VOA was estimated to have an audience of 100 million, about 70 million of whom lived in communist countries (Hansen, 1984). In 1948 the United States-owned Radio Free Europe, based in Munich, West Germany, was established. It specialized in news for and about Eastern Europe. In 1953 another United States-owned station, Radio Liberty, was also set up in Munich. It specialized in programs for and about the Soviet Union. Latin America's equivalent to Radio Liberty is Radio Free Cuba (also known as Radio Marti) whose task, according to President Reagan, is "to break Fidel Castro's monopoly on news and information within Cuba".

The USIA did not exactly heap honor and fame on itself in Vietnam, although there were enormous funds made available for propaganda there. Senator Fulbright (1970) estimated that some 2,800 people were employed on public relations for the Department of Defense, with the military public relations campaign targeted at the entire United States population. On the reporting of Vietnam Fulbright wrote: "It came as no great shock to me when I learned that some films were 'staged'. It was almost inevitable that fakery would be needed to portray war scenes that guaranteed that the Administration's efforts would be put in the best light" (p. 103). Some of USIA's propaganda work in Vietnam was simply bungled. Great store was set, for example, in the supposed effectiveness of leaflets. According to Chandler (1981) during its 7 years' activity in Vietnam USIA "littered the countryside of the North, South, and the Ho Chi Minh Trail in Laos and Cambodia with nearly 50 billion leaflets -- more than 1,500 for every person in both parts of the country -- trying to create a solid anti-Communist nationalism among the population. Political posters, banners, newspapers, magazines, brochures, cartoon books, bumper stickers, matchbook covers, and other kinds of printed matter inundated the South" (p. 3). As Chandler (1984) put it, "the Viet Cong and North Vietnamese armed forces hold the dubious honor of being targets of the most massive propaganda campaign in the history of warfare. Billions upon billions of leaflets were dumped on them from the air, and thousands of hours of loudspeaker broadcasts from airplanes, boats, and the ground penetrated their jungle hiding places in attempts to persuade them to give up the fight" (p. 39).

A spectacular American propaganda failure was the worldwide television extravaganza "Let Poland Be Poland", which featured Frank Sinatra crooning "Ever Homeward" in pidgin Polish. In Time's (September 9, 1985) assessment, this program drew howls of ridicule. It was relayed by satellite to more than 30 countries on January 31, 1982, reaching an estimated 170 million people. Additionally, the 90-minute production was distributed on video cassette and in seven languages -- English, French, Spanish, Portuguese, German, Italian and Arabic (Hansen, 1984). The object was to pillory the harsh policies of the Soviet and Polish governments. In fact, it only served to damage the reputation of American information work abroad.

Hansen (1984) criticized the USIA during both the hostage situation in Iran and the Soviet invasion of Afghanistan, claiming it failed "to be immediately responsive to requests from overseas posts in developing countries for television programs . . . on these subjects. Had such materials been available, they could easily have been placed on leading news shows in many friendly countries" (p. 39). Later, however, the USIA greatly influenced world public opinion about events in Afghanistan. Along with other Western countries, they equipped the resistance fighters with video cameras so they could conduct international PR with pictures of the fighting.

Recently the USIA has given particular attention to developing countries because of their importance to the U.S. economy (Hansen, 1984). According to Hansen, the USIA had been incorrectly using television, the most effective vehicle now available to public diplomacy in developing countries. Countries like Germany, Sweden, or Britain had no interest in USIA TV programs because they could produce enough of their own or had the financial resources to buy them on the open market, whereas developing countries are short of money and can produce few programs of their own, making them ripe for USIA television activities.

The best-selling novel The Ugly American (Lederer & Burdick, 1959) harshly criticized the way the American image is cultivated in developing countries. Using a fictitious developing country (but meaning Cambodia), the authors showed how poorly the Americans performed in the propaganda war compared to communists. The book's main message, according to Lederer and Burdick (1958) is: "the Red world is far better at public relations than is the free world". For instance, as dramatically presented in the novel, members of the American Foreign Service very often do not speak the language of the country to which they are assigned. The authors quoted James Reston, who had reported in The New York Times on March 18, 1958 that 50% of the entire Foreign Service officer corps did not have a speaking knowledge of any foreign language.

This is not to say that the USIA is incompetent or tends to squander money. The fact is that in public discussion in the United States, the negative examples are addressed first so as to learn from mistakes. There is comparatively little public discussion of the subtle and successful operations of the USIA. Bogart (1976) reported on one such example: The Americans, through the USIA, tried to encourage the members of the engineering and medicine faculties at Cairo University to use the American library or materials prepared by the Americans. The problem was that this target group had strong communist leanings. Clearly, however, they would watch a film about, say, new surgical techniques developed in America or certain engineering techniques currently being used. The obvious aim of such films was to impart useful and usable information. The hidden aim was to encourage the scientists to gather more knowledge about their particular areas expertise, perhaps prompting them to use the American library. At the very least, however, they would gain a positive impression of American science.

Image Cultivation by the CIA

The Bible quotation chiseled into the wall of the marble entrance lobby of the CIA in Langley, Virginia -- "And ye shall know the truth and the truth shall make you free" (John 8:32) -- cannot, of course, be taken as the guiding principle of the Agency's activities. In their 1974 book The CIA and the Cult of Intelligence, censored by the CIA, Marchetti and Marks argued that the CIA (and this is nothing unusual for a secret service) was involved in disinformation campaigns. Koschwitz (1988) reported that the former head of the CIA, William Colby, admitted that the CIA had manipulated news. False "stories" had been planted in the foreign press, for example exaggerating the strength of small pro-Western resistance groups.

Whereas is held to high standards the USIA with regard to the truthfulness of the information it disseminates, not so with the CIA. The CIA goes into action whenever the Washington government needs to implement an information policy but does not wish to be identified as the information source. Koschwitz (1988) reported CIA sources as explaining that the Agency concentrates its efforts on the behavior of enemies of the United States in the world. It claims to prevent the suppression of news that it perceives to be of no value. Hence, they will disseminate truth but only in such a way that it is of strategic value to United States interests. According to Koschwitz, a practical implementation of this policy, for example, is the Afghanistan war, which the CIA wanted to keep in the world public awareness. The "briefings" held Tuesdays in New Delhi or Islamabad up to 1988, at which correspondents of the international news agencies and representatives of other media were informed about events in Afghanistan, were based on information provided by the CIA.

As to the willingness of journalists to cooperate with the CIA, Koschwitz (1988) wrote: "As late as into the 70s it succeeded in winning a considerable number of American journalists as collaborators (at least 30, probably up to 100). At least 22 United States media, without knowing about it, at that time had foreign correspondents under contract which at the same time were on the payroll of the CIA" (p. 72). That the CIA can help make journalists' work easier and offer them evaluations of complex situations that they could not get elsewhere contributes to the readiness of journalists to collaborate with the CIA. The Agency even ran its own information service called Forum World Features which from 1966 to 1975 placed political articles in international print media. It supplied information as many as 150 newspapers, including such prestigious ones as the Washington Post (Agee, 1987).

One of the main goals of any secret service is to build up a network of trusted people and collaborators in the foreign media. According to Koschwitz (1988), the CIA had some 800 "propaganda assets" in the 1970s ready to be used in covert media projects. The method used to place a report in the international press was as follows: First one attempted to get a lesser known foreign paper to publish the report. From there the report would climb higher and higher up the media hierarchy until it arrived in the internationally renowned media. Horrock (1976) described the way wrong information was planted: "You place a story in Bangkok, for instance, in a small paper, maybe one with CIA support, and it gets picked up by a larger paper and then, possibly by a foreign news service, or Paris Match. The next step will see it used by Reuters or an American news service and coming back to the United States" (The New York Times, February 9, 1976). In this context Koschwitz noted that the Reuters agency was suspected in 1976 of disseminating wrong information planted by the CIA. Agee (1987) asserted that the CIA had infiltrated Associated Press, and that the following media enterprises served the CIA: The New York Times, CBS, Time Inc., ABC, NBC, UPI, Newsweek and the Wall Street Journal. However, his references as to the kind of relationships are vague. And in fact, The New York Times ran a series about the CIA's influence on world public opinion. According to Agee, a "witness," an unnamed staff member of a 1975 Senate inquiry who had read the files about CIA media operations, testified that there was an "incredible" (p. 50) network of relationship.

Koschwitz (1988) summarized the findings of a study that examined how the U.S. government is assumed to have persuaded European journalists to report positively on the then new and highly controversial neutron weapons and at the same time to evaluate the position of the Soviet Union negatively. Public protest against the neutron bomb snowballed in the latter half of 1977, probably due at least in part to the fact that Soviet propaganda against the "neutron killer warhead" was extraordinarily successful in Western Europe. In early 1978 the U.S. government, through the CIA, decided to run a campaign against the Soviet antineutron bomb campaign by stimulating the appearance of newspaper articles in the Western European press that supported Washington's position on the neutron bomb. The government programme aimed only at press coverage. There was no intention to prevent the renting of assembly halls or anything similar. The campaign had been chosen as a way of complementing the open activities such as the instruction to have talks with European journalists. The CIA believed that more favorable press coverage could persuade the European public that it was not the intention of the United States to disturb any nuclear balance, but rather that the neutron bomb was a legitimate modernization move, much like the Soviet Union's stationing of SS20 rockets. In fact, the comparison with the SS20s became the focal point of the campaign's argument.

To implement the program the CIA intended to rely on sympathetic journalists, but also to pay them fees. Because the action was carried out secretly, which journalists were influenced under which conditions cannot, of course, be documented. But in a great deal of published opinion, especially in the United Kingdom and West Germany, there was a swing toward greater support for the American view in the controversy. Koschwitz (1988) pointed out that some West German and British newspapers began either to relate the SS20 threat to the neutron bomb or to ridicule the Soviet propaganda campaign. The opinion swing was caused not only by the CIA activities, but also by the fact that some top West European politicians (e.g., foreign minister Genscher and chancellor Schmidt in Germany, and prime minister Callaghan in Britain) began to speak critically in public about the Soviet position.

A standard procedure followed by many intelligence services is to finance books for propaganda or image cultivation purposes. According to Agee (1987) between 1947 and 1967 the CIA itself published or subsidized publication of more than 1,000 books. One example is The Foreign Aid Program of the Soviet Bloc and Communist China. An Analysis (New York 1964/1967) by the West German, Kurt Müller (Marchetti & Marks, 1974). According to Marchetti and Marks' informant, the genesis of this book, which is very critical of communist development aid, was as follows: "The agency had found out that Müller was interested in communist foreign-aid programs, encouraged him to write a book which would have a strong anti-communist slant, provided him with information and then helped to get the book published and distributed" (p. 176). Another, particular importance, was the Penkovsky Papers, which were to show to the world at large that a Western agent had spied on the Soviet Union. The Penkovsky Papers became a world bestseller. To this day, however, rumors persist that they are not authentic but were fabricated by the CIA (Marchetti & Marks, 1974). Although they do contain authentic information, the "diary" as published was not written by Penkovsky. Agee (1987) claimed that the Penkovsky Papers were put together from CIA materials after Penkovsky was captured and executed.

For a long time the CIA's relationship to the media was very distant (cf. Marchetti & Marks, 1974), although there were always some journalists in its service. According to Marchetti and Marks, the CIA was also "looking for possible recruits in the press corps or hoping to place a CIA reporter under 'deep cover' with a reputable media outlet" (p. 354). One journalist, dispatched to Moscow for the CIA, was told "that the agency is willing to release certain top-secret information to you in order that you try and obtain certain information for us" (p. 355). Under Richard Helms, who took over the Agency in 1966, CIA relations with the press changed markedly. Helms, who had worked as a journalist himself, started a series of breakfasts, lunches, and occasional cocktail and dinner parties for individual and groups of reporters. At these functions, the CIA issued no press releases but leaked information to support its own case and serve its own purposes (Marchetti & Marks, 1974, p. 360).

The CIA scored one of its greatest successes when it managed to circulate a partially changed version of a speech given in 1956 to the 20th congress of the Soviet communist party. All foreign delegates had been barred from hearing it. Through a Polish communist party official, the CIA got hold of a copy of the speech, which copy Moscow, however, had prepared especially for circulation in Eastern Europe and so lacked 34 passages about foreign policy. The CIA prepared a second version that contained the missing 34 passages. Koschwitz (1988) reported: "Through various news channels, for example the Italian agency ANSA, the 'completed' draft was then disseminated worldwide. Since then the CIA has been feting the confusion in Moscow over this coup as one of its greatest triumphs" (p. 82).

According to Koschwitz's (1988) research, although he was able to cite only one newspaper item as his source, the CIA also tried to heat up the Sino-Soviet conflict. Radio transmitters claiming to be located in the People's Republic of China broadcast programs attacking leading Soviet politicians. Most of the reports were monitored in Hong Kong and fed from there into the world news network. The CIA also seized at post offices newspapers from the People's Republic of China addressed to foreign recipients. Articles were removed and exchanged for others written by the CIA. The altered papers were printed and then sent on. The CIA inserts were circulated around the world as authentic news from the People's Republic of China. The Agency also launched balloons in Taiwan that dropped leaflets, newspapers, and pamphlets over the People's Republic, all implying that they were being distributed by dissident groups within the country. The aim was to shake the internal balance of power in China.

For months during 1985/1986, the Libyan leader Qadaffi was shown on television in connection with terrorism acts. Qadaffi became the symbol of evil, helping the White House to mobilize public support for the American attack on Libya. The bombardment of Libya, a reprisal for terrorist bombing, took place on April 14, 1986. In August 1986 the Reagan administration started a disinformation campaign against Qadaffi, aimed at convincing him that the United States would bomb Libya again, thereby fomenting unrest in hopes of inciting a coup d'etat against him (Smith, 1988; Spoo, 1987). In an article in the Washington Post, Bob Woodward revealed that the plan, developed in a three-page memo by John Poindexter, the president's security adviser, was accepted in the White House on August 14, 1986. As outlined in the memorandum, one of the key elements of the plan was that it combine real and illusory events, with the basic goal of persuading Qadaffi that there was a high degree of internal opposition to him within Libya, that his key aides were disloyal, and that the United States was about to move against him militarily. One of the main goals of the action was to depict Qadaffi as ineffective and paranoid so that forces within Libya that desired his overthrow would be emboldened to act. The American media was guided by the Reagan administration to depict Libya as the heart of the international network of terrorism and as the legitimate target for anti-terrorist action. Qadaffi was depicted as the manipulator of world terrorism and built up as the villain for the American public.

On August 25, 1986, a report appeared in the Wall Street Journal claiming that Qadaffi was planning new attacks, that the United States and Libya were again headed for collision, and that the Pentagon was preparing plans for another bombardment of Libya. The report was described as "authoritative," that is, as being reliably sourced, by the spokesman for the White House, Larry Speakes. Other newspapers followed with reports that Libya was sponsoring terrorist activities and that there was the possibility of renewed confrontation with the United States According to Smith (1988), George Shultz, the Secretary of State, said: "Frankly, I don't have any problems with a little psychological warfare against Qaddafi" (p. 448), then recalled Churchill's justifying deceptions against Hitler during World War II: "In time of war, truth is so precious, it must be attended by a bodyguard of lies".

United Fruit and the CIA: The Coup in Guatemala

It is often hard to tell the difference between the international PR of governments and that of individual transnational corporations. One case in particular is that of United Fruit (called United Brands since 1975). The PR activities of United Fruit are well documented. Thomas P. McCann, the company's PR chief for many years (he joined the firm in 1952), in 1976 wrote a book about his working life. And Bernays (1965), PR counselor to United Fruit, reported in his memoirs about his work for the company: "Communist penetration, Mayan excavations, worldwide revolutionary movements, celiac disease and bananas engaged my interest for almost 20 years, beginning in the early 1940s when I first became counsel on public relations to the United Fruit Company, working closely with its president, Samuel Zemurray. . . . As a first step I organized the 'Middle America Information Bureau, conducted by the United Fruit Company', set up in our office. We corresponded actively with 25,000 Americans -- group leaders and opinion molders. We tried to interest them in Middle America; we supplied them with facts and points of view" (p. 749).

United Fruit's biggest land holdings were in Guatemala. For more than 50 years the company drew large profits from the country. Then Jacobo Arbenz Guzmán was elected president in 1950, assuming office on March 15, 1951. From the company's perspective Guzmán had an alarming flaw: He intended to reform land ownership and, by a decree of June 1952, to expropriate land owned by United Fruit. According to McCann (1976), the most urgent PR task was "to get out the word that a Communist beachhead had been established in our hemisphere" (p. 45). To Bernays (1965) it was clear in 1950 who was behind the unrest in the Caribbean: "I thought then such events were Communist furthered" (p. 757). As Bernays saw it, communism was advancing, particularly in Guatemala. In January 1950, for example, the correspondent of the New York Herald Tribune reported that President Arévolo was tolerating communists in important posts in the press, radio, and ruling party. Moreover, the correspondent alleged, Arévolo was conducting anti-American propaganda. Bernays imputed the following statement to then defense minister Arbenz Guzmán: "You people are doing things for your workers that we won't be able to do for 50 years. That's why I hate you" (p. 757).

Bernays had good contacts at The New York Times, whose publisher, Arthur Hayes Sulzberger, he acquainted with the Guatemalan situation in 1951. At United Fruit's invitation Sulzberger visited the country to see for himself. While he was in the capital city, the first "communist riot" occurred. McCann (1976) commented: "Even from the perspective of two decades later, the timing seems extraordinary. Bernays deserves credit for a first-class public relations coup" (p. 46). But Bernays (1965) told it differently: "In 1949-50 Mr. and Mrs. Arthur Hays Sulzberger of the Times went to Guatemala on a visit to their good friend Ambassador Richard Patterson. While they were there, the Communists staged an anti-American demonstration, which induced Mr. Sulzberger to investigate the situation thoroughly" (p. 758). Bernays continued: "I saw Arthur Hays Sulzberger . . . in late April 1951. I told him about Guatemala's unrest, Communist attempts at infiltration of the Guatemalan government, and our own fears of expropriation" (p. 758).

Bernays' (1965) strategy was to choose the most important American mass media -- newspapers like The New York Times, major magazines, the news agencies, and the electronic networks -- and bombard their journalists with "the company's version of the facts". Journalists were given guided tours of the tropics, generally flying first to Bogota, then Panama, Costa Rica, Honduras, and Guatemala -- all managed and paid for by United Fruit (Bernays, 1965, p. 761). According to McCann (1976), "These trips were billed as 'fact-finding' tours, and there was very little selling done, once the journalists had agreed to go. The trips were ostensibly to gather information, but what the press would hear and see was carefully staged and regulated by the host" (p. 47). Bernays remarked on the effect of these trips: "After their return, as I had anticipated, public interest in the Caribbean skyrocketed in this country" (p. 761).

In the meantime E. L. Bernays (1965) had also been active at another level. In order to decisively improve United Fruit's information situation, he suggested to Samuel Zemurray, the company president, that a "strategic intelligence department" (p. 762) be set up whose task would be to observe political developments and evaluate them so as to prevent events taking the company by surprise over and over again. Bernays by his own account took action on the matter in spring of 1952: "I urged . . . the company to support the anti-Communist democratic forces in Guatemala and to launch an attack on the Communist elements seeking power" (p. 762). This is a prime example of the "logic" of the American enemy-image of an alleged communist conspiracy. As Franck and Weisband (1971) characterized it, "The doublethink runs like this: communism is aggression. Therefore an attack on Guatemala is self-defense if it saves the Guatemalan people from their own leftist regime" (p. 50).

Implementing Arbenz Guzmán's 1952 decree, the government began expropriating United Fruit land in March 1953. But no land planted with bananas, oil palms, or other fruits was expropriated, nor were mahogany forests, dairy pastures, and building sites. A total of 178,000 acres was to be taken over by the government. United Fruit demanded $16 million for it; the Guatemalan government offered only $525,000, precisely the value of the company as reported for taxation purposes.

At the same time this was happening, United Fruit distributed several hundred copies of a "Report on Guatemala" which spoke of a "Moscow-directed Communist conspiracy in Central America" (McCann, 1976, p. 49). It argued further: "Any Guatemalan who loves his country so much that he wishes to protest publicly against its being under the yoke of the Kremlin -- now or ever -- must face the startling fact that he is held to be subversive. It may be considered the official government viewpoint" (McCann, 1976, p. 49). This 235-page work, published anonymously, was sent to every member of the United States Congress and to every major opinion molders in the United States. Ed Whitman, also responsible for the PR campaign and McCann's superior, gave a great many lectures, in which he used to say: "Whenever you read United Fruit in Communist propaganda, you may readily substitute United States."

Ed Whitman's statement was quite accurate; United Fruit indeed had very close relations to the government in Washington. McCann (1976) listed a number of people who had special relations to United Fruit or were on its payroll as advisers. By his estimation the communists could have had some influence on the unrest in Guatemala. But likely what ultimately brought down the Arbenz Guzmán government was United Fruit's PR efforts.

Of course, United Fruit's PR successes were depended on the readiness of the American press to spread their views,decisively influencing American public opinion against Guatemala. The American press expressed indignation at Arbenz Guzmán's announcement that United Fruit land was to be expropriated. And the U.S. Department of State sent the Arbenz Guzmán government a memorandum stating the U.S.' position on protecting private property and issuing an ultimatum for immediate restoration of the land to the company. At the same time, just a few hours after the expropriation, two tropical junkets were laid on for journalists from Time, Life, Newsweek, and the news agencies, among others, resulting in a wave of coverage siding with United Fruit. The company also circulated a weekly "confidential" Guatemala newsletter to 250 American journalists reporting economic and political developments. According to McCann (1976), these newsletters were so successful that later they were expanded to cover Honduras, Costa Rica, and Panama as well. McCann reported that a large number of the reports about Central America that appeared in the North American media from 1953 to 1960 comprised news that had come from the PR department of United Fruit.

In an operation named "El Diablo" (The Devil), the Eisenhower administration gave the order to topple the allegedly communist government of Guatemala. The CIA planned a secret invasion of the country and, according to McCann (1976), United Fruit was involved in all stages. Even the CIA's arms shipments were said to have been made in United Fruit vessels. Colonel Carlos Castillo Armas was the leader of the revolution and was headquartered on land owned by United Fruit along the border between Guatemala and Honduras, on Honduran territory. That was also where the invasion troops were marshaled. In mid-June 1954 began what The New York Times was later to call "the CIA-engineered revolution against the Communist-oriented President of Guatemala, Jacobo Arbenz Guzmán" (Franck & Weisband, 1971, p. 49), under the pretext of a declaration against communism threatening American republics, adopted in March 1954 in Caracas by the Tenth Inter-American Conference of the Organization of American States. Arbenz Guzmán was overthrown within a few days. Under the new Castillo Armas government United Fruit immediately received the expropriated land back. McCann (1976, p. 60) reported that manipulated photos, showing corpses allegedly mutilated by government troops, were used to discredit the Arbenz Guzmán government. According to McCann, however, the bodies were of unknown origin; they could have been killed by the people mounting the coup d'etat, or in an earthquake.

A few weeks after the Guatemalan government was overthrown, the United States Justice Department initiated action against United Fruit for alleged violation of antitrust laws (McCann, 1976). Bernays quickly developed a strategy for the new battle. A series of editorials, all remarkably similar, appeared in the press. They questioned why the same government that had received so much help from United Fruit to fight the communist threat in Guatemala was suddenly intent on taking action against its patriotic helper. Remember here that 1954 was at the peak of the McCarthy "communist" witchhunting era. At that time it was fairly easy to sell to Americans the idea that communist infiltration had been so successful in Washington -- especially in the Justice Department -- that the antitrust case against United Fruit was nothing but a Kremlin opportunity to strike a blow at the company. The United Fruit PR department went all out to exploit this image, even producing a film called Why the Kremlin Hates Bananas.

McCann (1976) reported an outstanding example of how adroitly United Fruit handled journalists. In early 1972 he spoke to Dick Severo, the new Latin America editor of The New York Times, who was relatively inexperienced in the job. He suggested to Severo that he visit the estates in Honduras, ensuring that Severo got all the literature he needed, that he got to see all the right things and meet all the right people. The result was excellent coverage: In April the report appeared on the front page. In McCann's words, "Severo wrote the best story United Fruit has ever received" (p. 171), depicting United Fruit as one of the most socially responsible Western enterprises. McCann further remarked: "I'm sure Severo believed every thing he saw, and I'm sure he believed everything he wrote. I'm equally sure he didn't see very much. The part that frightened me was that Eli Black believed it too" (p. 171). (Eli Black was then the main shareholder and most powerful man in the United Fruit Company.)

IMAGE POLICY OF THE SOVIET UNION

A Short History of Soviet Propaganda

The Soviet Union was the first state to use propaganda as a regular tool of international relations. The Communist International (commonly known as "Comintern") set up in 1919 was the first comprehensive, permanent international propaganda organization. Nominally an association of national communist parties, it claimed to have no links with the Soviet government, directing only the foreign parties. At the same time the Soviet state security services set up a "disinformation desk" to conduct propaganda. According to Barron (1963) that propaganda achieved spectacular successes in influencing public opinion and hence government policymaking in the West. Even visitors to the Soviet Union were duped into believing the Soviet Union was the workers' paradise. As Barron observed:

> Viewed in retrospect, the results . . . achieved surely must be classified as brilliant. At a time when the secret political police were murdering hundreds of thousands of Soviet citizens, and when countless others were being herded into concentration camps where ghastly conditions ensured the deaths of most, famous Western authors, scholars, journalists and lawyers acclaimed Soviet feats of "human regeneration" and "social correction". Even as millions perished from deliberately caused famines, playwright Bernard Shaw praised Stalin for blessing the Soviet people with plenty. (p. 243)

Barghoorn (1964) may have said it best:

> Words and pictures have played a more continuous and perhaps more vital role than bullets or rubles in Moscow's struggle to undermine the social order of capitalism and to reconstruct society on Marxist-Leninist foundations. (p. 3)

Soviet propaganda from the outset was very aggressive as it was meant to support world revolution. In the Soviet view the working class had a global historical mission to fulfill. It was perceived as the first class of world peoples to have a consistent international goal: to smash capitalism. Trotsky believed that supporting world revolution was a moral duty. Nikolay Bukharin, a prominent figure in Comintern, put it like this in his Programme of the World Revolution: "We must pursue the tactics of universal support of the international revolution, by means of revolutionary propaganda, strikes, revolts in imperialist countries, and by propagating revolts and insurrections in colonies of these countries". Indeed, in 1923 Foreign Secretary Lord Curzon issued an ultimatum to the Soviet Union to cease Bolshevist propaganda in the British empire within 10 days. This was by no means an isolated incident (Whitton & Larson, 1964). Beginning in 1926 "Radio Odessa" on the Black Sea attacked the Romanian government in nightly broadcasts calling for revolution. The Romanians tried to disrupt the broadcasts whereupon the Soviets set up a new, stronger station at the Soviet-Romanian border. In 1927 China and France protested about the communist propaganda there. France even withdrew its ambassador from Moscow and expelled the Soviet ambassador. In 1930 radio programs were broadcast in German against which the Reich government protested to no avail. The Soviets maintained that the broadcasts were directed at Germans living in Russia, certainly not a plausible argument as Germans were being called on to revolt. The broadcasts ended with the slogan: "Lang lebe die deutsche Sowjetrepublik" (Long live the German Soviet Republic). That same year a letter by Maksim Gorky was read aloud on the radio in which French and British workers were called on to support the Soviets and to resist interventions in foreign countries. Again, the British foreign secretary protested.

According to Chase (1953) Soviet post-World War II propaganda pursued four main objectives: (a) Spreading the idea of the revolution in other countries, (b) breaking up existing alliances against the Soviet Union by exploiting differences in interests between the allies, (c) weakening individual Western countries by stirring up internal tensions there, and (d) paralyzing the power to resist by spreading an image of the Soviet Union as an invincible power based on an invincible idea. The main aim of Soviet propaganda was to demoralize, to wear down the West's self-confidence, to implant a sense of pessimism about its ability to maintain its values in a global competition against alternative values. The propaganda was aimed at segments of Western societies disenchanted by their political systems, such as peace movements, nuclear arms opponents, certain religious movements, and intellectuals.

The Soviet Union began a special "Hate America" campaign on January 21, 1951, building on false documents, photographs, alleged eyewitness testimony, historical reports, and statistics. (Chase, 1953). The Soviet propaganda attacked America but was not addressed to Americans. As Chase observed, "When a Russian delegate at the United Nations looks at a United States delegate and proceeds to charge Washington with the most dreadful crimes, he is not really talking to the United States delegate and is well aware the charges are untrue. He is talking to a ragged peasant listening to the village radio somewhere in Burma or Iran. He is trying to fix in that peasant's mind a list of evils which will thereafter be associated with America" (p. 213).

Soviet foreign propagandists used many different image-cultivation approaches: publishing and distributing books in foreign languages, distributing newspapers and periodicals (e.g., the weekly Moscow News), broadcasting propaganda reports over Radio Moscow, the activities of news agencies (TASS and Novosti Press Agency), sporting events and cultural Soviet diplomacy, aimed at building up a more positive attitude to Soviet culture. According to Kruglak (1962), TASS encouraged a "good guys against bad guys" image of East-West relations: "The impression to be gained from an examination of the TASS World Service reports and the Moscow press is that there is unanimity among the countries of the Soviet bloc, discord and strife in the Western bloc, and friendship toward the USSR among the neutral nations" (p. 147).

The Soviet efforts to make the 1988 "Millennium of Christianity in Russia" an international media event is an excellent example of their use of culture as propaganda, intending to convey cultural tradition and religious tolerance. Scientists, artists, writers, painters, musicians, and so on were regarded as active fighters on the ideological front. However, in the culture struggle the USSR was at a decisive disadvantage vis à vis the United States: Mass culture was and is still firmly in the grip of the West. Television series such as "Dallas," "Dynasty," "Bonanza", "Baywatch" are distributed worldwide. (It may be quite possible, however, that such TV series create a negative image of America, for characters like J.R. and others are not exactly the sort to generate allround empathy.) Hollywood films still dominate the world market, Western pop music and fashion are popular worldwide, and Western products, from cigarettes to high-tech equipment, often have something approaching magical images in former East Bloc countries.

The attractiveness of the West often presented an image problem within a country's own population. For example, in a confidential paper to the Polish party leadership, Mieczyslaw Rakowski, politburo member, discussed the Polish people's dwindling attraction to socialism and its slogans, in large part because of heavy exposure to the capitalist system via the mass media. As Rakowski told party leaders, to the ordinary person living under socialism, the image of capitalism imparted by the media ultimately is positive: "Unemployment and the other diseases of capitalism, which they have never got to know about, don't interest them. Their relationship to capitalism rests on superficial feelings. Looking at the capitalist everyday they come to the conclusion that capitalism is a system in which both the workers and the bourgeois have the opportunities to enjoy the advantages of technical development and competition" (Der Spiegel, No. 29, 1988).

Many inhabitants of communist countries rarely believed anything reported in their media, often leading to some bizarre situations. For instance, Soviet visitors to the United States were occasionally shocked at the notion of unemployment in America (Time, September 9, 1985). Because the Soviet media bombarded them constantly with reports about the enormous joblessness in the United States, they believed just the opposite, namely that there was no unemployment at all.

Disinformation Campaigns of the KGB

Disinformation means covertly feeding a carefully assembled false news item into the opponent's communications system to influence decision-making processes and/or public opinion in the country concerned. Disinformation is one way of spreading propaganda, which is aptly described by the saying "Propaganda is a long word for the short word lie". As Lenin wrote in 1921 in a memorandum to Foreign Affairs Commissar Tchitcherin, "To tell the truth is a petty bourgeois habit whereas for us to lie is justified by our objectives." A disinformation department was set up in the KGB in 1959. Its task was to influence public opinion. The great advantage the KGB had over Western secret services is that most Western democracies are open societies in which even foreign journalists can move about almost at will. In the late 1970s more than half the KGB's agents abroad used the journalist's profession as their cover. The United States Department of State (1987) maintained: "While 35 to 40 percent of the Soviets stationed abroad are KGB, 50 percent of the journalists are KGB" (p. 27). The reasons for preferring journalists are obvious: Journalists are in touch with important decision makers and with other journalists, so they have easy access to information. It is estimated, for example, that about 70% of the journalists sent abroad by the TASS news agency were KGB agents (Koschwitz, 1988).

The KGB's media operations had as their purpose to selectively stir up in Western countries, unrest and feelings of insecurity or bewilderment; to disorientate; to destabilize the climate of social opinion in central domestic and foreign issues; selectively to disrupt the relationship between population and leadership or even to incite important segments of the population against the leadership; and to provoke wrong reactions and decisions at government level by calculated deceptions (Koschwitz, 1988). They also were aimed at presenting the policies of the Soviet Union and the countries it dominated in a positive light, mobilizing supporters for these policies, and moving foreign decision makers bit by bit to meet the will of these supporters. A speciality of Soviet disinformation policy was the defamation of leading political personalities in order to place them in a bad light in front of their own publics. For example, the KGB supposedly defamed President Sadat of Egypt using false materials (Koschwitz, 1988), though this technique is hardly unique to the KGB.

Some characteristic examples of a false news item placed in the foreign press by the KGB are as follows: When in October 1981 a Soviet submarine ran aground in Swedish territorial waters off Karlskrona, 10 journalists working in Washington received a telegram signed by an official of the State Department offering them information on the text of a secret agreement which allowed the United States to use this Swedish base for military purposes (Koschwitz, 1988). Another Soviet propaganda lie is that in the spring of 1982, it was reported by the mass media of India, Egypt, Pakistan, and The Philippines that when the astronaut Neil Armstrong was on the moon, he heard the word azan sung. Later he learned that this was the Muslim call to prayers, and because of this metaphysical experience became a Muslim, forcing the NASA to dismiss him. To fight this lie, which was aimed at damaging the U.S. image in Islamic countries and creating the impression that Muslims were discriminated against in the United States, the USIA arranged a telephone conference between Armstrong and foreign journalists. Armstrong asserted that he had voluntarily left NASA in 1971 and was never a Muslim (Fialka, 1983).

There was quite some excitement in 1983 over the case of the Greek newspaper To Ethnos. According to Koschwitz (1988) it had become obvious that the Athenian newspaper with the largest circulation (200,000) was taking an anti-Western line. Its journalists were publicly accused of being financed and controlled by the KGB. Koschwitz concluded that for the first time in the history of their secret service the Soviets had managed, for the price of $3 million, covertly to control a supposedly independent Western newspaper.

In February 1983, just before a conference of the nonaligned nations in New Delhi, the text of a speech allegedly by Jeanne Kirkpatrick, United States ambassador to the United Nations, was distributed to journalists and several Indian newspapers reported on it (Fialka, 1983). In the "speech," Kirkpatrick supposed to have said, among other things, that Third World countries should depend more on "free enterprise" and less on "foreign aid," that their governments bore a great share of responsibility for their own backwardness because of the incompetence of their leaders, and that India should be balkanized. She supposedly also complained about "inexcusable equivocations" in Mexico's economic policy and asserted that the support of the South African government was the "main goal of this administration". The speech that never was was even to be debated in the Indian parliament until they discovered it was a forgery.

In October 1984 TASS reported that the Pentagon was poisoning the Amazon River. Also in 1984 there were reports about a letter from the American ambassador in Austria, Helene von Damm, sent to Austrian defense minister Frischenschlager, asking on behalf of the American government how the republic of Austria could stand by the West in case of a Soviet atomic attack. In July 1985 the Soviet press published a letter allegedly from an American army general to the Chilean dictator Pinochet, welcoming Chilean troops to fight in El Salvador. According to Koschwitz (1988), the Soviet Union even tried to exploit the atomic disaster of Chernobyl in spring of 1986 to malign the United States. The KGB spread the text of a letter, supposedly written by an American government official, asserting that in order to damage the Soviet Union the reactor accident had to be played up in Western media, and that especially in the United States reports about radioactive rain in Europe should be exaggerated.

Under Secretary-General Yuri Andropov, a former head of the KGB, Soviet disinformation policy was greatly expanded. Only between 1972 and 1975 were there no significant KGB disinformation activities against the United States. An explanation for this was offered by Ladislav Bittman, former deputy chief of the Disinformation Department of the Czechoslovak Intelligence Service: "The Watergate scandal and the following investigation of United States intelligence activities supplied the American as well as foreign mass media with such an enormous volume of damaging information that forgeries were not necessary" (Martin, 1982, p. 59). One notion planted in the world media by the KGB was the so-called ethnic weapon. Since 1980 the Soviet media had been making the downright ridiculous claim that the United States was working on the development of weapons that killed only non-White people. In this context, they attempted again and again link the United States and South Africa and/or Israel. For instance, TASS maintained on January 4, 1984 that the South African racists are actively developing an 'invention' by United States criminals derived from medicine, so-called chemical 'ethnic weapons' with a 'selective factor of application' against the people of Africa. Then on August 13, 1984, TASS again claimed that the United States and South Africa were developing carefully selected pathogenic viruses which are practically harmless to whites and mortally dangerous to Africans, Asians, and 'coloreds'. The South Africans were allegedly testing the virus on captured Blacks. The same report claimed that Israel was testing the virus on Arab prisoners (cf. USIA, 1988).

The list of KGB-generated false news seems endless. For example, the United States is supposed to have been involved in the murders of former prime ministers Olof Palme (Sweden), Indira Gandhi (India) and Aldo Moro (Italy), as well as the attempted assassination of Pope John Paul II. The shooting down by the Soviets of the Korean airliner KAL 007 in September 1983 was allegedly planned by the United States as a deliberate provocation. I discuss here in more detail two KGB campaigns aimed at damaging the U.S. image that got worldwide attention: the baby organs trade campaign and the AIDS campaign.

In August 1988 a globally distributed false report about an alleged trade in baby organs played a decisive part in the secret service rivalry in the mass media. The report claimed that babies from South American countries were abducted or "adopted" from developing countries and then sold in the United States as living organ donors. Comprehensive documentation of how this report was propagated was prepared by the USIA in 1988. In West Germany, for example, on August 9, 1988 the nationally circulated left-liberal <u>Frankfurter Rundschau</u> ran a front-page story entitled "Babies Adopted for Organ Bank?" The story said that according to revelations by a judge, police in Paraguay had prevented seven babies being sold as living organ suppliers to laboratories in the United States There the infants, aged 3 - 6 months, were to have been killed in organ banks, judge Angel Campos was quoted as saying in Asunción. Baby traffickers had abducted the seven boys from Brazil to Paraguay to sell them there to United States organ banks under cover of adoption by American parents for about $15,000 per baby. Campos was also quoted as explaining how the police managed to track down the gang. When they found out that the alleged adoptive parents wanted any baby, even a deformed one, they got suspicious; typically, Judge Campos was quoted as saying, people look for the prettiest and healthiest children.

The <u>Frankfurter Rundschau</u>'s version of events originated from the British news agency Reuters in Asunción (USIA, 1988). The Reuters correspondent, Luis Mauro, had the previous day read a report about the baby organ trade in the newspaper <u>El Diario</u>, which quoted Judge Campos as saying: "Imagine, for example, the child of a multi-millionaire suffering from a kidney disease. That father would without doubt pay millions for a new kidney to save the life of his child." Mauro confirmed the remarks with Campos and wired his report to the Reuters head office in London. From there it went around the world. Many newspapers picked up the scandalous story, convinced that surely Reuters would not fall for a bogus story. In Germany it appeared in Munich's Merkur, in the reputable nationally circulated Süddeutsche Zeitung, also of Munich, and its biggest circulation daily, the tabloid Bild. Bild went on better: It faked a picture it claimed was of the infants saved from "slaughter".

The United States embassy in Ascunción denied the report immediately (USIA, 1988). The USIA commented that Judge Campos had repeated totally untenable rumors that had been circulating since January 1987 and that the rumors had been initiated by the KGB. The rumor began on January 2, 1987 in the capital of the Republic of Honduras, Tegucigalpa. A high-ranking staff member of the state welfare council, Leonardo Villeda Bermudez, told the newspaper La Tribuna: "Many people wanted to adopt physically handicapped children. At first it was thought that the adopting parents were well-meaning people who took in the children because they liked them and wanted to help them; but then it was discovered that the parents intended to sell them as spare parts. Thus the children's eyes were taken out, for example, to be given to other children who needed new eyes." On the same day, Reuters reported Bermudez's comments worldwide. On January 3, Bermudez, in an interview with the newspaper El Heraldo, also published in Tegucigalpa emphasized, that he was not used to giving interviews to the press, and that he had only passed on a rumor, to draw attention to the problems connected with the adoption of babies. In a letter to the editor in *La Tribuna*, Bermudez denied that the baby trafficking he had mentioned was fact. And on January 8, the state welfare council denied that there was a baby trade. Reuters ran the denial on the same day.

On February 5, a comparable rumor surfaced in Guatemala (USIA, 1988). The newspapers Prensa, Libre, El Grafico, and others quoted the chief of the intelligence and narcotics section of the Treasury Police, Baudillo Hichos-Lopez, as saying that a woman arrested for baby trading had told him that in some cases the babies would be used as organ donors. This report, too, was immediately rejected as false, by Hichos-Lopez himself. But the press spread the rumor at first in Latin America and then it turned up in Europe on April 7, in the Volkskrant of Holland. Two days earlier, on April 5, Pravda had picked up the story, with its Mexico correspondent asserting that "thousands of children have been sent to the United States from Honduras to serve as organ donors for the children of rich families; eyes, kidneys, hearts, lungs -- in short, anything transplantable -- are in circulation". TASS spread the Pravda article, which then was printed in communist newspapers in Finland, India, Italy, and Cuba. L'Humanité, the newspaper of the French communist party, ran an article on April 14, entitled "Children's Hearts for Sale: Children Abducted in Honduras, Guatemala and El Salvador and Sold to Secret Laboratories in the United States".

In January 1987 and August 1988 several hundred articles appeared on this topic, all of which ignored the denials of the alleged witnesses. The USIA was unable to stop the disinformation campaign, despite the fact that no article contained verified facts; all of them just put forth claims and ignored denials. The fact that journalists worldwide apparently believed the baby trade story to be true certainly suggests that their image of the United States needed some repair work.

The AIDS disinformation campaign began in 1985 whereby the United States was blamed worldwide for the outbreak of the disease. This report, although dismissed as absurd by all experts, including Soviet medical scientists, met with much positive response, especially in African countries. For example Afrique Novelle, a weekly newspaper very close to the Catholic church, reported: "According to an authorized scientific source, the AIDS virus was developed in the research center at Fort Detrick, Maryland, where it was grown at the same time as other viruses to be used in biological weapons. It was then tested on drug addicts and homosexuals" (U.S. Department of State, 1987b, p. 71). In August 1986 a study conducted by biophysicist Professor Jakob Segal, his wife Dr. Lilli Segal, and Dr. Ronald Dehmlow of Humboldt University in East Berlin became public. The study claimed that at Fort Detrick in 1977, the United States had synthetically manufactured the AIDS virus by combining two naturally occurring viruses, VISNA and HTLV-I. Experts agree that this hypothesis is untenable, but it circulated nonetheless in the media of Africa, South Asia, and the Soviet Union. Indeed, it was discussed extensively at the 8th conference of the Nonaligned Movement at Harare in September of that year. Both Pravda and Izvestiya have repeatedly printed articles alleging that AIDS was created in laboratories at Fort Detrick as part of alleged attempts by the United States to create new biological weapons (Walker, 1988). The Soviet media later warned against American soldiers spreading AIDS in other countries. The obvious intention of such reports was to spread mistrust of the American military, but it also affected tourists, businesspeople, and so forth. Indeed, the newspaper Sovyetskaya Rossiya reported on January 23, 1987 that in Western Europe AIDS was most prevalent in places where United States troops were based.

Gorbachev's PR Offensive

The methods by which the U.S.S.R. communicates with the world public have changed greatly in recent years. A turning point in the propaganda war between the United States and the USSR was the public relations regarding treatment of the shooting down of Korean Airlines flight 007 in September 1983 in which 269 people were killed. The conversation between the Soviet pilot and his controllers was recorded by the USIA and used for propagandistic attack against the Soviet Union (Blyskal & Blyskal, 1985). The USIA produced a 10-minute video tape that documented how coldly and unscrupulously the Soviet air force shot down the passenger plane. The tape also documented the recorded conversation: "I see [the target], visually and on radar." "The air navigation lights are burning. The strobe light is flashing." "I'm dropping back. Now I will try a rocket." "I am closing on the target." "I have executed the launch." "The target is destroyed."

Prior the U.N. debate about the shooting down of the airliner, the USIA obtained permission from the U.N. administration to install TV monitors in the Security Council chambers. Blyskal and Blyskal (1985) reported that installation was delayed until the Soviet duty officer was relieved so that a monitor could be installed "right behind the seat Soviet Ambassador Oleg Troyanovsky would occupy, providing a perfect photo opportunity for the media, a Reagan administration trademark" (p. 210). The entire American PR exercise was a success. Ambassador Kirkpatrick attacked the Soviet action in front of the U.N. Then the video produced by the USIA was shown, and the showing itself photographed. Time's September 19, 1983 ran this cover: "The photo of Troyanovsky icily staring into the distance and ignoring the damning video screen over his shoulder" with the comment "A memorable image of stonewalling," not realizing, like every other news organization, that the picture had been carefully staged by the USIA (Blyskal & Blyskal, 1985, p. 210).

The Soviet response to the KAL 007 crisis ushered in a new phase of Soviet international public relations. Marshal Nikolay V. Orgakov held a press conference via satellite with foreign reporters. In front of a large map on which flight routes were marked, he argued that the Korean airliner was out to spy. Soviet television also interviewed the pilot who had shot the airliner down; he insisted that he had warned the plane several times and had wanted to force it to land.

Steps to change the international image of the Soviet Union followed. In October 1984 Constantin Chernienko, the Soviet president, gave the Washington Post an interview. But the major image turnaround was achieved by Gorbachev (helped, of course, by his wife Raissa, also a media star). Following the signing of a declaration in Geneva in January 1985 by foreign ministers Gromyko and Shultz, in which the first summit meeting between Reagan and Gorbachev was announced, intensive communication began between the Soviet Union and the United States. Three examples deserve special attention:

1. In April 1985 the Soviet Union distributed to a target group of political decision makers and journalists in Western capitals 70,000 copies of a document printed in six languages, entitled "Star Wars -- Delusion and Dangers". The publication explained the Soviet position on the Strategic Defense Initiative (SDI) plans and exposed the "war machinery" of the United States. The document attempted, by its selection of data, to depict the Soviet Union as merely responding to a threat created by the West. In April 1984 the Americans countered with their publication entitled "Soviet Military Power," which addressed the Soviet Union's increased armament and strategic intentions from the American point of view. This document, too, was distributed in Western capitals.

2. On November 5, 1985, the government newspaper Izvestiya ran two full pages on President Reagan's responses to questions from four Soviet journalists. He put forth his views on SDI, his security policy plans, the aims and readiness to negotiate of his administration, and so on. On November 9, Reagan addressed the Soviet population over the Voice of America; the audience was said to have numbered 23 million. The information department of the Soviet embassy in Washington for its part placed a Pravda editorial as an advertisement in the August 13, 1985 edition of The New York Times, outlining for the American public the Soviet point of view as to what was blocking progress in the Geneva talks. On September 9, 1985, Time printed several pages of interview with Gorbachev. Later in his book Perestroika, Gorbachev (1987) described this interview as having been a very important element of his foreign policy and expressed the hope that it made clear to the United States public his views on Soviet-American relations and what needed to be done to improve them.

3. Televised New Year's messages to each other's populations by Reagan and Gorbachev on January 1, 1986, lasting 5 minutes each, were seen by an estimated 150 million people in the USSR and about 110 million in the United States. Both addresses aimed at improving the foreign policy

> climate and regaining mutual trust. Arms control ideas were put forward and a fundamental readiness to continue the dialogue for peace and understanding was emphasized. Gorbachev said he regarded the chance to address the American people as a hopeful sign that relations between the Soviet Union and the United States would improve. Ronald Reagan, who watched Gorbachev's speech on TV, told the Soviet press immediately after the two speeches had been aired that he welcomed Gorbachev's message as a continuation of the Geneva talks.

These events clearly belong in the field of public diplomacy and image cultivation. Each government used the other country's mass media to communicate messages and in all cases resorted to public relations counsel. Such foreign policy publicity by political leaders had never happened before in world history. The high-level mutual exchanges of information were designed to attract the greatest possible public attention, aiming at world public opinion. In August 1988 Lev Alexandrovich Voznessensky, commentator for Soviet television, was appointed chief government spokesman of the Soviet Union. In an interview, he said the newly created position was to help those in political responsibility better recognize the new Soviet reality, and to give the public at large the chance to control the work of the leading institutions (Der Spiegel, August 8, 1988).

Of central importance to the new Soviet PR activities, internally and externally, was the already mentioned (1987) book Perestroika by Mikhail Gorbachev. Its importance at home is ignored here except to note that Perestroika also means abandonment of the attempt at self-deception. Suddenly talked about in Soviet media were problems that had always existed in socialist everyday life: alcoholism, crime, unemployment, poverty and need, revanchism, strikes, and so on. History was reexamined: the massacres by the Red Army in Lithuania and Poland (Katyn); the assassination in 1940 of Leon Trotsky, Stalin's chief rival for power. Gorbachev made the foreign-political relevance of perestroika quite clear when he wrote: "In writing this book it has been my desire to address directly the peoples of the USSR, the United States, indeed every country. I have met government and other leaders of many states and representatives of their public, but the purpose of this book is to talk without intermediaries to the citizens of the whole world about things that, without exception, concern us all" (p. 9). He pointed explicitly to another reason for writing the book: "Many want to understand what is actually happening in the Soviet Union, especially since newspapers and television in the West continue to be swept by waves of ill-will toward my country" (p. 10).

"As for the official circles and most of the mass media in the West," Gorbachev (1987) continued, "at first there was very little belief in the feasibility of the reforms we announced in April 1985. Caustic remarks were abundant" (p. 125). But even in his own estimation the situation had clearly improved: "We see that many in the West did not expect such frank and in-depth discussion, such large-scale constructive measures" (p. 125). Gorbachev complained, however, that what he called "extreme right-wing quarters" (p. 127) do not attempt to hide their hostility to perestroika: "They have even tried to discredit openness and democratization. For example, they report false news from the U.S.S.R., quoting the Soviet press as the original source. But it soon transpires that nothing of the kind has ever been printed in Soviet publications" (p. 127).

Gorbachev (1987) took the view that improved communication ameliorates conflicts. A "constructive and wide-ranging dialogue" (p. 13) was needed: "That is what we intend when we arrange television links between Soviet and American cities, between Soviet and American politicians and public figures, between ordinary Americans and Soviet citizens. We have our media present the full spectrum of Western positions, including the most conservative of them" (p. 13). With a view to foreign image cultivation, he argued: "It has to be recognized that foreign policy proposals in this age of mass information and mass interest in international problems are always accompanied by propaganda. They must 'impress'. American leaders, for example, begin to advertise their intended international moves long before they announce them officially and always present them as 'major', 'historic', 'crucial', etc." (p. 159).

Gorbachev's many travels abroad were also part of the image cultivation process. And the Soviet leader was cultivating image when he ordered political prisoners released, allowed the formerly internally exiled dissident, Andrei Sacharov, to visit America, and suggested that in 1991 an international conference on human rights should be convened in Moscow. In West Germany, at any rate, an opinion poll of a representative sample of the population (Der Spiegel, No. 35, August 1988) found Gorbachev very highly regarded. Overall, the West Germans polled also trusted the peace and disarmament policy of the Soviet Union more than that of the United States. There is no doubt that Gorbachev's popularity was largely generated by his skilful image policy. A new variety of image cultivation was the full-page advertisement placed on June 30, 1989 in British newspapers, including The Times, with the head "Astronaut wanted -- no experience necessary". It was placed by the Soviet space authority, Glavcosmos, on the advice of the advertising agency, Saatchi & Saatchi.

In connection with the Gorbachev image drive it must not be overlooked, however, that he has also called the West the Soviet Union's unchanged enemy that he told a congress of Soviet writers on June 19, 1986, was trying to harm the Soviet Union by all possible means (published in the newspaper of the Italian communists, L'Unita on October 7, 1986). According to Wettig (1988), who examined the speeches and publications of top Soviet politicians from a political science point of view, Moscow regarded as a tremendous success "that it has been possible to make great inroads in public opinion in Western Europe which Washington had always regarded as its very own sphere of influence" (p. 382). According to Wettig, the Soviets put this success down to "Soviet foreign policy having fully and completely armed itself with the principle of publicity (glasnost)" (p. 382). The decisive change in Soviet PR in the West was that the audience was no longer just protesters and opponents, but the public at large. As Wettig observed, in a speech at the start of the 19th Party conference, Gorbachev stressed the great importance of contact with representatives of other countries, from heads of state and government to ordinary citizens. He explicitly mentioned authorities in science and culture, outstanding writers, leaders and delegations of political parties, social organizations, and movements, trade union leaders and Social Democrats, religious dignitaries and parliamentarians.

CHAPTER 8

Image Policy During Wartimes: Theoretical Considerations and the Gulf War

CARL VON CLAUSEWITZ AND PARADOXICAL COMMUNICATION: THE NECESSITY OF CENSORSHIP

The French Revolution changed the character of warfare. As in former times, war was again the concern of the people, not solely the business of specialists, of professional soldiers. The first military historian and theoretician to recognize this was the Prussian general, Carl von Clausewitz (1780 - 1831). In his *Vom Kriege* (On War), published posthumously in 1832, von Clausewitz argued that Napoleon's military success was due mainly to the enthusiasm of the French people. According to von Clausewitz, war is an act of violence aimed at forcing the enemy to accept our will. The central aspect of warfare, he suggested, however, is not physical force, but morale. The goal of war, then, is to break the enemy's morale. The von Clausewitz' theory of war takes the following factors into consideration: (a) the government that defines the war aims, (b) the army that is fighting, and (c)the people.

Von Clausewitz already knew what Sir Arthur Ponsonby later said in 1935: "The point is that propaganda is as much a weapon of war as a gun, and far more effective." Propaganda in wartime means that information not favorable to one's own cause is suppressed. During war the lie becomes a kind of patriotic duty or even a virtue

(Ponsonby, 1928). Important to understanding the theoretical foundation of censorship is the environment in which military actions are taking place. This environment is characterized by danger, highest physical strain and confusion. Von Clausewitz (1832/1873) called this *friktion*, which means that all plans developed during maneuvers have to be changed in real war. All is simple in war, but the simple is difficult and nothing is certain. Camouflage and deception are the norm. Most intelligence is not secure and very often is wrong. Indeed, von Clausewitz argued, in war most news is false. Secrecy becomes most important because the enemy has to be deceived.

The ideas of von Clausewitz were relevant even during the Gulf War. Imagine what would have happened if the media had reported about the thousands of dead the Allies had expected but did not get, because they succeeded in deceiving the Iraqis by instrumental use of the media. Reporting the truth of war might not only give the enemy advantages but also weaken the morale of one's own population and/or troops. Lying and propaganda are important instruments of warfare. If journalists can be instrumentalized, that is, can be manipulated to do propaganda, then they are useful. But reporting the truth in most cases is dangerous for the successful achievement of war aims.

According to von Clausewitz (1832/1873) lying and deceiving are necessary in war. Mastery of deceit and hypocrisy is decisive for successful military actions because the aim has to be to surprise the enemy. The German sociologist Simmel (1922) argued that during war the basis of social life must be undermined. The enemy must be confronted with unexpected situations. Simmel made the following assumption: "All relationships between people are self-evidently based on their knowing something about each other" (p. 256). People have expectations regarding the behavior of others and know that those they are dealing with also have such expectations. Stable social relations are based on the formation of "expectations of expectations", which makes social behavior predictable. In a war situation one has to deceive the enemy's expectations of one's behavior and, as a result, to undermine the foundations of human coexistence.

Communication is interaction through messages. Communication means, then, that information is passed from one person to another. In times of war, communication with the enemy means that we try to pass false intelligence to the enemy -- and the enemy knows that this is our intention. It is a situation of paradoxical communication (Watzlawick, 1976). Decision making in war, then, means making paradox predictions: The higher the probability of a certain action, the lower the chance the enemy will mount it. The lower the probability of an action, the higher the probability the enemy will act that way.

The art of disinformation assumes highest importance for survival in times of war. Successful disinformation means the enemy treats false information as credible. A famous example of successful disinformation is *Operation Mincemeat*, under which in 1943 British intelligence deceived the Germans about the place of the Allied landing in the Mediterranean. Fake documents were planted on the corpse of a Major Martin to convince the Germans that the landing was intended not to take place in Sicily but in Greece or Sardinia (Masterman, 1972; Montagu, 1945). The documents stated that for military reasons Sicily was so obviously the place to land, the Allies would choose another place. The Allies made the Germans believe that the truth was a lie and the lie was the truth. One of the fake documents contained a hint that the Germans should be deceived in the following way: out of reasons of camouflage the impression should be created that Sicily was the place chosen for the landing operation. Furthermore it was said that Husky, the code word for the landing in Sicily was the code word for the landing in Greece.

The logic of disinformation is as follows: What does the enemy think, that I think, what he thinks, and so on (Watzlawick, 1976). The idea is to feed the enemy wrong intelligence, taking care that he will not find out it is wrong until it is too late. One must imagine oneself in the position of the enemy and take over his or her ways of thinking and perceiving. The normal rules of communication are turned upside down -- it is the world of double cross. To summarize: Censorship in times of war is necessary in order not to loose the advantage of surprise and not to inform the enemy about one's own weakness, strength, or intentions.

PUBLIC OPINION IN WARTIME

Three more reasons for institutionalizing censorship during wartime are (a) the morale of the soldiers, (b) the morale of the population, and (c) world public opinion. Any nation-state waging war has to find stories that justify and ennoble the cause. These are the stories to be disseminated, whereas those that tell of the horrors of war from the soldiers' point of view should be suppressed. The German sociologist Tönnies (1922) argued that in a country at war, people believe in the just cause of the war, which was forced upon the country by the enemy. Hume (1749/1985), discussing the nature of love and hatred, wrote:

> When our own nation is at war with any other, we detest them under the character of cruel, perfidious, unjust and violent: But always esteem ourselves and allies equitable, moderate, and merciful. If the general of our enemies be successful, 'tis with difficulty we allow him the figure and character of a man. He is a sorcerer: He has a communication with daemons; as is reported of *Oliver Cromwell* and the *Duke of Luxembourg*: He is bloody-minded, and takes pleasure in death and destruction. But if the success be on our side, our commander has all the opposite good qualities, and is a pattern of virtue, as well as of courage and conduct. His treachery we call policy: His cruelty is an evil inseparable from war. In short, every one of his faults we either endeavour to extenuate, or dignify it with the name of that virtue, which approaches it. (p. 348)

In order to justify war the Nazis, for example, invented a legendary past to vindicate their acts. In other countries, the past was newly edited to conform to war slogans. Some examples of the dialectic contortions warmongering states have used to put the public in a war mood are "Holy War", "ad majorem dei gloriam", "Fatherland War" (the description in Russian history writing of the war of 1812), "liberation war", "preventive war", "defensive war", "enforced war", "war of opportunity", "war that broke out coincidentally as a result of unexpected fatal conflicts or a rapid series of unexpected events", "concluding war", "last war", "war on war", "death to the executioners", "destruction of the murderous barbarians", and "violence against perpetrators of violence".

To stabilize belligerent public opinion, the government stigmatizes the enemy as aggressor or as a nonhuman monster. President Bush, who characterized Saddam Hussein as another Hitler, argued: "Saddam tried to cast this conflict as a religious war, but it has nothing to do with religion per se. It has, on the other hand, everything to do with what religion embodies: good vs. evil, right vs. wrong" (Time, March 11, 1991, p. 24). A review of newspaper editorial coverage of the Gulf Crisis concluded that Saddam Hussein proved to be the quintessential *bad guy* (LaMay, 1991). A counting of keywords that appeared in news stories between August 1, 1990 and February 28, 1991 reveals that the American media covered the Gulf War as "a sort of new millennium crusade" (LaMay, 1991, p. 41). Talbott (1992) argued that in his feud with Saddam Hussein, George Bush was trying to be Gary Cooper in the climactic scene from High Noon: "As the lanky sheriff faces down the archvillain, frightened townspeople peek out of the windows to see who will be left standing in the dusty street" (Time, February 10, 1992, p. 23).

During war it is of vital interest to the supreme command or the government to control public opinion. In Germany during World War I the motto of the military PR was: "We cannot say all, but what we say is the truth". One must add, though, not the whole truth and this in fact means a lie. So the German World War I defeat at the Marne, which was most decisive for the war, was never reported truthfully in the German press while the war was still on.

Kaiser Wilhelm on his birthday, January 27, 1915, congratulated the journalists: "My compliments. Your articles are great. I thank you very much. You are doing a great service. I enjoy reading your articles -- they are full of patriotism. It is also of great value to our people in the trenches when we can send them things like this."

On February 16, 1913, Theodore Roosevelt spoke to journalist John C. O'Laughlin about his view of the conflict between journalists and the military (specifically, the Navy) during war times: ". . . I would choose the correspondent and treat the correspondent on the theory that he is for the time being a part of Uncle Sam's military force, in a position of high responsibility both to the Navy and to the country, and as honorably bound to meet his service and national obligations as is the officer himself" (O'Laughlin, 1913, p. 11). And journalist Palmer saw as the main task of journalism at the outbreak of a war the creation of patriotic solidarity: "A two-edged sword, the correspondent -- use him against the enemy" (O'Laughlin, 1913, p. 16).

During World War I all countries taking part in the war had institutions responsible for lying, that is, for handling the press. The author of the French war communiques, Jean de Pierrefou, was called the biggest liar in the whole country. But, as one might say: There are normal lies, there are sacred lies, and the biggest lies are official war communiques.

Stigmatizing the enemy has a long tradition. The Gulf War was not the first war in the Arab region during which the Western mass media built an Arab leader up as the enemy. It happened also during the war Spain waged from 1922 to 1927 in Morocco, part of which was then its protectorate (the rest was French), in response to Abd el Krim's (1880 - 1963) defeat of the Spanish army at Annoual in 1921. The German military historian Roth (1990) observed: "The proclamation of an Islamic republic posed a serious challenge to European colonial rule and at the same time impinged considerably on the strategic interests of the great powers in the Mediterranean region" (p. 11). Marshal Hubert Lyauteuy, France's representative in Morocco, saw the war as "the biggest threat to civilisation and the peace of the West" (Roth, 1990, p. 19). With the proclamation of the Islamic republic the entire European colonial policy was called into question, with the Kabyles claiming the right to self-determination proclaimed by the League of Nations.

The Spanish dictator, Primo de Rivera (1870 - 1930), who called the war a crusade and the revenge of the cross on the crescent, said arrogantly: "We want to do them [the Riffians] good, but they don't let us" (Woolman, 1969, p. 143). In mid-1925 France and Spain made a peace offer, but it was rejected. Kunz and Müller (1990) treated the offer as a tactical political move to placate world public opinion (and the Rif tribes). France and Spain's goal was to make the public believe they were ready for peace and that Abd el Krim was the warmonger who would not accept a sensible compromise. He was depicted as the threat to Western civilization. Woolman (1968/1969) wrote: "Most of the journalists, even those who admired Abd el Krim and perhaps believed in the justice of his rebellion, felt that Spain had the situation well under control. They could not, or would not, accept the possibility that a parcel of crude barbarians, however intelligently guided, could outmaneuver and outfight the soldiers of a European power" (p. 141). On April 5, 1924 Lieutenant Colonel Repington, correspondent of the London Daily Telegraph, described Abd el Krim as "that interesting bandit" (Woolman, 1968, p. 142).

Reporting was subject to strict censorship. Journalists for the most part did not even get into the fighting area. In fact, some were also there for other reasons. For example, Harris, the Morocco correspondent for The Times of London, was an agent of the British secret service. Abd el Krim (1927) noted in his memoirs: "Harris, the correspondent of the Times betrayed me, he was my evil spirit" (p. 106). He wrote that Harris talked him into believing "that the Spaniards and the French will never succeed to penetrate the Rif. He incessantly incited me to wage war on France by telling me over and over -- as also did the American consul and the American correspondents -- that internally and externally French politics were in a terrible bind and that all the French could do was to try to cope with their own problems" (p. 106). (Harris, 1927, depicted events differently.) Woolman (1968/1969), who analyzed the articles of foreign correspondents, concluded that they knew nothing about what was really going on in the fighting area. The reports merely reproduced the official statements of the Spanish supreme command. The crime of the gas warfare remained hidden from the public -- but then, perhaps they were not interested in it, anyway, because in fact a few newspapers did report that poison gas had been used. But this was the first to be decided by poisonous gas (Kunz & Müller, 1990). In 1925, when the Spaniards had signed the Geneva Protocol forbidding first use of poisonous gas in war, systematic use of gas began in the Kabylie in whose mountain valleys it was especially devastating

In the Algerian War, which began in 1954 and lasted 8 years, France also strictly filtered information (Knightley, 1975). At first the uprisings were presented as minor internal difficulties. When reports from Algeria became increasingly frequent the French government changed its press policy, resorting to censorship, propaganda, and political pressure. The insurgents were maligned as rebellious barbarians ungrateful for having been able to enjoy French culture these many years. The proud army of the Grande Nation had allegedly been dragged into a filthy war. The propaganda message was that France would stand firm and not yield a centimeter, that its duty was to defend Christian civilisation. In August 1955 Francois Mitterand, later France's president, argued that in Algeria the only negotiation was war (Knightley, 1975). According to Knightley, not just the French, but also the American and British publics were subjected to the French propaganda because there were hardly any reporters in Algeria.

PUBLIC RELATIONS IN WARTIME: THE GULF WAR II

The PR agency Hill & Knowlton played a major part in the preparations for the Gulf War. Shortly after the invasion of Kuwait in August 1990, Hill & Knowlton signed a contract with an interest-lobbying group called Citizens for a Free Kuwait (CFK; financed by $17,861 in contributions from individuals and $11,852,329 from the Government of Kuwait; MacArthur, 1992; Trento, 1992). The account brought the agency an estimated $10 million to $12 million. According to MacArthur, H & K organized a Kuwait Information Day on college campuses on September 12, September 23 became a national day of prayer, and September 24 was declared by 13 governors a national Free Kuwait Day. Thousands of media kits extolling the virtues of Kuwaiti society were distributed. Media events featuring Kuwaiti "resistance fighters" and businesspeople were organized. Meetings with newspaper editorial boards were arranged. Video news releases from the Middle East were produced. According to Trento, H & K arranged a press conference with a Kuwaiti "freedom fighter" in early September to offset the view that Kuwaitis were fleeing their country and to outline the activities of Kuwaiti resistance: "H & K spent over $600,000 to produce and distribute video news releases that were sent to outlets reaching millions of people" (p. 381). Press conferences like these, according to Trento, were arranged to present the image of a strong, gallant Kuwaiti resistance and to counter reports of young Kuwaitis partying the war away in Cairo discos.

Hill & Knowlton tried to remind members of Congress that Kuwait was a democracy by showing copies of its constitution (Roschwalb, 1994). There is no doubt that Kuwait had certain problems with its image in the United States. MacArthur (1992) observed: "In August 1990, the Bush dministration's task was to sell two images -- an ugly one of Hussein and a handsome one of Kuwait -- to the American people" (p. 43). MacArthur went on to give an account of the dominant image of Kuwait theretofore: human rights violations, exploitation of foreign workers, breaking up of prodemocracy movements, being an unreliable ally of the United States. MacArthur commented: "The unsavory facts about Kuwaiti society made the task of presenting a martyred nation to the American public a delicate one. The selling of Kuwait as a modern-day analogy to pre-World War II Czechoslovakia would take some doing" (p. 45). Trento (1992) emphasized that "a month before the Iraqi invasion, Amnesty International issued a report that stated that Kuwaiti authorities arrested dissidents and torturede them without trial" (p. 380).

During the Gulf Crisis antiwar demonstrators in the United States attacked oil companies and carried posters reading "NO BLOOD FOR OIL". Senator Howard Metzenbaum, Democrat from Ohio, said: "We are protecting their oil with American boys" (Metzenbaum in Time, February 25, 1991, p. 60). But Bush maintained: "It's not about oil! It's about naked aggression!" (Time, February 25, 1991, p. 60). Kellner (1992) pointed out in this context that another issue was decisive in mobilizing support against Saddam, who was called an "environmental terrorist" by President Bush, referring to the oil spills that had killed so many animals (the picture of the oil-smeared cormorant was aired worldwide). According to Kellner the media never really investigated who was responsible for the oil spills, but accepted the web of deception and disinformation sold by the military and the Administration to the media; that is, they assumed the Iraqis were solely responsible. Kellner regarded the Gulf oil spill as the greatest propaganda victory of the war for the coalition force, because "many who had been sympathetic to the plight of the Iraqis were now angry with the images of dead birds and oil pouring onto the Saudi beaches. The powerful images of environmental damage intensified hatred of Saddam Hussein and demoralized the peace movement, many of whose members were strong environmentalists" (p. 227).

H & K also used atrocity propaganda. MacArthur (1992) emphasized that of all the accusations made against Saddam Hussein, none had more impact on the American public than the one about Iraqi soldiers removing 312 babies from incubators and letting them die. According to Cutlip (1994), Robert Keith Gray, then head of Hill & Knowlton sent a memo to Citizens for a Free Kuwait calling for atrocity stories. In October 1990 the Congressional Human Right's Caucus held a public hearing on conditions in

Kuwait under Iraqi occupation. Trento (1992) reported that George Hymel of H & K and his staff "provided witnesses, wrote testimony, and coached the witnesses for effectiveness. The PR staff produced videotapes detailling the atrocities and ensured that the room was filled with reporters and television cameras" (p. 381). Nayirah, a 15-year-old Kuwaiti girl, whose last name was kept secret to protect her family in Kuwait, testified: "I volunteered at the al-Addan hospital . . . While I was there, I saw the Iraqi soldiers come into the hospital with guns, and go into the room were 15 babies were in incubators. They took the babies out of the incubators, took the incubators, and left the children on the cold floor to die" (MacArthur, 1992, p. 58). None of the members of Congress knew that Nayirah in fact was the daughter of the Kuwaiti ambassador to Washington. As Cutlip (1994) commented: "H & K sent its own camera crew to film this hearing that it had helped cast and direct. It then produced a film that was quickly sent out as a video release used widely by a gullible media. Too late some alert reporter unmasked the story as a hoax and revealed that Nayirah was the Kuwaiti Ambassador's daughter living in Washington. Once more the press served as patsies for the public relations staged event"[1] (p. 771). H & K also ensured that the video was aired by about 700 TV stations. On October 10, 1990, about 53 million Americans watched the tearful testimony on ABC's "Nightline".

[1] Cutlip (1994) was referring to Susan B. Trento's (1992) *The Power House: Robert Keith Gray and the Selling of Access and Influence in Washington* and to John R. McArthur's *Remember Nayirah, Witness for Kuwait?* (in *The New York Times* op-ed page, January 6, 1992), but in the meantime some new evidence has been published and Cutlip's argument has to be modified. (For H & K's version of the Kuwait account, see Pratt, 1994). Roschwalb (1994) pointed out that the story of Iraqi soldiers removing hundreds of babies from incubators "was shown to be almost certainly false by an ABC reporter, John Martin, in March 1991 after the liberation of Kuwait" (p. 271). MacArthur emphasized that Nayirah was the daughter of the Ambassador, had been brought to the Committee by H & K, and that H & K did not respond to the question whether she was in Kuwait in August and September 1990 when the alleged atrocities took place.

According to H & K the substance of Nayirah's testimony was true; using her as a witness was a stylistic move. The Ambassador did verify that Nayirah indeed had been in Kuwait, and Kroll Associates, a private investigative company, inquired on behalf of the Kuwaiti government about the alleged atrocities and concluded "that multiple incubator atrocities had taken place and that Nayirah was a witness to one of them" (Pratt, 1994, p. 289). MacArthur (1992) argued that the main result of the investigation was that Nayirah did not work in the hospital, came to the hospital by accident, and did not see babies taken out of incubators.

According to Roschwalb (1994), the atrocity story "seriously distorted the American debate about whether to support military action. Seven senators cited the story in speeches backing the January 12 resolution authorizing war" (p. 271). Decisive in supporting the credibility of the baby incubator story was the fact that on December 19, 1990 Amnesty International published a report on human rights violations in occupied Kuwait. The report included the baby incubator story: "In addition over 300 premature babies were reported to have died after Iraqi soldiers removed them from incubators, which were then looted. Such deaths were reported at al-Razi and al-Addan hospitals, as well as the Maternity Hospital" (MacArthur, 1992, p. 66). President Bush made heavy use of the atrocity story, too. On October 15, 1990 he said: "I met with the Emir of Kuwait. And I heard horrible tales: newborn babies thrown out of incubators and the incubators then shipped off to Baghdad" (MacArthur, 1992, p. 65). MacArthur also quoted a speech of Bush to the troops, which he characterized as Bush's best imitation of an H & K press release: "It turns your stomach when you listen to the tales of those that have escaped the brutality of Saddam the invader. Mass hangings. Babies pulled from incubators and scattered like firewood across the floor" (p. 65).

When questioned whether the testimony of Nayirah was decisive in mobilizing of support to enter the war, Frank Mankiewicz, vice-president of H & K, answered that he had been against the war from the beginning and the decision for war was the President's (<u>Der</u>

Spiegel, No. 40, 1990). But Mankiewicz also called Kuwait a success for his company. Because the White House, Pentagon, and State Department controlled all information they gave to the media and the public, Trento (1992) argued that it remains a question whether or not H & K's effort on behalf of Kuwait was technically necessary or effective. But, and this is the point, it did demonstrate that a PR firm behaved like a warmonger, distorting facts, distributing atrocity propaganda, presenting violators of human rights as democrats, and so on. Bertolt Brecht characterized scientists as a species of inventive gnomes to be hired by everyone; just replace scientist with PR counselor and you have the ethics of PR during the Gulf War.

CHAPTER 9

Consequences of Image Polishing

The conclusion to be drawn from the research findings and the experiences of the practitioners is that clearly the best form of image cultivation for nation-states is for them to be democratic, to observe human rights, and to pursue policies of openness. Because this is so, Panama under General Noriega, Iran under Ayatollah Khomeini, Romania under Ceaucescu, North Korea under Kim il Sung, Ethiopia under Mengistu Haile Mariam, or East Germany (which had to lock in its citizens) had no chance of acquiring a positive image in the Western media. All the same, there are structural reasons that make PR necessary to cultivate image. Probably one of the most important instruments in this context is of the national news agency, if one exists, to provide coverage adequate to news values. Active participation in news pools and/or news exchanges, for example of TV news, is recommended without limitations. This holds true for any kind of program exchange.

In fairly general terms, there is a three-phase approach to building up a positive or breaking down a negative image (Manheim & Albritton, 1984):

1. Phase 1 is to do a situation analysis, that is, to gather information about the actual image one's country has abroad in general or in a particular country. If it is a negative image one should try to disappear from media attention, if need be by initially actively restricting information. This "submerging" is to create quiet necessary to prepare Phase 2. The governmental information and communication apparatus

must be coordinated; that is, embassies and consulates abroad must be prepared for their future communicative work (e.g., how to produce materials for the press, how to write up facts in news agency style, how to present picture materials and longer term background information). Here, attention should also be given to the peripheral arenas of image cultivation, such as postage stamps, which can spread information about a country and its people. Austria in particular has used this avenue to present itself as a cultured nation, depicting painters, sculptors, architects, musicians, writers, works of art, and cultural events on its stamps.

2. In Phase 2 one moves from reacting to acting on one's own initiative. This transition should be slow and inconspicuous because there is always the danger of a boomerang effect. Two aspects must be given particular attention here: First, a "side entry" through cultural activities (e.g., exhibitions, visits by artists, etc.) is recommended. By image transfer one can try to use the aura of famous persons to cultivate a country's image. Second, it is important to unobtrusively win the trust of journalists. Personal contacts should be made and cultivated. In relating to journalists one should be aware that as a rule they know that what they write is based on inadequate research, and that they are not out to report only the negative. Usually they gladly accept background information as long as they are not given the impression that someone is trying to manipulate them.

3. In Phase 3 positive information can be more widely conveyed, transitioning smoothly to continuous image cultivation. Important to this is building up symbols of identification -- for example, the statesman who fights corruption and, of course, cultural activities. Always important is long-term cultivation of contacts with people who influence public opinion, politics, and business, or will

so in future. Apart from journalists these should include up and coming young politicians, young managers in the business community, intellectuals, and influential politicians in international organizations.

As my final remark I emphasize once more that image cultivation begins at home, in one's own country, in the way one deals with one's people and one's journalists. The best image cultivation is observance of human rights, establishment of a democratic form of state, and a free press.

References

Abbott, W. C. (1915). Germany and the Prussian propaganda. The Yale Review, 4.

Abd el-Krim. (1927). Mémoires d'Abd-el-Krim [Memoirs of Abd el-Krim]. Paris: Libraire des Champs Elysées.

Adelman, K. L. (1981). Speaking of America: Public diplomacy in our time. Foreign Affairs, 59.

Adorno, T. W., et alii (1950). The authoritarian personality. New York: Harper.

Agee, P. (1987). Central Intelligence Agency: Massenmedien als Transportmittel für U.S.-Interesssen. In E. Jürgens & E. Spoo (Ed.), Unheimlich zu Diensten. Medienmissbrauch durch Geheimdienste. Göttingen, Germany: Steidl.

Ainsworth, G. (1939). The New York World's Fair: Adventure in promotion. Public Opinion Quarterly, 3.

Albritton, R. B. (1985). Public relations efforts for the Third World: Images in the news. Journal of Communication, 35.

Albritton, R. B., & Manheim, J. B. (1983). News of Rhodesia: The impact of a public relations campaign. Journalism Quarterly, 60.

Alexandre, L. (1987). In the service of the state: Public diplomacy, government media and Ronald Reagan. Media, Culture and Society, 9.

Allport, F. H. & Simpson, M. M. (1946). Broadcasting to an enemy country: What appeals are effective, and why. Journal of Social Psychology, 23.

Allport, G. W. (1958). The nature of prejudice. Garden City, NY: Doubleday. (Original work published 1954)

Almond, G. A. (1963). Public opinion and the development of space technology: 1957 - 60. In J. Goldsen (Ed.), Outer space in world politics. New York: Praeger.

Almond, G. A. & Verba, S. (1963). The civic culture. Princeton, NJ: Princeton University Press.

Amaize, O. & Faber, R. J. (1983). Advertising by governments in leading United States, Indian and British newspapers. Gazette, 32.

August, T. G. (1985). The selling of the empire: British and French imperialist propaganda, 1890 - 1940. Westport, CT: Greenwood.

Baker, R. S. (1968). Woodrow Wilson: Life and letters. Facing war, 1915 - 1917. Garden City, NY: Doubleday.

Barghoorn, F. C. (1960). The Soviet cultural offensive: The role of cultural diplomacy in Soviet foreign policy. Princeton, NJ: Princeton University Press.

Barghoorn, F. C. (1964). Soviet foreign propaganda. Princeton, NJ: Princeton University Press.

Barron, J. (1983). KGB today: The hidden hand. New York: Readers' Digest Press.

Bateman, J.C. (1963, August). Techniques of managing the news. Public Relations Journal.

Bauer, W. (1930). Die öffentliche Meinung in der Weltgeschichte. Potsdam, Germany: Athenaion.

Beaverbrook, Lord. (1925). Politicians and the press. London: Hutchinson.

Befu, H. (1980). The group model of Japanese society and an alternative. In C. S. Drake (Ed.), The cultural context: Essays in honor of Edward Norbeck. Rice University Studies, Vol. 66, No. 1.

Bender, M., & Javits, M. (1976, February 27). Issue focuses unwelcome spotlight on publicizing of foreign clients. New York Times.

Benn, G. (1938). Wie Miß Cavell erschossen wurde: Bericht eines Augenzeugen über die Hinrichtung der englischen Krankenschwester. In W. Jost & F. Felger (Eds.), Was wir vom Weltkrieg nicht wissen (2nd ed.). Leipzig, Germany: Fikentscher.

Bernays, E. L. (1923). Crystallizing public opinion. New York: Boni & Liveright.

Bernays, E. L. (1965). Biography of an idea: Memoirs of public relations counsel Edward L. Bernays. New York: Simon & Schuster.

Bernays, E. L., & Hershey, B. (Eds.). (1970). The case for reappraisal of U.S. overseas information policies and programs. New York: Praeger.

Bernays, W. (1970). Dimensions of the problem. In E. L. Bernays & B. Hershey (Eds.), The case for reappraisal of U.S. overseas information policies and programs. New York: Praeger.

Bernstorff, Count J. H. (1920a). Deutschland und Amerika: Erinnerungen aus dem fünfjährigen Kriege, Berlin: Ullstein & Co..

Bernstorff, Count J. H. (1920b). My three years in America. London: Skeffington & Son.

Bettelheim, B., & Janowitz, M. (1950). Dynamics of prejudice. New York: Harper.

Blake, D. H., & Toros, V. (1976). The global image makers: It's time for a high profile for multinational corporations. Public Relations Journal, 32.

Blyskal, J., & Blyskal, M. (1985). PR: How the public relations industry writes the news. New York: Morrow.

Bogart, L. (1957). Measuring the effectiveness of an overseas information campaign: A case history. Public Opinion Quarterly, 21.

Bogart, L. (1976). Premises for propaganda: The United States Information Agency's operating assumptions in the Cold War. New York: The Free Press.

Boorstin, D. (1961). The image: A guide to pseudo-events in America. New York: Harper & Row.

Boot, W. (1991, May/June). The pool. Columbia Journalism Review.

Borchard, E., & Lage, W. P. (1940). Neutrality for the United States (2nd ed.). New Haven. CT: Yale University Press.

Botan, C. H., & Hazleton, V. H. (Eds.). (1989). Public relations theory. Hillsdale, NJ: Lawrence Erlbaum Associates.

Boulding, K. E. (1956). The image. Ann Arbor: University of Michigan Press.

Boulding, K. E. (1967). The learning and reality-testing process in the international system. Journal of International Affairs, 21.

Boulding, K. E. (1969). National images and international systems. In J. N. Rosenau (Ed.), International politics and foreign policy. New York: The Free Press.

Boyd-Barrett, O. (1980). The international news agencies. London: Constable.

Brinkley, A. (1982). Voices of protest: Huey Long, Father Coughlin, and the Great Depression. New York: Knopf.

Bronfenbrenner, U. (1961). The mirror-image in Soviet-American relations: A social psychologist's report. Journal of Social Issues, 17, 45 - 56.

Brown, J. A. C. (1963). Techniques of persuasion: From propaganda to brainwashing. Harmondsworth, England: Penguin.

Bryan, W. J. (1925). The memoirs of W. J. Bryan. Chicago: Winston.

Bryce Report (1915). Report of the Committee on Alleged German Outrages. London: Printed under the authority of His Majesty's Stationery Office by Eyre and Pottiswoode, Ltd.

Buchanan, W. & Cantril, H. (1953). How nations see each other. Urbana: University of Illinois Press.

Buchli, H. (1962/66). 6000 Jahre Werbung: Geschichte der Wirtschaftswerbung und der Propaganda (Vols. 1 - 3). Berlin: Walter de Gruyter.

Buie, J. et alii (1983, October). Foreign governments are playing our press. Washington Journalism Review, 5.

Buitenhuis, P. (1987). The great war of words: British, American, and Canadian propaganda and fiction, 1914 - 1933. Vancouver: University of British Columbia Press.

Burgess, J. et alii (1977). The great white hoax: South Africa's international propaganda machine. London: Africa Bureau.

Burke, K. (1935). Permanence and change. New York: New Republic Books.

Burke, P. (1992). The fabrication of Louis XIV. New Haven, CT: Yale University Press.

Campbell, J. (1978). The German Werkbund: The politics of reform in the applied arts. Princeton, NJ: Princeton University Press.

Cantor, M. G., & Cantor, J. M. (1985). American television in the international marketplace. Communication Research, 13.

Cantril, H. (1958). The politics of despair. New York: Collier Books.

Cardozo, A. R. (1970). A modern American witch-craze. In M. Marwick (Ed.), Witchcraft and sorcery. Harmondsworth, England: Penguin.

Carter, R. E. & Sepolveda, O. (1965). Some patterns of mass media use in Santiago de Chile. Journalism Quarterly, 42.

Chamberlain, H. S. (1925). Die Grundlagen des 19. Jahrhunderts (14th ed.). Munich, Germany: F. Bruckmann. (Original work published 1900)

Chandler, R. W. (1981). War of ideas: The U.S. propaganda campaign in Vietnam. Boulder, CO.

Chase, S. (1951). Roads to agreement. New York: Harper.

Chase, S. (1954). Power of words. New York: Brace & World.

Choate, P. (1990a). Agents of influence: How Japanese lobbyists are manipulating Western political and economic Systems. New York: Knopf.

Choate, P. (1990b, October). Political advantage: Japan's campaign for America. Harvard Business Review, 87 - 103.

Christiansen, B. (1959). Attitudes towards foreign affairs as a function of personality. Oslo: The Norwegian Research Council for Sciences and the Humanities.

Conacher, J. B. (1968). The Aberdeen Coalition: 1825 - 1855. A study in mid-nineteenth-century party politics. London: Cambridge University Press.

Considine, D. (1994). Media literacy and media education. Telemedium: The Journal of Media Literacy, 40.

Cooper, K. (1942). Barriers down. New York: Farrar & Rinehart.

Creel, G. (1920). How we advertised America. New York: Harper.

Creel, G. (1941, November 1). The truth shall make you free. Collier's, 108.

Cutlip, S. M. (1987). Pioneering public relations for foreign governments. Public Relations Review, 13.

Cutlip, S. M. (1994). The unseen power: Public relations. A history. Hillsdale, NJ: Lawrence Erlbaum Associates.

D'Amore, L. J. (1988, May/June). Tourism: A vital force for peace. The Futurist.

Daniels, J. (1944). The Wilson era: Years of peace, 1910 - 1917. Chapel Hill: University of North Carolina Press.

Darrow, R. W., Forrestal, D. J., & Cookman, A. O. (1967). The Dartnell Public Relations Handbook (rev. ed.). Chicago: Dartnell.

Davison, W. P. (1965). International political communication. New York: Praeger.

Davison, W. P. (1971, November). Some trends in international propaganda. Annals of the American Academy of Political and Social Science, 398.

Davison, W. P. (1973). International and world public opinion. In I. de Sola Pool et alii (Eds.), Handbook of communication. Chicago: Rand McNally College Publishing.

Davison, W. P. (1974a). Mass communication and conflict resolution. New York: Praeger.

Davison, W. P. (1974b). News media and international negotiation. Public Opinion Quarterly, 38.

Davison, W. P. (1975). Diplomatic reporting: Rules of the game. Journal of Communication, 25.

de Sola Pool, I. et alii (Eds.). (1973a). Handbook of communication. Chicago: Rand McNally College Publishing.

de Sola Pool, I. (1973b). Public opinion. In I. de Sola Pool et alii (Eds.), Handbook of communication. Chicago: Rand McNally College Publishing.

de Tocqueville, A. (1946). Democracy in America (Vol. 2). London: Oxford University Press. m

Deutsch, K. W. (1969). Nationalism and its alternatives. New York: Knopf.

Deutsch, K. W., & Merritt. R. L. (1965). Effects of events on national and international images. In H. C. Kelman (Ed.), International behavior: A socio-psychological analysis. New York: Holt, Rinehart & Winston.

Dilenschneider, R. L., & Forrestal, D. J. (1990). The Dartnell public relations handbook (3rd ed.). Chicago, IL: Dartnell.

Doerries, R. R. (1989). Imperial challenge: Ambassador Count Bernstorff and German-American relations, 1908 - 1917 (C. D. Shannon, Trans.). Chapel Hill: University of North Carolina Press.

Domatob, J. K. (1985). Propaganda techniques in Black Africa. Gazette, 36, 193 - 212.

Donsbach, W. (1991). Medienwirkung trotz Selektion. Einflußfaktoren auf die Zuwendung zu Zeitungsninhalten. Cologne, Germany: Böhlau

Drake, F. V. (1968). Why we are fighting in Asia. In A. Casty (Ed.), Mass media and mass man. New York: Holt, Rinehart & Winston. (Original work published 1965)

Dresser, M. (1989). Britannia. In R. Samuel (Ed.), Patriotism: The making and unmaking of British national identity (Vol. 3). London: National Fictions.

Duijker, H. C., J. & Frijda, N. H. (1960). National character and national stereotypes. Amsterdam: North-Holland.

Ellul, J. (1965). Propaganda: The formation of men's attitude. New York: Knopf.

Erzberger, M. (1920). Erlebnisse im Weltkrieg. Stuttgart, Germany: Deutsche Verlagsanstalt.

Everth, E. (1931). Die Öffentlichkeit in der Außenpolitik von Karl V. bis Napoleon. Jena, Germany: Gustav Fischer.

Fabian, R. (1970). Die Meinungsmacher: Eine heimliche Großmacht. Hamburg, Germany: Hoffmann & Campe.

Fialka, J. J. (1983, December 15). Tales of imagination in the foreign press give U.S. headaches. Wall Street Journal.

Fishbein, M. (Ed.). (1967). Readings in attitude theory and measurement. New York: Wiley.

Fisher, G. (1987). American communication in a global society (rev. ed.). Norwood, NJ: Ablex.

Forbath, P. (1977). The river Congo. Boston: Houghton Mifflin.

Ford, G. S. (1919). America's fight for public opinion. Minnesota Historical Bulletin, 3.

Fosdick, R. B. (1932, January). America at war. Foreign Affairs.

Foster, H. S. (1935). How America became belligerent: A quantitative study of war news, 1914 - 17. American Journal of Sociology, 40, 263 - 271.

Foster, H. S. (1937). Charting America's news of the world war. Foreign Affairs, 15.

Foster, H. S. (1939). The official propaganda of Great Britain. Public Opinion Quarterly, 3.

Franck, T. M., & Weisband, E. (1971). Word politics: Verbal strategy among the superpowers. New York: Oxford University Press.

Freud, S. (1921). Group psychology and the analysis of the ego. In J. Strachey (Ed. and Trans.), The standard edition of the complete psychological works of Sigmund Freud, (Vol. 18). London: Hogarth.

Fulbright, J. W. (1970). The Pentagon propaganda machine. New York: Liveright.

Galician, M. L., & Vestre, N. D. (1987). Effects of "good news" and "bad news" on newscast image and community image. Journalism Quarterly, 64.

Gallup, G. (1970). Image of the United States abroad in 1969: A report. In E. L. Bernays & B. Hershey (Eds.), The case for reappraisal of U.S. overseas information policies and programs. New York: Praeger.

Galtung, J., & Ruge, M. H. (1965). The structure of foreign news. Journal of Peace Research, 1, 64 - 91.

Gilbert, M. (1991). Churchill: A life. New York: Holt.

Goebbels, J. (1936). Bolshevism in theory and practice. Berlin: M. Müller & Sohn.

Goebbels, J. (1937). Die Wahrheit über Spanien. Munich: Zentralverlag der NSDAP, F. Eher Nachfahren.

Goldman, Eric. F. (1948). Two-waystreet: The emergence of the public relations counsel. Boston: Bellman.

Gorbachev, M. (1987). <u>Perestroika: New thinking in our country and the world</u>. London: Collins.

Grattan, C. H. (1969). <u>Why we fought</u>. (K. L. Nelson, Ed.). New York: Bobbs-Merrill (Original work published 1929)

Greider, W. (1992). <u>Who will tell the people: The betrayal of American democracy</u>. New York: Simon & Schuster.

Grivas, G. (1962). <u>General Grivas on guerilla warfare</u> (A. A. Pallis, Trans.). New York.

Grunig, J. E. (1993). Public relations and international affairs: Effects, ethics and responsibility. <u>Journal of International Affairs, 47</u>.

Grunig, J. E. (1989). Symmetrical presuppositions as a framework for public relations theory. In C. H. Botan & V. Hazleton (Eds.), <u>Public relations theory</u> (pp. 17 - 44). Hillsdale, NJ: Lawrence Erlbaum Associates.

Grunig, J. E., & Hunt, T. (1984). <u>Managing public relations</u>. New York: Holt, Rinehart & Winston.

Hagemann, W. (1948). <u>Publizistik im Dritten Reich</u>. Hamburg, Germany: Heitmann.

Hainsworth, B. E. (1987). Retrospective: Ivy Lee and the German Dye Trust. <u>Public Relations Review, 13</u>.

Halberstam, D. (1979). <u>The powers that be</u>. New York: Knopf.

Hallam, E. (Ed.). (1989). <u>Chronicle of the crusades</u>. New York: Weidenfeld & Nicolson.

Hansen, A. C. (1984). <u>U.S.I.A.: Public diplomacy in the computer age</u>. New York: Praeger.

Hapgood, N. (1928). <u>Professional patriots</u>. New York: Albert & Charles.

Harris, W. B. (1927). France, Spain and the Rif. London: E. Arnold.

Hayakawa, G. L. (1950). Recognizing stereotypes as substitutes for thought. Revue of General Semantics, 7.

Head, D. (1992). Made in Germany: Corporate identity of a nation. London: Hodder.

Heckscher, A. (1991). Woodrow Wilson. New York: Macmillan.

Hedin, S. (1916). Nach Osten!. Leipzig, Germany: F. A. Brockhaus.

Hertz, J. H. (1982). Political realism revisited. International Studies Quarterly, 25.

Hess, S. (1981). The Washington reporters. Washington, DC: Brookings Institution.

Hiebert, R. E. (1966). Courtier to the crowd: The story of Ivy Lee and the development of public relations. Ames: Iowa State University Press.

Hilton, J. (1987). How to meet the press: A survival guide. New York: Dodd Mead.

Himmelweit, H. T., Oppenheim, A. N., & Vince, P. (1958). Television and the child. New York: Oxford University Press.

Hitler, A. (1962). Mein Kampf (R. Manheim, Trans.). Boston: Houghton Mifflin.

Hofstätter, P. R. (1957). Gruppendynamik. Reinbek, Germany: Rowohlt.

Holsti, O. (1962). The belief system and national images: A case study. Journal of Conflict Resolution, 6.

Holsti, O. (1967). Cognitive dynamics and images of the enemy. Journal of International Affairs, 21.

Holtman, R. B. (1950). Napoleonic propaganda. Baton Rouge: Louisiana State University Press.

Houston, David F. (1926). Eight years with Wilson's Cabinet. 1913 - 1920 (Vol. 2). Garden City, NY: Doubleday.

Hovland, C. I. (1954). Effects of the mass media of communication. In G. Lindzey (Ed.), Handbook of social psychology. Reading, MA: Addison-Wesley.

Hovland, C. I., Lumsdaine, A. A., & Sheffield, F. D. (1965). Experiments on mass communication. New York: Wiley. (Original work published 1949)

Howard, C. M. (1986/87, Winter). How to say „No" without alienating reports. Public Relations Quarterly.

Hume, D. (1958). A treatise of human nature (L.A. Selby-Bigge, Ed.). London: Clarendon. (Original work published 1749)

Huttenback, R. A. (1970). G. A. Henty and the vision of empire. Encounter, 35 (1), 46 - 53.

Hyman, H. H., & Sheatsley, P. B. (1947). Some reasons why information campaigns fail. Public Opinion Quarterly, 11.

Inkeles, A., & Levinson, D. J. (1969). National character: The study of modal personality. In G. Lindzey & E. Aronson (Eds.), Handbook of social psychology (Vol. 4, 2nd ed.). Reading, MA: Addison-Wesley.

Isaacs, H. (1958). Scratches on our minds: American images of China and India. New York: Day.

Isaacson, W. (1992). Kissinger: A biography. London: Faber & Faber.

James, H. A. (1989). German identity 1770 - 1990. London: Weidenfeld.

Janis, I. L., & Smith, M. B. (1965). Effects of education and persuasion on national and international images. In H. C. Kelman (Ed.), International behavior: A socio-psychological analysis. New York: Holt, Rinehart & Winston.

Jowett, G. S. (1993). Propaganda and the Gulf War. Critical Studies in Mass Communication, 10.

Jowett, G. S., & O'Donell, V. (1992). Propaganda and persuasion (2nd ed.). Newbury Park, CA: Sage. (Original work published 1986)

Jürgens, E., & Spoo, E. (Eds.). (1987). Unheimlich zu Diensten: Medienmissbrauch durch Geheimdienste. Göttingen, Germany: Steidl.

Kaemba, L. F. (1968). Building the image of a new nation. In J. Lee (Ed.), The diplomatic persuaders: New role of the mass media in international relations. New York: Wiley.

Karl, P. M. (1982). Media diplomacy. In G. Benjamin (Ed.), The communications revolution in politics. Proceedings of the Academy of Political Science, 34 (No. 4).

Katz, D., & Braly, K. W. (1958). Verbal stereotypes and racial prejudice. In E. E. Maccoby, T. M. Newcomb, & E. L. Hartley (Eds.), Readings in social psychology (3rd ed.). New York: Holt, Rinehart & Winston.

Keenan, J. (1943). A steel man in India. New York: Duell, Sloan & Pearce.

Kellner, D. (1992). The Persian Gulf TV war. Boulder, CO: Westview Press.

Kelman, H. C. (Ed.). (1965). International behavior: A socio-psychological analysis. New York: Holt, Rinehart & Winston.

Kendall, P. L., & Wolf, K. M. (1949). The analysis of deviant cases in communications research. In P. F. Lazarsfeld & F. N. Stanton (Eds.), Communications research 1948 - 1949. New York: Harper & Row.

Kennedy, P. M. (1971). Imperial cable communications and strategy, 1870 - 1914. English Historical Review, 86, 728 - 752.

Kepplinger, H. M. (1983). Fuktionswandel der Massenmedien. In M. Rühl & H. W. Stuiber (Eds.), Kommunikationspolitik in Forschung und Anwendung. Düsseldorf, Germany: Droste.

Keune, R. (1981). Television in a North-South perspective. Bonn, Germany: Friedrich-Ebert-Stiftung.

Keune, R. (1985). Electronic media and the Third World. Bonn, Germany: Friedrich-Ebert-Stiftung.

Keune, R. (1991). Introduction: Who's leading whom up the garden path? Report of the 5th International Broadcast News Workshop. Ottawa.

Kipling, R. (1940). Rudyard Kipling's verse. New York: Doubleday. (Original work published 1899)

Kircheisen, G. (Ed.). (1912). Memoiren der Frau von Stael [Memoirs of Frau von Stael]. Berlin: Morawe & Scheffelt.

Kissinger, H. (1969). American foreign policy: Three essays. New York: Norton.

Kissinger, H. (1979). White House years. Boston: Little, Brown.

Klapper, J. T. (1960). The effects of mass communication. Glencoe, IL: The Free Press.

Knightley, P. (1975). The first casualty: From the Crimea to Vietnam. The war correspondent as hero, propagandist, and myth maker. New York: Harcourt Brace Jovanovich.

Knorr, K. D. (1980). Die Fabrikation von Wissen. In N. Stehr & V. Meja (Eds.), Wissenssoziologie. Kölner Zeitschrift für Soziologie und Sozialpsychologie, Sonderheft 22. Opladen, Germany: Westdeutscher Verlag.

Koschwitz, H. J. (1984). Massenmedien und publizistische Propaganda in der internationalen Politik: Analyse am Beispiel des Nahost-Konfliktes. Publizistik, 29.

Koschwitz, H. J. (1988). Der verdeckte Kampf: Methoden und Strategien geheimer Nachrichtendienste zur Manipulation der Auslandsmedien. Publizistik, 33.

Kotler, P., & Levy, S. J. (1969). Broadening the concept of marketing. Journal of Marketing, 33.

Krauze, E. (1994, October 10). Violence: Legend and reality. Time.

Krech, D., Crutchfield, R. S. & Ballachey, E. L. (1962). Individual in society. New York: McGraw-Hill Book.

Kriesberg, M. (1949). Dark areas of ignorance. In L. Markel (Ed.), Public opinion and foreign policy (pp. 49 - 64). New York: Harper.

Kruglak, T. E. (1962). The two faces of TASS. Minneapolis: University of Minnesota Press.

Kunczik, M. (1990a). Images of nations and international public relations. Bonn, Germany: Friedrich-Ebert-Stiftung.

Kunczik, M. (1990b). Die manipulierte Meinung: Nationale Image-Politik und internationale Public Relations. Cologne, Germany: Böhlau.

Kunczik, M., Heintzel, A., & Malmström, A. C. (1995). Public Relations in Schweden: Historische und aktuelle Aspekte. prmagazin, 26 (3), 33 - 40.

Kunczik, M., & Weber, U. (1994). Public diplomacy and public relations advertisements of foreign countries in Germany. The Journal of International Communication, 1.

Kunz, R., & Müller, R. D. (1990). Giftgas gegen Abd el Krim: Deutschland, Spanien und der Gaskrieg in Spanisch-Marokko 1922 - 1927. Freiburg i. B., Germany: Raubach Freiburg.

La May, C., FitzSimon, M., & Sahadi, J. (Eds.). (1991). The media at war. New York: Gannett Foundation.

Lansing, R. (1935). War memoirs of Robert Lansing. New York: Bobbs-Merril.

Lara, F. J. (1968). The fight against misunderstanding. In J. Lee (Ed.), The diplomatic persuaders: New role of the mass media in international relations. New York: Wiley.

Lasswell, H. D. (1927). Propaganda technique in the World War. New York: Knopf.

Lasswell, H. D. (1942). Communications research and politics. In D. Waples (Ed.), Print, radio, and film in a democracy. Chicago: University of Chicago Press.

Lavine, H., & Wechsler, J. (1940). War propaganda and the United States. New Haven, CT: Yale University Press.

Le Bon, G. (1896). The crowd. London: T. Fisher Unwin.

Lederer, W., & Burdick, E. (1959). The ugly American. London: V. Gollancz.

Lee, J. (Ed.). (1968). The diplomatic persuaders: New role of the mass media in international relations. New York: Wiley.

Leites, N. (1953). A study of Bolshevism. Glencoe, IL: The Free Press.

Leonhard, W. (1955). Die Revolution entläßt ihre Kinder. Cologne, Germany: Kiepenheuer & Witsch.

Lerner, D. (1949). Sykewar. New York: Steward.

Lesly, P. (Ed.). (1978). Lesly's public relations handbook. Englewood Cliffs, NJ: Prentice-Hall.

LeVine, R. A. (1965). Socialization, social structure, and intersocietal images. In H. C. Kelman (Ed.), International behavior: A socio-psychological analysis. New York: Holt, Rinehart & Winston.

Lindzey, G., & Aronson, E. (Eds.). (1968 - 1969). Handbook of social psychology (2nd ed.). Reading, MA: Addison-Wesley.

Link, A. S. (1954). Woodrow Wilson and the progressive era: 1910 - 1917. New York: Harper.

Link, A. S. (1960). The struggle for neutrality, 1914 - 1915. Princeton: Princeton University Press.

Lippmann, W. (1922). Public opinion. New York: Harcourt Brace.

Lippmann, W. (1947). The cold war: A study in U.S. foreign policy. London: Hamish Hamilton.

Lobsenz, A. (1984, August). Representing a foreign government. Public Relations Journal, 40.

MacArthur, J. R. (1992). Second front: Censorship and propaganda in the Gulf War. New York: Hill & Wang.

Macnair, J. I. (Ed.). (1954). Livingstone's travels. London: J. M. Dent & Sons.

Manheim, J. B. (1986). Public relations in the public eye: Two case studies of the failure of public information campaigns. Political Communication and Persuasion, 3.

Manheim, J. B. (1987). Insurgent violence versus image management: The struggle for national images in southern Africa. British Journal of Political Science, 17.

Manheim, J. B. (1990). Rites of passage: The 1988 Seoul Olympics as public diplomacy. Western Political Quarterly, 43.

Manheim, J. B. (1991). All of the people all the time: Strategic communication and American politics. Armonk, NY: M. E. Sharpe.

Manheim, J. B. (1994). Strategic public diplomacy and American foreign policy: The evolution of influence. Oxford, England: Oxford University Press.

Manheim, J. B., & Albritton, R. B. (1984). Changing national images: International public relations and media agenda setting. American Political Science Review, 78.

Manson, M. (1991, May/June). Another front. Columbia Journalism Review.

Marchetti, V., & Marks, J. D. (1974). The CIA and the cult of intelligence. London: Cape.

Martin, D. W. (1959). Die österreich-ungarische Propagandatätigkeit in den USA 1914 - 1917. Unpublished doctoral dissertation.

Martin, L. J. (1982). Disinformation: An instrumentality in the propaganda arsenal. Political Communication and Persuasion, 2.

Masaryk, T. G. (1969). The making of a state: Memories and observations, 1914 - 1918. New York: Howard Fertig. (Original work published 1927)

Masterman, J. C. (1972). The double-cross system in the war of 1939 to 1945. New Haven, CT: Yale University Press.

Masterman, L. (1968). C. F. G. Masterman: A Biography. London: Frank Cass. (Original work published 1939)

Matthias, L. L. (1964). Die Kehrseite der U.S.A.. Hamburg, Germany: Rowohlt.

Mazrui, A. A. (1986). The Africans: A triple heritage. London: BBC Publications.

McAdoo, W. G. (1931). Crowded years: The reminiscences of William G. McAdoo. Boston: Houghton Mifflin.

McCann, T.P. (1976). An American Company: The tragedy of United Fruit. New York: Crown.

McClung Lee, A. M., & Lee, E. B. (1939). The fine art of propaganda: A study of Father Coughlin's speeches. New York: Harcourt Brace.

McGuire, W. J. (1964). Inducing resistance to persuasion. In L. Berkowitz (Ed.), Advances in experimental social psychology (Vol. I). New York: Academic Press.

McGuire, W. J. (1969). The nature of attitudes and attitude change. In G. Lindzey & E. Aronson (Eds.), Handbook of social psychology (Vol. 3, 2nd ed.). Reading, MA: Addison-Wesley.

McNamara, R. (1995). Retrospect: The tragedy and lessons of Vietnam. New York: New York Times Books.

Mead, M. (1947, February). The application of anthropological techniques to cross-national communication. Transactions of the New York Academy of Sciences, Series II, 9 (4).

Mead, M. (1958). Cultural determinants of behavior. In A. Roe & G. G. Simpson (Eds.), Behavior and evolution. New Haven, CT: Yale University Press.

Merriam, A. P. (1961). Congo: Background of conflict. Evanston, IL: Northwestern University Press.

Merton, R. K. (1987). Three fragments from a sociologist's notebook: Establishing the phenomenon, specified ignorance, and strategic research materials. Annual Review of Sociology, 13.

Meyer, W. G. (1968). The challenge of South Africa. In J. Lee (Ed.), The diplomatic persuaders: New role of the mass media in international relations. New York: Wiley.

Michels, R. (1949). Political parties. Glencoe, IL: The Free Press.

Milbrath, L. W. (1965). Political participation. Chicago: Rand McNally.

Milgram, S. (1961). Nationality and conformity. Scientific American, 205.

Miller, N. (1992). Theodore Roosevelt: A life. New York: Quill.

Millis, W. (1935). Road to war: America 1914 - 1917. New York: Houghton Mifflin.

Mitchell, G. (1992). The campaign of the century: Upton Sinclair's race for governor of California and the birth of media politics. New York: Random House.

Mock, J. R., & Larson, C. (1939). Words that won the war. Princeton, NJ: Princeton University Press.

Montagu, A. (1974; first 1942). Man's most dangerous myth: the fallacy of race. London: Oxford University Press.

Montagu, E. E. P. (1953). The man who never was. London: Evans Bros.

Müller, K. (1967). The foreign aid program of the Soviet bloc and communist China: An analysis. New York: Walker. (Original work published 1964)

Nagashima, A. (1970). A comparison of Japanese and U.S. attitudes toward foreign products. Journal of Marketing, 34, 68 - 74.

Newsom, D., Scott, A., & VanSlyke Turk, J. (1989). This is PR: The realities of public relations (4th ed.). Belmont, CA: Wadsworth.

Nicholson, I. (1931, May). An aspect of British official wartime propaganda. Cornhill Magazine, 70.

Nyerere, J. K. (1973). Freedom and development. London: Oxford University Press.

Obasanjo, O. (1994, September 23). Wie ein Schaf auf der Schlachtbank. Die Zeit, 39.

O'Keefe, K. J. (1972). A thousand deadlines: The New York City press and American neutrality, 1914 - 1917. The Hague, Netherlands: Nijhoff.

Olasky, M. N. (1985, Spring). A reappraisal of 19th-century public relations. Public Relations Review, 11.

O'Laughlin, J. C. (1913). The relation of press correspondents to the Navy before and during the war. Washington, DC: U.S. Government Printing Office.

Onkvisit, S., & Shaw, J. J. (1989). International marketing. Analysis and strategy. Columbus, OH: Merrill.

Opie, R. (1985). Rule Britannia: Trading on the British image. Harmondsworth, England: Penguin.

Östgaard, E. (1965). Factors influencing the flow of news. Journal of Peace Research, 2.

Palmer, F. (1934). With my own eyes: A personal story of battle years. London: Jarrolds.

Paneth, E. (1926). Die Entwicklung der Reklame vom Altertum bis zur Gegenwart. Munich: R. Oldenbourg.

Parker, G. (1918, March). The United States and the war. Harper's Monthly Magazine, 136.

Pavlik, J. V. (1987). Public relations: What research tells us. Beverly Hills, CA: Sage.

Pendergrast, M. (1993). For God, country, and Coca-Cola. The unauthorized history of the great American soft drink and the company that makes it. New York: Collier.

Peterson, H. C. (1939). Propaganda for war: The campaign against American neutrality, 1914 - 1917. Norman: University of Oklahoma Press.

Peterson, S. (1981). International news selection by the elite press: A case study. Public Opinion Quarterly, 45.

Platon (1970). Politeia. Reinbek, Germany: Rowohlt.

Pohle, H. (1955). Der Rundfunk als Instrument der Politik. Zur Geschichte des deutschen Rundfunks von 1923 - 38. Hamburg, Germany: Hans-Bredow-Institut.

Pollmann, T. (1991). Kolonialgewalt als "Polizeiaktion". Der niederländische Krieg gegen die indonesischen Nationalisten, 1945 - 1949. In M. van der Linden & G. Mergner (Eds.), Kriegsbegeisterung und mentale Kriegsvorbereitung. Interdisziplinäre Studien. Berlin: Duncker & Humblot.

Ponsonby, A. (1928). Falsehood in wartime. London: Allen & Unwin.

Pratt, C. B. (1994). Hill & Knowlton's two ethical dilemmas. Public Relations Review, 20.

Rakowski, M. (1988). Unser System ist veraltet. Der Spiegel, 29.

Ratliff, W. E. (1987a). The New York Times and the Cuban revolution. In W. E. Ratliff (Ed.), The selling of Fidel Castro: The media and the Cuban revolution (pp. 1 - 37). New Brunswick, NJ: Transaction Books.

Ratliff, W. E. (Ed.). (1987b). The selling of Fidel Castro: The media and the Cuban revolution. New Brunswick, NJ: Transaction Books.

Reagan, M. D. (1971). Business, power, influence. In Rothschild, K. W. (Ed.), Power in economics. Harmondsworth: Penguin Books.

Révész, L. (1974). Recht und Willkür in der Sowjetpresse. Eine presserechtliche und pressepolitische Untersuchung. Freiburg, Switzerland: Universitätsverlag Freiburg/ Switzerland.

Rhoodie, E. (1983). The real information scandal. Pretoria, South Africa: ORBIS SA (PTY) Ltd.

Richards, J. (1973). Visions of yesterday. London: Routledge & Kegan Paul.

Robinson, J. P. (1967). World affairs information and mass media exposure. Journalism Quarterly, 44.

Roetter, C. (1974). The art of psychological warfare, 1914 - 1945. New York: Stein & Day.

Roschwalb, S. A. (1994). The Hill & Knowlton cases: A brief on the controversy. Public Relations Review, 20.

Ross, I. (1959). The image merchants. Garden City, NY: Doubleday.

Roth, G. (1990). Preface. In R. Kunz & R. D. Müller (Eds.), Giftgas gegen Abd el Krim. Deutschland: Spanien und der Gaskrieg in Spanisch-Marokko 1922 - 1927, Freiburg i. B., Germany: Raubach Freiburg.

Rothmyer, K. (1980, April 19). The South Africa lobby: Americans for sale. The Nation.

Said, E. W. (1994). Culture and imperialism. London: Vintage. (Original work published 1993)

Sanders, M. L. (1975). Wellington House and British propaganda during the First World War. Historical Journal, 18.

Sanders, M. L. & Taylor, P. M. (1982). British propaganda during the First World War. London: Macmillan.

Schmid, A. P., & de Graaf, J. (1982). Violence as communication: Insurgent terrorism and the Western media. London: Sage.

Schwarzkopf, H. N. (1993). It doesn't take a hero. New York: Bantam.

Schweiger, G. (1992). Österreichs Image in der Welt. Ein Vergleich mit Deutschland und der Schweiz. Vienna, Austria: Service Fachverlag.

Seagrave, S. (1986). The Soong dynasty. New York: Harper Collins.

Sears, D. O., & Whitney, R. E. (1973). Political persuasion. In I. de Sola Pool et alii (Eds.), Handbook of communication. Chicago: Rand McNally College Publishing.

Secord, P. F., & Backman, C. W. (1974). Social psychology. New York: McGraw-Hill.

Shaheen, J. (1981). Images of Saudis and Palestinians: A review of major documentaries. In W. C. Adams (Ed.), Television coverage of the Middle East. Norwood, NJ: Ablex.

Sherif, M., & Sherif, C. W. (1956). An outline of social psychology. New York: Harper & Row.

Sigal, L. V. (1973). Reporters and officials. Lexington, MA: Heath.

Signitzer, B., & Coombs, T. (1992). Public relations and public diplomacy: Conceptual convergences. Public Relations Review, 18.

Silber, J. C. (1932). The invisible weapons. London: Hutchinson.

Simmel, G. (1920). Soziologie [Sociology] (2nd ed.). Munich, Germany: Duncker & Humblot.

Singer, E., & Ludwig, J. (1987). South Africa's press restrictions: Effects on press coverage and public opinion toward South Africa. Public Opinion Quarterly, 51.

Singer, M. (1972). When a great tradition modernizes: An anthropological approach to Indian civilization. New York: Praeger.

Smith, D. C. (1986). H. G. Wells: Desperately moral. A biography. New Haven, CT: Yale University Press.

Smith, D. D. (1973). Mass communications and international image change. Journal of Conflict Resolution, 17.

Smith, H. (1988). The power game: How Washington works. New York: Random House.

Solzhenitsyn, A. (1980). Misconceptions about Russia are a threat to America. Foreign Affairs, 58.

Sorensen, T. C. (1968). The word war: The story of American propaganda. New York: Harper & Row.

Spanier, J. W., & Nogee, J. L. (1962). The politics of disarmament: A study in Soviet-American gamesmanship. New York: Praeger.

Spellman, R. L. (1994). Transnational public relations: De Lesseps promotes the Panama Canal. Gazette, 53.

Spoo, E. (1987). Geheimdienste und Medien: Wie internationale Beziehungen vergiftet werden. In E. Jürgens & E. Spoo (Eds.), Unheimlich zu Diensten. Medienmissbrauch durch Geheimdienste. Göttingen, Germany: Steidl.

Squires, J. D. (1935). British propaganda at home and in the United States from 1914 to 1917. Cambridge, MA: Harvard University Press.

Sreberny-Mohammadi, A. (1984). Results of international cooperation. Journal of Communication, 34.

Sreberny-Mohammadi, A. (1985). Foreign news in the media. International reporting in 29 countries. Paris: Unesco.

Sreberny-Mohammadi, A. et alii (1980). The world of the news - the news of the world (Final Report of the Foreign Images Study) London: International Association for Mass Communication Research of UNESCO.

Staar, R. F. (Ed.). (1986). Public diplomacy: U.S.A. versus U.S.S.R.. Stanford, CA: Hoover Institution Press.

Star; S. A., & Hughes, H. M. (1950). Report on an educational campaign: The Cincinnati plan for the United Nations. American Journal of Sociology, 55, 389 - 400.

Steinbach, U. (1992). Der Islam und die Moderne. Der Spiegel, 4.

Steinbiss, F., & Eisermann, D. (1988). "Wir haben damals die beste Musik gemacht." Über Goebbel's Propaganda-Jazzband "Charlie and his orchestra". Der Spiegel, 16.

Stephan, W. (1949). Joseph Goebbels: Dämon einer Diktatur. Stuttgart, Germany: Union Deutsche Verlagsgesellschaft.

Stevenson, R. L. (1988). Communication, development, and the Third World: The global politics of information. New York: Longman.

Stoldt, H. U. (1988, October 10). Die unendliche Legende: Baby-Organ-Handel. Die Karriere einer Falschmeldung. Die Zeit, 44.

Stone, P. H. (1979, April 14). Muldergate on Madison Avenue. The Nation,

Strenski, J. B. (1975). Problems in international public relations. Public Relations Journal, 31 (5).

Sturminger, A. (1938). Politische Propaganda in der Weltgeschichte: Beispiele vom Altertum bis in die Gegenwart. Salzburg, Austria: Das Bergland Buch.

Sturminger, A. (1960). 3000 Jahre politische Propaganda [Three thousand years of political propaganda]. Vienna, Austria: Herold.

Sumner, W. G. (1906). Folkways. Boston: Ginn.

Surel, J. (1989). John Bull. In R. Samuel (Ed.), Patriotism: The making and unmaking of British national identity (Vol. 3). London: National Fictions.

Swanberg, W. A. (1972). Luce and his empire. New York: Scribner's.

Tansill, C. C. (1938). America goes to war. Boston: Little, Brown.

Taylor, E. (1947). Richer by Asia. Cambridge, MA: Riverside Press.

Taylor, P. M. (1978). Cultural diplomacy and the British Council, 1934 - 1939. British Journal of International Studies, 4.

Taylor, P. M. (1981). The projection of Britain: British overseas publicity and propaganda. Cambridge, England: Cambridge University Press.

Taylor, P. M. (1983). Propaganda in international politics, 1919 - 1939. In K. R. M. Short (Ed.), Film and radio propaganda in World War II. London: Croom Helm.

Thierfelder, F. (1940). Englischer Kulturimperialismus: Der "British Council" als Werkzeug der geistigen Einkreisung Deutschlands. Berlin: Junter & Dünnhaupt.

Thomas, W. I., & Thomas, D. S. (1928). The child in America. New York: Knopf.

Tönnies, F. (1922). Kritik der öffentlichen Meinung. Berlin: Springer.

Trento, S. B. (1992). The power house: Robert Keith Gray and the selling of access and influence in Washington. New York: St. Martin's Press.

Ume-Nwagbo, E. N. (1982). Foreign news flow in Africa. Gazette, 29, 41 - 56.

U.S. Department of State (1987a, March). Contemporary Soviet propaganda and Disinformation. A conference report. Washington, DC: U.S. Government Printing Office.

U.S. Department of State (1987b, October). Soviet influence activities: A report on active measures and propaganda. Washington, DC: U.S. Government Printing Office.

USIA (1988, March). Soviet active measures in the era of Glasnost. Report to the Congress by the United States Information Agency.

Valone, R. P., Ross, L., & Lepper, M. R. (1985). The hostile media phenomenon: Biased perception and perceptions of media bias in coverage of the Beirut massacre. Journal of Personality and Social Psychology, 49, 577- 585.

Viereck, G. S. (1930). Spreading germs of hate. New York: H. Liveright.

Virilio, P. (1986). Krieg und Kino: Logistik der Wahrnehmung. Munich, Germany: Hauser.

von Clausewitz, C. P. G. (1873). On war. (J. J. Graham, Trans., Vols. 1 - 3). London: N. Trübner. (Original work published 1832)

von Studnitz, H. G. (1950). Presse und auswärtige Politik. Aussenpolitik, 1.

Walker, F. E. (1988, May). Recent changes in the Soviet propaganda machine. Journal of Defense & Diplomacy.

Wallach, J. P. (1987). Fidel Castro and the United States press. In W. E. Ratliff (Ed.), The selling of Fidel Castro: The media and the Cuban revolution (pp. 129 - 155). New Brunswick, NJ: Transaction Books.

Walworth, A. C. (1965). Woodrow Wilson (Vols. 1 - 2, 2nd rev. ed.). Boston: Houghton Mifflin.

Wanderscheck, H. (1940). Die englische Lügenpropaganda im Weltkrieg und heute. Berlin: Junker & Dünnhaupt.

Watzlawick, P. (1976). How real is real? Confusion, disinformation, communication. New York: Random House.

Weimann, G. (1990). "Redefinition of image": The impact of mass-mediated terrorism. International Journal of Public Opinion Research, 2, 16 - 29.

Weiss, W. (1969). Effects of the mass media of communication. In G. Lindzey & E. Aronson (Eds.), Handbook of social psychology (2nd ed., Vol. 5) (pp. 77 - 195). Reading, MA: Addison-Wesley.

Wettig, G. (1988). Friedenssicherung, Klassenkampf und neues Denken in Gorbatschows Westpolitik. Aussenpolitik, 39.

White, L., & Leigh, R. D. (1946). Peoples speaking to peoples. Chicago: University of Chicago Press.

White, T. H. (1978). In search of history: A personal adventure. New York: Harper & Row.

Whiteman, D. (1983). The press and the neutron bomb. Unpublished manuscript, Harvard University, Kennedy School of Government, Cambridge, MA.

Whitton, J. B., & Larson, A. (1964). Propaganda: Towards disarmament in the war of words. Dobbs Ferry, NY: Oceana Publications.

Wilcox, D. L., Ault, P. H., & Agee, W. K. (1986). Public relations: Strategies and tactics. New York: Harper & Row.

Wilke, J. (1993). Deutsche Auslandspropaganda im Ersten Weltkrieg: Die Zentralstelle für Auslandsdienst. In S. Quandt & H. Schichtel (Eds.), Medien Kommunikaton Geschichte: Der Erste Weltkrieg als Kommunikationsereignis (pp. 95 - 157). Gießen, Germany: Justus-Liebig-Universität.

Wilkinson, E. (1981). Misunderstanding: Europe vs. Japan. Tokyo: Chuokoron-sha.

Wilson, W. (1913). The new freedom: A call for the emancipation of the generous energies of a people. Leipzig, Germany: Bernhard Tauchnitz.

Wilson, W. (1918). War addresses of Woodrow Wilson (with an introcution and notes by Arthur Roy Leonard). Boston: Ginn.

Witcover, J. (1989). Sabotage at Black Tom: Imperial Germany's secret war in America,1914 - 1917. Chapel Hill, NC: Algonquin Books.

Wolff, K. H. (Ed.). (1950). The sociology of Georg Simmel. New York: The Free Press.

Wolfsfeld, G. (1983). International awareness, information processing, and attitude change: A cross-cultural experimental study. Political Communication and Persuasion, 2, 127 - 146.

Woll, A. L. (1980). The Latin image in American film (rev. ed.). Los Angeles: UCLA Latin America Center Publications.

Woolman, D. (1969). Rebels in the Rif: Abd el Krim and the Rif rebellion (2nd ed.). London: Oxford University Press. (Original work published 1968)

Wright, M. R. (1897). Picturesque Mexico. Philadelphia: Lippincott.

Wulfemeyer, K. T. (1985). How and why anonymous attribution is used by Time and Newsweek. Journalism Quarterly, 62, 81 - 86.

Wulfemeyer, K. T., & McFadden, L. L. (1986). Anonymous attribution in network news. Journalism Quarterly, 63, 468 - 473 .

Yakobson, S., & Lasswell, H. D. (1949). Trend: May Day slogans in Soviet Russia, 1918 - 1943. In H. D. Lasswell et alii (Eds.), Language of politics: Studies in quantitative semantics.Cambridge, MA: MIT Press.

Zeman, Z. A. B. (1964). Nazi propaganda. London: Oxford University Press.

Index

A

Abd el Krim, 273
Abu Dhabi, 33
Académie Francaise, 158-159
Acheson, Dean, 126
Advertisements, 30-34, 55, 63, 67,
    69-70, 76-80, 94-95, 138, 140,
    142-143, 185, 212-213, 218,
    220, 223-224, 265, 268
Advertising, 12, 25-26, 28, 65, 67,
    77-78, 95, 124, 132, 181, 187,
    210, 268
Afghanistan, 114, 238, 240
AFP, *see Agence France Press*
Africa, 11, 22, 24, 30, 47-48, 59-
    61, 103, 119-120, 259, 263
    Black Africa, 119
    Central Africa, 60, 103, 119
    East Africa, 11
    South Africa, *see South Africa*
    West Africa, 24
    African, 47, 59-61
    Senate Subcommittee on
    African Affairs, 216
    East African Dependencies
        Trade and Information
        Office, 63
    Africans, 47, 259
Agence France Press, 62
Agnelli, Giovanni, 46
Aidid, 96
AIDS campaign, 25, 260
AIDS disinformation campaign,
    262
Air India, 55

Albert, Heinrich, 180
Alexander the Great, 114, 124, 154
Algeria, 81, 277
Algerian, 47, 81
Algerian War, 81, 277
Algerian War of Independence, 47
Allen-Edmonds Shoe Corporation,
    138
Allied Syndicates, Inc., 211
Alsop, Joseph, 206
America, 6, 8, 23, 29, 31-35, 44,
    48, 62, 75, 80, 98, 100, 117,
    121-122, 129, 135-138, 143,
    146, 166, 169-171, 174-177,
    180, 186-188, 199, 205-209,
    227-229, 233-236, 239, 246,
    249-250, 254-256, 268
American Defense Society, 121
American Enterprise Institute,
    33
American Express, 79
American image, 227-228; 232
American image cultivation,
    236
American mass media, 53, 88,
    200, 245, 250, 274
American Partizipation
    Program, 231
American propaganda, 235, 238
American public, 30, 65, 100,
    125, 135, 206, 211, 245,
    263, 278-279
American public opinion, 122,
    136, 139, 169, 175, 180,
    182, 201, 226, 249

Americans, 8, 15, 29, 35, 38,
    43-44, 52, 97, 117-118, 121,
    125, 132, 137, 143, 174-
    176, 181-183, 198, 206-207,
    210-211, 230-233, 239, 246,
    251, 254, 265, 267, 280
    „Buy American" campaign, 137
    „Hate America" campaign, 254
Amin, Idi, 60, 119
Amnesty International, 19, 27-28,
    279, 281
Andropov, Yuri, 259
Anglo American Corporation, 223
Angola, 93, 220
Anonymous attributions, 88
AP, see Associated Press
Arab, 14-16, 130-135, 275
Arabia, 129-134
Arab League, 132
Arafat, Yasser, 46, 80
Arbatov, Georgi, 118
Archibald, James, 186
Argentina, 76, 201-204
Armas, Carlos Castillo, 250
Armstrong, Neil, 232, 257
Arnett, Peter, 97, 99
Asia, 52, 54, 77, 138, 198-199, 207-
    209
    Asians, 259
    Asian tigers, 59
    South Asia, 263
    Southeast Asia, 137
Asis, Tarik, 57
Assad, Hafis, 133
Associated Press, 23, 211, 241
Asylum, 80, 131
Athenian, 153-154, 257
Atlantic Richfield, 28
Atrocity campaigns, 189
Atrocity propaganda, 72, 159, 166,
177, 188, 279, 283
Attitude change, 42, 190, 206

Attitudes, 13, 16, 19, 38, 45, 52,
    61, 73, 86, 110, 146-152, 203,
    234
Australia House, 63
Austria, 14, 73, 79-80, 106-109,
    156, 165-166, 195-196, 258,
    284
    Austria-Hungary, 179, 188
    Austro-Hungarian, 183
Author's Manifesto, 172
Autostereotypes, 38, 41-42

B

Baby organs, 260
Baby organs trade campaign, 260
Baghdad, 14, 96-99, 281
Bahamas, 6
Baker, 34
Baker, James, 126
Banco do Brasil, 76
Band wagon, 113
Bangemann, Martin, 222
Bank of America, 218
Bank of Credit & Commerce
    International, 32-33
Barbarossa, 155
Barnard, Christian, 217
Sydney S. Baron & Associates, 217
Barrie, James, 171
Baxter, Leone, 121
Bay of Pigs, 57
BCCI, see Bank of Credit &
    Commerce International
Beaverbrook, William M. A., 174
Beethoven, Ludwig van, 110, 172,
    182
Belgian, 65-66, 180
Belgian Congo, 60
Belgium, 44, 65-66, 73, 170

Belize, 6
Beltagui, Mamdough, 78
Bergman, Ingrid, 209
Bernays, Edward L., 13, 27, 89-90, 188-189, 193, 198-201, 233-234, 246-248
Bernhard of Clairvaux, 155-156
Bhutto, Benazir, 90-91
Bible, 152, 240
Bismarck, Otto von, 69, 114-115, 166-167
Bittman, Ladislav, 259
Black Death, 55
Black, Eli M., 14, 251
Black-and-white explanation, 57
Boer War, 168
Boers, 168
Bokassa, Jean Bedel, 60, 119
Bolivia, 6
Bolshevism, 121, 127
Bolshevists, 120
Boomerang effect, 68, 111, 147, 179, 284
Boone Co., 138-139
Boot, William, 98
Bophuthatswana, 213, 216
Bosnia, 91, 94
Botswana, 59
Boyd-Barrett, Oliver, 22
Boys' papers, 9
Brecht, Bertolt, 282
Britannia, 69-70
British, 8, 10-11, 38, 59, 63-64, 68-69, 80-84, 92, 100, 115, 162-168, 171, 173, 177-181, 183, 277
    British Commonwealth, 63
    British Council, 63, 87
    British empire, 59, 69, 253
    British Lion, 69
    British propaganda, 84, 170, 173-175, 177, 186

Britons, 43; 116; 173; 175
Broadcasting, 14-15, 196-197, 254
Bryan, William Jennings, 185
Bryant, John, 139
Bryce-Bericht, 179
Bukharin, Nikolay, 253
Bull, John, 69
Burke, P, 102, 160-162
Burkina Faso, 47
Burma, 6, 254
Burrough, Edgar Rice, 11
Burson-Marsteller, 125
Burton, Richard, 131
Burton, Sir Richard Francis, 130
Burundi, 214
Bush, George, 29, 98-99, 125, 274, 278-279, 281
Buthelezi, Gatsha, 213
Byoir, Carl, 191
    Carl Byoir & Associates, 191

C

California, 121-122, 216
Callaghan, James, 243
Callisthenes of Olynthus, 154
Cambodia, 237, 239
Campaign of Truth, 233
Campos, Angel, 260-261
Canaan, 153
Canada, 73-74, 118
Canada House, 63
Card stacking, 113
Cardinal Richelieu, 159
Carl XVI Gustaf, 67
Carter, Jimmy, 96, 234
Caruso, Enrico, 188
Castro, Fidel, 5, 57, 237
Categorical statements, 38
Cavell, Edith, 185

CBS News, 24
Censorship, 99, 134, 174, 223-225,
    270-273, 276-277
Central Powers, 188
CFK, *see Citizen for a Free Kuwait*
Chamberlain, Houston S., 40
Charlie and His Orchestra, 148
Chase Manhattan Bank, 79
Ché Guevara, 5
Chechenya, 57
Checkpoint Charlie, 229
Chernienko, Constantin, 264
Chesterton, G. K., 172
Chiang Kai-Shek, 205-211
Chile, 108
China, 4, 28-29, 52-54, 74, 91,
    134-136, 205-209, 211, 243,
    245, 253
    China lobby, 209-210
    China Ventures, 28
    People's Republic of China, 14,
        244
Chinese, 11, 52-53, 77, 118, 136,
    208-210
    Chinese tortures, 52
Choate, Pat, 137, 142
Churchill, Winston, 54, 105, 120-
    123, 148, 154, 246
CIA, 98, 126, 129, 198, 231, 234,
    240-246, 250
Ciller, Tansu, 91
Cisalpine Republic, 165
Citicorp bank, 79
Citizen for a Free Kuwait, 278
Clinton, Bill, 96
Club of Ten, 220
CNN, 94, 96-101
Coca-Cola, 68, 125
Cognitive selectivity, 104
Colby, William, 240
Cold War, 27, 56-57, 117, 123-
    126, 220, 227, 230-231, 235

Colonialism, 10, 40, 47, 60
Colonies, 63-65, 72, 253
Comintern, *see Communist
    International*
Commercial intelligence, 64
Commercials, 25
Commissioner Sanders, 10
Committee of Fairness in Sports,
    218
Committee on Public Information,
    186-188
Communism, 31, 41, 46, 56, 120-
    121, 124, 200, 205, 229, 233,
    247-250
Communist International, 252-253
Compromise, 116-117, 142, 276
Concentration camps, 179, 252
Confucius, 53
Congo, 44, 47-48
    Belgian Congo, 60
Congress, 31-34, 92, 126, 179-182,
    189, 207-208, 210, 215, 230,
    249, 278-280
Copenhagen, 72, 166
Corcoran, Thomas G., 207
Corneille, 160
Costa Rica, 248, 250
Council on Foreign Relations, 192
Country of origin effect, 68-69, 73
CPI, *see Committee on Public
    Information*
Credibility, 16, 24, 74, 106, 110-
    111, 145-147, 166, 170, 176,
    190, 204, 233, 236, 281
Credible, 107, 171, 234, 236, 272
Creel Committee, 186
Creel, George, 186-188
Cretans, 154
Crichton, Michael, 136-137
Crimean War, 97
Croatia, 41
Crusade for Freedom, 31

Crusades, 31, 155-156, 164, 276
Cuba, 20, 57, 237, 262
Cultural bias, 22
Cultural identity, 29, 42, 48
Currency exchange rates, 74
Current of history, 46, 145
Czechoslovakia, 14, 90, 114, 189,
    227, 279

D

Daniels, Josephus, 175, 182
Dark areas of ignorance, 4
d'Estaing, Valérie Giscard, 231
de Gobineau, Arthur, 40
de Lesseps, Count Ferdinand, 35
de Pierrefou, Jean, 275
de Rivera, Primo, 276
de Tocqueville, Alexis, 29
Deaver and Henkel, 230
Decisions in international politics,
    50
Declaration of the 93, 172
Thomas J. Deegan Co., 125
Defense of Realm Act, 170
Definition of situations, 58
DeGaulle, Charles, 80
Delacroix, Eugène, 130
Demag, 31-32
Democracy, 29, 31, 41, 59, 76, 79,
    90, 95, 111-113, 116-118, 122,
    125-126, 134, 153-154, 198-
    199, 231-233, 278
Deng Xiaoping, 29
Denmark, 23
Department of Defense, 98, 237
Dernburg, Bernhard, 180, 182
Descarte, René, 61

Developing Countries, 16, 22, 26,
    86, 119-120, 201, 204, 232,
    238-239, 260
Development aid, 58-60, 243
Dewey, Thomas E., 209
Dietrich, Marlene, 209
Dilenschneider and Forrestal, 33-
    34
Diouf, Abdou, 59
Diplomacy, 12, 77, 85-87, 167,
    219, 254
    Media diplomacy, 86
    Public diplomacy, 62, 86, 90,
        228, 231-232, 235, 239, 266
Diplomat, 4; 47; 51; 63; 86-88
Diplomatic correspondents, 87
Disinformation, 25; 99; 231; 252;
    256; 272; 279
    Disinformation campaign,25;
        89; 240; 245; 256; 262
    Disinformation policy, 257-259
Distortions of reality, 150
Dixon, William Macneile, 174
D mark, 75
Doctor No, 11
Dollar, 17, 33-34, 75, 121, 126,
    191, 205
Dollfuss, Engelbert, 195-196
Domatob, Jerry Komia, 117, 119
Dominican Republic, 217
Domino theory, 124
Donsbach, Wolfgang, 104-107
DORA, see Defense of Realm Act
Dover, Lia, 27
Doyle, Sir Arthur Conan, 172
Dreadnought, 169
Drucker, Peter, 137-138
Dulles, John Foster, 56, 122-123
Dumba, Konstantin, 183
Dumba-Archibald affair, 183
Dunlop Tyres, 69
Dutch, 136, 154, 162

Dykstra, Peter, 92

E

Earth Summit, 19, 141
East-West Center, 231
Eastman Kodak, 33
EC, *see European Community*
Economic policy, 33, 258
Economy, 27, 65, 68, 77-79, 223
Education, 2, 13, 63-64, 77-78,
    110, 200
Edward VII, 70
EFE, 24
Effects of foreign propaganda, 145
Egypt, 78, 130-133, 148, 153, 164-
    165, 257
Egyptians, 59, 165
Eisenhower, Dwight D., 235, 250
El Diablo (The Devil), 250
El Salvador, 258, 262
Elites, 18-19, 60, 86- 90, 158, 165,
    201
Empire of evil, 56
Ems telegram, 114-115
Enemy-image, 118-129, 133-138,
    148, 166, 248
England, 8, 69-72, 80, 165-168,
    172, 177, 187-188, 220-221
English, 9-10, 38, 45, 130, 163-
    165, 167, 169, 176, 181
EOKA, *see Ethniki Organosis*
    Kypriakou Agonos
Erzberger, Matthias, 173, 181
Establishment of Trust, 74
Estonia, 76, 95
Ethiopia, 119, 283
Ethnic identity, 45
Ethnic weapon, 259

Ethniki Organosis Kypriakou
    Agonos, 81
Ethnocentrism, 40
European balance, 115-116
European Community, 25
Evil empire, 50, 118, 126
Exchange rate,75-76
Expectations of expectations, 271

F

False stories, 240
Fascist, 80, 112-114, 119, 150
Father Charles Edward Coughlin,
    112
Fenton Communications Inc., 125
Fifth column, 95
Fireside summit, 230
Fleming, Ian, 11
FLN, 81
Folkways, 40
Fonda, Henry, 209
Ford automobiles, 68
Ford Company, 31
Ford, Gerald R., 88, 216-217
Ford, Henry, 31
Foreign affairs community, 87
Foreign Images Study for the
    UNESCO, 21-23
Foreign policy, 16, 20, 27, 56-57,
    62, 85-96, 116, 138, 167, 210,
    214, 228-229, 233-234, 244,
    265,268
    Foreign Policy Association, 192
Foreign reporting, 20
Fortune magazine, 125, 205-206
Forum World Features, 241
Fouché, Joseph, 165
Fourie, Bernardus G., 212

France, 24, 41, 46, 62-64, 72-75, 92, 114-115, 129-131, 149-150, 158-166, 173, 188, 213, 221, 253, 275-277
Franco, 95, 193
Frank, Hans, 195
Frankenstein Germany, 173
Frederick I, *see Barbarossa*
Frederick II, 156
French colonies, 47, 64
French Revolution, 115, 163, 165, 270
French, 24, 45-46, 100, 114, 162-163, 166, 253, 270, 276
Freud, Sigmund, 193
Friktion, 271
Fu-Manchu, 11
Fugger, 158
Fujimori, Alberto, 78
Fulbright, 237
    Fulbright-Hays Act, 232
    Fulbright Program of academic exchanges, 231

G

Galsworthy, John, 172
Galtung and Ruge, 20
Gandhi, Indira, 231, 259
Gandhi, Mahatma, 54-55, 82, 92-93
Gates, Robert, 126
Gaydar, Yegor E., 32
Gazette, 159
Genghis Khan, 52, 154
Genscher, Hans Dietrich, 243
George, Lloyd, 120
Germany, 2, 4, 23, 32, 62-63, 68-74, 95, 104, 116-118, 120-122, 127-130, 135, 138, 144, 149, 158, 164, 167-173, 177, 179-185, 188, 192, 195, 197-198, 222, 225, 239, 243, 261, 274
    East Germany, 101, 283
    Nazi Germany, 12, 109, 191
    West Germany, *see West Germany*
German-Austrian radio, 195
German Dye Trust, 191
German image, 72, 130
German Information Bureau, 181
German-made, 72
German mark, 75-76
German propaganda, 170, 176, 180-182, 185, 193
German Reich, 109, 115, 188, 196
German Tourist Information Office, 191
German Werkbund, 71
Germania, 152
Germans, 2-4, 11, 32, 39, 42-45, 58, 63, 73-74, 116, 128, 148, 152, 168, 173, 178, 181, 184, 195, 253, 268, 272
Ghana, 47, 61
Glasnost, 117, 268
Glemp, Cardinal Josef, 129
Glittering generality, 112
Gloire (Glory), 160
Goebbels, Joseph, 14, 118, 127, 148, 194, 197
Goethe, Johann Wolfgang von, 172, 179
Gold Coast, 10, 47, 63-64
Gorbachev, Michail, 117-118, 230, 263-268
Gorky, Maksim, 253
Gray and Company, 93, 97

Great Britain,40, 62-69, 131, 149, 169, 172, 174, 212-213, 221
Greek-Cypriot, 81
Greenpeace, 19, 27, 91-92, 140-141
Grenada, 237
Grey, Sir Edward, 171, 189
Grivas, Georgios, 81-84
Gromyko, Andrei A., 264
Guardpost Collier, 229
Guatemala,246-251, 261-262
Gulf War, 96-101, 270, 274-275, 277, 282
Gutenberg, Johannes, 158
Guzmán, Jacobo Arbenz, 246-250
Gynt, Peer, 131

H

H & K, *see Hill & Knowlton*
Habicht, Theo, 196
Habsburg, 159
Hadamovsky, Eugen, 148
Haiti, 6
Hale, William Bayard, 182
Hamburg, 164, 221
Handling journalists, 5
Hannibal, 154
Harmand, Jules, 40
Hassan II, 97
Hayworth, Rita, 209
Hearst, William R., 182
Hedin, Sven, 173
Heimkehr ins Reich, 195
Helms, Richard, 244
Henkel, Bill, 229
Hennenhofer, Gerd, 222-223
Henty, George Alfred, 8-9
Herodotus, 152-153
Herzog, Chaim, 16, 36

Highway of Death, 100
Hill & Knowlton, 6, 28, 278-282
Hilmy, Amin, 132
Himmler, Heinrich, 127
Hindu, 54-55
Hinduism, 54
Historians, 47, 143
History, 40-46, 50-52, 57, 90, 120, 126, 128, 143, 152-153, 169, 189, 197, 229, 238, 252, 258, 266
Hitler, Adolf, 14, 40, 46, 58, 109, 119, 122, 150, 191-196, 246, 274
Ho Chi Minh, 237
Holland, 221, 262
Hollywood, 8, 131-132, 209, 227, 230, 255
Holtman, R. B., 163-166
Holy Roman Empire of the German Nation, 158, 160
Honduras, 248, 250-251, 261-262
Hong Kong, 59, 244
Hoover, Edgar, 121
Hostile media phenomenon, 103-104
Human rights, 28, 36, 202, 268, 283, 285
    Human rights violations, 22, 120, 225, 278, 281-282
    Universal Declaration of Human Rights, 117
    Congressional Human Rights' Caucus, 279
Hume, David, 273
Hun, 121, 177
Hungary, 15, 75-76, 114, 149-150, 195, 227
    Hungarian uprising, 15, 149-151
    Hungarians, 165
Huns, 45

Hussein, Saddam, 95-96, 99-100, 274, 278-279

I

I.G. Farben, *see German Dye Trust*
IBM, 68
Ibsen, Hendrik, 131
Ideology, 13, 56, 76, 114
IESC, *see International Executive Service Corps*
Image building, 2-3, 51, 91, 120, 123, 161
Image changes, 45, 102, 106-107
Image cultivation, 1, 4, 12, 16, 18, 25-26, 62, 106-107, 111, 125, 152, 160, 169, 188, 195, 198, 203, 205, 225, 227-230, 232, 236, 240, 243, 266-268, 283-285
Image of the international system, 49
Image policy, 75, 113, 160-161, 212, 252, 268, 270
Image polishing, 29, 61-63, 143, 283
Image transfer, 68, 284
Images, 1, 3, 6-7, 16, 20-21, 25, 36-54, 57, 68, 96, 99, 102, 106, 148-149, 201, 204
    Images of nations, 2, 5, 8, 23, 36-39, 42, 107, 201, 203
    International images, 3, 17, 92, 147, 223, 264
    Literary images, 49, 52
    Negative images, 26, 39-41, 68, 120, 145, 202
    Stability of images, 144, 148
IMF, *see International Monetary Fund*

Imperial studies, 64
Imperial, 9-10, 57
Imperialism, 9, 113-115, 119
Imperialist movement, 64
India, 9, 31-32, 52-55, 59, 82, 198-201, 257-259
Indo-China, 64
Indonesia, 124, 136, 201-204
Influence brokers, 28, 79
Information, 1, 6-7, 12, 15, 21-25, 35, 44-45, 49-51, 58, 64-67, 72, 77, 83-89, 93, 97-102, 104-107, 111, 159, 170-171, 184, 188, 192, 198-200, 205, 214-228, 232-237, 239-244, 248, 256-259, 266-272, 277, 282-284
Ingroups, 39
Institute for Propaganda Analysis, 112
Instrumentalizing media, 99
International behavior, 21
International economic organizations, 27
International Executive Service Corps, 228
International Monetary Fund, 30
International PR agencies, 28
International Public Relations, 12, 25-30, 61, 74, 80, 95, 158, 189, 191, 238, 246, 264
International social organizations, 27
International System, 12, 37, 49-51
International Visitor Program, 234
Inter-Press Service, 28, 203
Involvement, 203
IPS, *see Inter-Press Service*
Iran, 48, 58, 95, 238, 254, 283
Iranians, 57
Iraq, 57, 95, 99
Ireland, 64
Irish, 47, 180-181

Iron Curtain, 23, 123-124, 220
Isaacs, Harold, 52-54
Ishihara, Shintaro, 140
Israel, 14, 36, 133, 215, 236, 259
Israeli, 46, 80, 104, 133
Italians, 43, 67, 74, 154
Italy, 46, 74, 113-114, 132, 135, 149-150, 165, 188, 259, 262
ITT, 28
IV, *see International Visitor Program*

J

Jahn, Friedrich Ludwig, 165
Janis and Smith, 105-106, 148
Japan Automobile Manufacturers Association, 142
Japan, 68, 74, 134-141, 143
Japanese, 11, 52, 59, 69, 98, 136-138, 142
Jelloun, Tahar Ben, 134
Jerusalem, 133-134, 156
Jewish-Bolshevist conspiracy, 116, 127-128
Jews, 3, 43, 109, 126-127, 137, 191-192, 196
Jinzhan, Peng, 135
Journalistic racism, 214
Jud Süss, 137

K

Kadar, Janos, 151
Kadoumi, Farouk, 134
Kaemba, L. F., 236
Kaiser, 3, 120, 167-168, 187-188, 275
Kaiserism, 173

KAL 007, 231, 259, 263-264
Kant, Immanuel, 172, 179
Karl XI of Sweden, 162
Karloff, Boris, 131
Keenan, John, 59
Kennedy, Jacqueline, 125
Kennedy, John F., 88, 116, 234
Kennedy, Paul, 143, 169
Kepplinger, Hans Mathias, 85
Kernel of Truth, 37-38, 42
Keune, Reinhard, 24, 101
KGB, 15-16, 25, 256-261
Khomeini, Ayatullah Ruhollah, 48, 283
Khrushchev, Nikita S., 116
Kipling, Rudyard, 9-11, 53-54, 177
Kirkpatrick, Jeanne, 258, 264
Kissinger, Henry, 28-29, 49, 79, 88
Kleinmann, Robert, 81
Kodjo, Edem, 60
Kohl, Helmut, 95
Kollek, Teddy, 134
Koppel, Ted, 99
Korea, 12, 90, 124, 198, 201, 204, 229
    North Korea, 229
    South Korea, 59
Korean Airlines flight 007, *see KAL 007*
Korean War, 211
Koschwitz, Hansjürgen, 131, 240-244
Krauthammer, Charles, 136
Krauze, Enrique, 7
Kroll Associates, 281
Krugman, Paul, 137
Krupp, 68
Kruppism, 173
Ku Klux Klan, 121
Kühnemann, Eugen, 181
Kuwait, 68, 95, 277-282
Kwa Zulu, 213

L

Lafayette, 29
Lang, Jacques, 24
Lansing, Robert, 176, 182-184
Lao-tzu, 53
Laos, 237
Lara, Franzisco J., 23
Latin America, 23-24, 237, 262
    Latin American, 8
League of American Women for
    Strict Neutrality, 182
League of Nations, 195, 276
Leaking, 89
Lebanon, 6, 133
LeBon, Gustave, 193
Lee, Ivy Lee, 75-76, 191-192
Lenin, Vladimir I., 256
Leopold I of Austria, 162
Lessing, Gotthold Ephraim, 131
LeVine, Robert A., 41
Li, K. C., 207
Library of the Congress, 181
Libya, 97, 245
    Libyans, 152
Lincoln, Abraham, 18-19, 118
Lippmann, Walter, 5, 38, 45, 102,
    123, 208
Lithuania, 266
Little Greeks, 152
Litvinov, Maxim, 192
Livingstone's Travels, 47
Loan, 75
Lobbyist, 62, 90, 137, 217
Logic of disinformation, 272
Lord Byron, 47
Lord Curzon, 63, 253
Lord Hailsham, 55
Löschnack, Franz, 79
Loti, Pierre, 130
Louis XIV, 159-162

Lowenbrau, 73
Luce, Henry R., 205-209, 211
Lusitania, 170, 184-186
Lyauteuy, Hubert, 275
Lying, 25, 111, 194, 235, 271, 275

M

MacArthur, Douglas, 98, 278-281
MacDonnel Douglas, 218
Macedonia, 114, 154
Made in Germany, 2, 69-70
Mademoiselle de Scudéry, 160
Mainz, 155
Mair, H. G., 174
Malaysia, 58, 77, 120, 124, 141
Manchuria, 69, 135
Mandela, Nelson, 224-225
Mangope, Lucas, 213
Manheim and Albritton, 36, 201-
    204
Manheim, J. B., 36, 50, 62, 90-91,
    139
Manipulate, 50, 115, 123, 128,
    137, 154, 158, 167, 177, 240,
    250, 271
    Manipulate media reporting, 15
    Manipulate the image, 151
    Manipulate the mass media,
    137
Manipulation, 5, 12-13, 16, 11,
    113, 152, 163, 175, 223, 235
Manipulative PR, 25
Mankiewicz, Frank, 93, 281-282
Mao Tse Tung, 52
Marco Polo, 52
Marshall plan, 126, 236
Marubeni, 143
Masaryk, Tomás Garrigue, 89-90,
    189

Mason, A. E. W., 171
Mass culture, 255
Mass psychology, 189, 193
Masterman, Charles F. G., 170-174, 189, 272
Matthews, Herbert, 5, 201
Maximilian I, 158
May, Karl, 129-130
McAdoo, William G., 170
McCann, Thomas P., 14, 246-251
McCann Erickson, 65
McCarthy, Joseph, 122, 233, 236, 251
McGoff, John, 215-216
McNamara, Robert, 51
Mead, Margaret, 41, 116
Meany, George, 217
Meciar, Vladimir, 58
Media diplomacy, 86
Media foreign policy, 167
Media image, 20, 133
Mediation of foreign policy, 85, 96
Mein Kampf, 193
Mercedes-Benz, 60
Merchandise Marks Act, 68
Mercouri, Melina, 125
Meri, Lennart, 94
Metzenbaum, Howard, 279
Mexicans, 43, 79, 186
Mexico, 6-7, 74, 79, 187, 201-204, 258, 262
Meyer, Kuno, 181
Meyer, Wilhelmus Gerhardus, 212
Middle America Information Bureau, 246
Mitchell, Greg, 122
Mitterand, Francois, 277
MNCs, see Multinational corporations
Mobil Corporation, 31
Mobuto Sese Seko, 60
Molière, 160

Mondale, 91
Monetary policy, 75
Money, 28, 58-59, 66, 73-75, 143, 167, 209-210, 216, 221, 228, 230, 239
Mongolian, 52
Monroe Doctrine, 35
Montagu, A., 40, 272
Moon landing, 227
Moral slogans, 114
Morita, Akio, 139
Moro, Aldo, 259
Morocco, 95-97, 134, 275-276
Mowrer, Edgar Ansel, 206
Mozart, 73, 108-109, 132
Mulder, Cornelius, 213, 215-216
Muldergate Scandal, 212-213, 223
Müller, Kurt, 243
Multinational corporations, 27-34
Munich Olympic Games, 80
Münsterberg, Hugo, 180
Mussolini, Benito, 122, 196
Muthesius, Hermann, 71-72
Mvubelo, Lucy, 213

N

Nagy, Imre, 150-151
Name calling, 112
Napoleon, 114, 130, 162-166
Napoleon III, 115
Nasser, Gamal Abdel, 133
Nation-states, 12-13, 27, 29, 68, 72, 74, 95, 201, 273, 283
National Character, 37, 72
National identity, 47, 77, 127
National image, 46, 65
National Security Agency, 231
National Socialists, 128, 193, 195
National Stereotypes, 37

Nationalism, 35, 45, 162, 237
NATO, *see North Atlantic Treaty Organization*
Nazi, 45, 63, 80, 107-111, 119, 122, 126-128, 137, 144, 148, 193-196, 273
    Nazi ideologie, 114
    Nazi Germany, 12, 109, 191
    Nazi propaganda, 128, 145, 192-197
Negativism, 22-23, 26
Nehru, Pandit, 55, 198-200
Nelson, 166
Neutral Press Committee, 173, 175
Neutron bomb, 242
New Year's messages, 265
New York Times, 5, 31, 53, 66, 98, 108, 138, 142, 170, 172, 191, 199-201, 204, 206, 214, 216, 220, 226, 239, 241, 247, 250-251, 263
New Zealand, 92, 213
News agencies, 16, 22-24, 62, 173, 211, 220, 240, 247-249, 254, 256, 260, 283-284
News event, 90, 92
News selection, 22-26, 80
News value, 21, 25, 89, 283
Newsom, Earl, 31
Newsweek, 19, 36, 42, 74, 94, 125-126, 134-137, 208, 212, 241, 249
Nicholson, 171-172
Nietzsche, Friedrich, 177
Nigeria, 59
Nixon, Richard, 88
Nkrumah, Kwame, 61
Nonaggression pact, 128
North American Free Trade Agreement (NAFTA), 7
North Atlantic Treaty Organization, 94, 213, 230

Novosti Press Agency, 254
Nozomi, 142
NSA, *see National Security Agency*
Nyerere, Julius, 61, 119

O

Obasanjo, Olusegun, 59
Observer, 27, 214, 221
„Off the record", 88
Olasky, M. N., 29-30
Olympic competitions, 197
1936 Olympic Games, 195-196
Olympics, 2, 12, 136, 197, 213
Onassis, Aristotle, 125
One-way argumentation, 110
Operation Mincemeat, 272
Orgakov, Nikolay V., 264
Orient, 41, 129-130, 207
Östgaard, Einar, 20-21
Ottoman Empire, 160
Outgroups, 39, 41
Oxford Pamphlets, 171, 176

P

Paderewski, Ignacy, 90
Palestinians, 80, 104, 134
Palme, Olof, 259
Palmer, Frederick, 173, 275
Pan-Hellenic idea, 114
Panama Canal Co., 35
Panama, 6, 35, 140, 250, 283
Papandreou, Andreas, 125
Paradoxical communication, 164, 270-272
Paraguay, 260
Parker, Sir Gilbert, 172, 174
Patterson, Richard, 247

Peace Corps, 227, 232
Peace propaganda, 185
Pearl Harbor, 136, 138
Penkovsky Papers, 243
Pentagon, 98, 245, 258, 283
Pére Joseph, 159
Peres, Shimon, 215
Perestroika, 117, 265-267
Perfidious Albion, 165
Pericles, 155
Perot, Ross, 138
Persians, 153
Peru, 78
Phaidros, 113
Philipp II, 114
Philippine Islands, 10, 65
Philippines, 58, 65, 201, 204, 257
Pickford, Mary, 209
Pinocchio, 3
Pinochet, Augusto, 258
Plain folks, 113
Plato, 51, 113
Player, Gary, 218-219
Poland, 75, 90, 129, 189, 238, 266
Ponsonby, Sir Arthur, 270-271
Pope Gregor XV, 13
Pope Gregor XVI, 30
Pope Gregory VIII, 155
Pope Gregory IX, 156
Pope Innocent III, 156
Pope Pius IX, 29-30
Pope Urban II, 155
Pope Urban VIII, 13
Portuguese, 26
Potemkin, Prince Grigory
    Aleksandrovich, 4
Powell, Colin, 100
PR, *see Public Relations*
    PR, 12-13, 19, 26, 29, 33, 64-
    67, 89,90, 97-98, 123-126, 142,
    159, 189-191, 198, 200, 205,

215, 217, 223, 228, 263, 274,
280-283
    PR activities, 32, 35-39, 65,
        125, 189, 198, 202-204,
        213, 217, 220, 246, 263
    PR agency, 27-28, 31, 36,
        65, 201, 225, 277
    PR campaigns, 25, 33, 35,
        64-66, 125, 142, 189, 198,
        211, 249
    International PR, 26-28, 30, 34,
        63, 74, 80, 95, 142, 158,
        238, 246
    Structural international PR,
        25
    Manipulative PR, 25
    National PR, 16
    Symmetrical PR, 189
    Voluntaristic PR, 29
Prejudices, 2-3, 21, 37-42, 45, 58,
    106, 141, 212
Press guidelines, 164
Press releases, 36, 78, 202, 217,
    224, 244
Prestowitz, Clyde, 144
PRO-International, 221-222
Project Truth, 234
Prokesch-Osten, 166
Propaganda, 12-17, 45, 63-65, 82-
    86, 95, 103, 106-107, 110-112,
    117-119, 133, 144-148, 153,
    156, 158, 162-164, 171-177,
    180, 184-189, 193-196, 206,
    210-211, 214-215, 223, 232-
    239, 243, 252-256, 263, 267,
    270-271, 277, 279
    Atrocity propaganda, 72,
        159, 166, 177, 188, 279,
        282
    Black propaganda, 15
    Grey propaganda, 15

Nazi propaganda, 128, 145, 192-195, 197
Soviet propaganda, 117, 128, 234, 242, 252-254, 257
White propaganda, 15, 234
Propaganda campaign, 64, 72, 102, 189, 170, 213, 238, 243
Propagandist, 13-15, 111-113, 153-154, 157, 163, 166, 174, 176-177, 180-182, 189, 194, 208, 223, 234-235, 254
Propagandistic catchphrases, 115
Propagandistic manipulation, 113
Protocol news, 24
Prussia, 114-115, 166
Prussian Pressbüro, 166
Pseudoevents, 91-93, 155
Public diplomacy, 62, 86, 90, 228, 231-232, 235, 239, 266
Public Opinion, 5, 18-19, 30, 32, 35, 42, 82-83, 90-95, 122, 133, 136, 139, 142, 150, 156, 159-160, 163-164, 169, 174-175, 180-189, 201-203, 215, 226, 234, 249, 252, 256, 268, 273-274, 284
Domestic public opinion, 18
World public opinion, 18-20, 81, 92, 195, 238, 241, 266, 273, 276
Public Relations, 2, 6-7, 30, 36, 80, 85, 89, 98, 100-101, 121, 132, 136, 171, 184, 189, 192, 201, 204, 210, 228, 233-234, 237, 239, 246-247, 263, 277, 280
Public Relations for States, 20, 85
International Public Relations, 12, 27, 61, 80, 158, 189, 191, 264

National Public Relations, 16
Public sentiment, 19

Q

Q8, 68
Qaddafi, Muammar, 25, 89, 97, 246
Qatar, 78
Quayle, Dan, 231
Queen Victoria, 70, 168
Quia Maior, 156

R

Racine, 160
Racism, 9, 40, 214
Radio Ceylon, 32
Radio Free Cuba, 237
Radio Free Europe, 15, 237
Radio Free Hungary, 15
Radio Liberty, 237
Radio war, 195, 237
Rainbow Warrior, 92
Rakowski, Mieczyslaw, 255
Ramdane, Abane, 81
Ratcliffe, S. K., 172
Reagan Administration, 25, 33, 89, 245, 264
Reagan, Ronald, 31, 49, 91, 118, 126, 140, 229-230, 232, 263, 265
Real, 76
Reciprocity of indifference, 23
Red Menace, 31, 120-121, 210
Reds, 121-122, 124
Reference groups, 39, 111
Regionalism, 22
Regnault, Henri, 131

Repington, 276
Report on Guatemala, 249
La réputation, 159
Resistance, 106-107, 125, 145,
 196, 201, 225, 238, 240, 278
Reuters, 23, 134, 241, 260-261
Reuters TV, 24
Rhodesia, 201-204
Rhoodie, Eschel, 213-233
Rio, 19, 141
Rockefeller, John D., 209
Rogers, Ginger, 209
Roh Tae Woo, 90
Romania, 79, 283
 Romanians, 79-80, 253
Rome, 144, 152, 157
Roosevelt, Franklin D., 113, 135-
 136, 148, 171, 180, 185-186,
 189, 192, 206-208, 210
Roosevelt, Theodore, 278
Roquelin, Jean-Baptiste, *see*
 Molière
Rosegger, Peter, 129
Rothmyer, K., 215-219
Rourkela, 31
Royal Family, 69-70, 99
Rudolf II, 158
Rumors, 6, 51, 115, 154, 164, 243,
 261
Russia, 2-4, 15, 32, 50, 57, 70, 74,
 95, 115, 121-123, 129, 135,
 149, 188, 199, 220, 253, 255
 Russians, 3-4, 15, 118, 128, 220
Russian foreign policy, 56

S

Saatchi & Saatchi, 28, 160, 268
Sabbah el-Ahmed el-Sabbah, 95
Sabena, 66

Sacharov, Andrei, 268
Sacra Congregatio de Propaganda
 Fide, 13
Sacramento Union, 216
Sadat, Anwar el, 133, 231, 257
Said, Edward W., 40, 47, 129
Sakurauchi, Yoshio, 143
Salinas, Carlos, 79
Sandinista, 228
Sarajevo, 91
Sato, Masao, 142
Saudi Arabia, 24, 31, 98
Schallberg, Wolfgang, 109
Schmidt, Helmut, 62, 231, 243
Schumacher, Fritz, 71
Schwarzkopf, Norman, 98-100
Science, 48-53, 59-63, 135, 140,
 191, 200, 232-233, 241, 268-
 269
SDI, *see Strategic Defense
 Initiative*
Seagrave, Sterling, 205-210
Second hand experiences, 12
Selective evaluation, 104
Selective perception, 102-107, 150
Self-Fulfilling Prophecy, 58-59
Sen, Beney Rayan, 199-201
Senghor, Leopold, 61
Servan-Schreiber, Jean-Jacques,
 221
Shaheen, Jack, 132
Shakespeare, William, 3, 11, 131
Sharif, Nawaz, 91
Shaw, George Bernhard, 174
Shaw, Peter, 97
Shell Oil International, 224
 Shell South Africa, 224
Shultz, George, 246, 264
Siad, Ali Ahmed (Adonis), 134
Side entry, 285
Siegel, Mark, 90
Simmel, Georg, 271

Simon, William, 217
Sinatra, Frank, 238
Sinbad, 131
Sinclair, Upton, 121-122
Singapore, 59
Singer, M., 54
Slater, 63
Snowcroft, Brent, 98
Sodom, 152
Solzhenitsyn, Alexander, 236
Somalia, 94, 96, 119
Somoza, 193
Sony, 139
Soong Chiang, May-ling, 206-210
Soong, T. V., 206-207, 210
Sorensen, Thomas C., 227, 232-236
South Africa, 68, 108, 203, 212-226, 259
    South Africans, 217-218, 221, 224-225, 259
Soviet Union, 15, 17, 32, 56, 92, 96, 114, 118-119, 123, 125-129, 139, 146-149, 192, 227, 37, 242-243, 252-258, 263-268
Soviets, 32, 92, 126, 234, 253, 256, 58, 268
Soweto, 220
Spain, 74, 132, 162, 164, 275-276
Spartans, 154
Speakes, Larry, 245
Spellman, Robert L., 35-36
Spiegel, 6, 58, 95, 99, 108-109, 34, 141-142, 214, 221-224, 66, 268, 282
Split image, 179
Sputnik, 149
Squires, James D., 170-171, 175-76
SS20, 242
St. Petersburg, 32

Stalin, Josef, 51, 119, 122-123, 26, 252, 266
Star Wars, 118, 126, 265
State Department, 87-88, 94, 198-99, 219, 230, 232, 237, 282
Steinbach, Udo, 135
Stereotypes, 3, 7, 38-39, 42, 45, 50, 3, 106, 137, 148
    Autostereotypes, 38, 41-42
    Heterostereotypes, 41
    National stereotypes, 37
Stigmatizing the enemy, 274
Stimulus-reaction model, 105, 189
Storm troops, 192
Strategic Defense Initiative, 265
Strauss, Richard, 132
Strauss, Robert, 126
Stürmer, 196
Suez Canal, 35, 132
Suez crisis, 59
Suggestibility, 193
Sulzberger, Arthur H., 247
Sunlight Soap, 70
Sweden, 67, 162, 239, 259
Swinehart, Gerry, 191
Swiss, 1, 187
Switzerland, 13, 67, 73
Swope, Herbert Bayard, 123
Symbolic, 12, 90, 158, 230
Synod of Clermont, 155
Syria, 133

T

Tactic of Withdrawal, 201-204
Taiwan, 14, 59, 74, 134, 206, 211, 17, 244
Takeshita, Noboru, 143
Talleyrand, 49
Tarzan, 11

TASS, 16, 254-259, 262
Tata Brothers, 59
Taylor, Elizabeth, 66, 131
Tchitcherin, Georgi W., 256
Television news exchange, 24
Tellez, Luis, 79
Temple, Shirley, 209
Terrorism, 36, 80, 202, 214, 245
Terrorist, 78, 80, 132, 245, 279
Testimonial, 112
Texaco, 34
Thailand, 124
Thatcher, Margaret, 231
The American Road, 31
The White Man's Burden, 10
Theatre of terror, 80
Third World, 22-26, 116, 234, 258
Third-party approach, 158, 181
Thomson, Meldrim, 220
Thucydides, 153
Thwaites, Norman G., 176
Tiananmen Square crackdown, 28, 50
Time, 5-6, 19, 27, 32-33, 46-49, 53-55, 59-60, 75-81, 89, 95, 97-99, 125-126, 129, 132, 136-140, 143, 205-206, 236, 241, 249, 256, 265, 274, 279
Times of London, 19, 276
Tiroleans, 165
To Ethnos, 257
Tokyo Olympics, 136
Tönnies, Ferdinand, 273
Toshiba Machine Co., 139
Tourism, 12, 26, 55, 62, 78, 225
Toyota Motor Co., 138
Tracy, Spencer, 209
Transfer, 68, 112, 117, 284
Transkei, 216
Trento, S. B., 93, 97, 278-280, 282
Trevelyan, George, 172
Trotsky, Leon, 253, 266

Troyanovsky, Oleg, 264
Truman, Harry S., 123, 209-210, 233
Trumbull, Robert, 199
Trust, 74-76, 107, 266, 284
Truth, 29, 42, 44, 49, 51, 84, 111, 126, 145, 152, 157, 162-163, 205, 233-235, 240, 246, 256, 271-272, 274
Tsushima, 135
Turkey, 28, 115
Turks, 132, 158
Turner, Ted, 97
Tutu, Desmond, 60
Two-way argumentation, 110

U

Uganda, 60, 119
Ugly American, 239
UN, *see United Nations*
UNESCO, *see United Nations Educational, Scientific, and Cultural Organization*
Union Carbide, 218
Union Jack, 69-70
United China Relief organization, 209
United Fruit, 14, 27, 36, 246-251
United Kingdom, 64, 68, 74, 242
United Nations, 16, 19, 80-83, 102-103, 107, 139, 144, 213, 218, 236, 254, 258
United Nations Educational, Scientific, and Cultural Organization, 27-28
United Press International, 23
United States, 2-6, 10, 15, 23, 26-36, 39-40, 44, 46, 50, 52, 56, 62, 65-68, 73-76, 79, 88, 90,

94-97, 107, 112, 118-126, 131-
139, 142-144, 148, 170-171,
175-179180-187, 191-193, 197-
200, 201-203, 206-213, 215,
218-221, 223, 226-238, 240-
243, 246, 248, 254-260, 262-
266, 268, 278-279
U.S. image, 5, 68, 150, 227,
257, 260, 262
United States Information Agency,
15-17, 230-240, 257-264
United Steelworkers of America
AFL-CIO, 34
UPI, *see United Press International*
Upper Volta, 47
USIA, *see United States
Information Agency*

V

Valentino, Rudolpho, 131
van den Bergh, Hendrik, 215
van Doren, Charles, 66
Vatican, 30
Venezuela, 23
Venice, 3, 158
Verdi, Giuseppe, 132
Versailles, 160-162
Viereck, George S., 175-176, 180,
182
Viet Cong, 238
Vietnam, 15, 44, 51, 98, 146-147,
227, 235-237
VOA, *see Voice of America*
Voice of America, 231-232, 236-
237, 265
von Bernhardi, Friedrich, 177
von Bernstorff, Count Johann, 180,
184
von Clausewitz, Carl, 270-271

von der Vogelweide, Walther, 157
von Hohenzollern-Sigmaringen,
Leopold, 115
von Leibniz, Gottfried Wilhelm
Freiherr, 4
von Papen, Franz, 183
von Ribbentrop, Joachim, 192
von Treitschke, 177
Vorster, John, 213-216, 220
Voznessensky, Lev Alexandrovich,
266

W

Wabenzi, 60
Wagner, Richard, 40
Waldheim, Kurt, 107-109
Wallace, Edgar, 10
War of Devolution, 161
War slogans, 274
Washington, George, 80
Washington Star, 216
Watanabe, Michio, 143
Watergate, 236, 259
We-group, 118
Weber, Max, 54, 141
Webster, William, 98
Wellington House, 170-176
Wells, Herbert George, 172-173,
177
West Germany, 62, 67, 73, 149,
221, 224-225, 237, 242, 260,
268
Western, 14, 22-26, 35, 41, 46, 48,
54, 59-61, 68, 129, 132-133,
148-149, 155, 205, 215, 221,
229, 236, 238, 240-243, 251-
258, 263, 266, 268, 275-276,
283
Western Sahara, 95

Whales, 139-140
Whaling, 91, 139-140
Whispering campaign, 184
Whitaker, Clem, 121
White House, 98, 100, 189, 207-210, 245, 282
White Man's Grave, 47
Whitman, Ed, 249
Wick, Charles, 231, 235-236
Wild West, 23
Wildermuth, Ron, 98, 100
Wilhelm I, 115
Wilhelm II, 3, 71, 167
Wilke, Jürgen, 181
Willert, Arthur, 174
Willkie, Wendell, 207-209
Wilson, Woodrow, 170, 179-189
Winick, Charles, 230
Witchhunters, 127
Woodward, Bob, 245
World's fair, 64, 71
World Bank, 27, 30
World of literary images, 49, 52
World public opinion, 18-20, 81, 92, 195, 238, 241, 266, 273, 276
World War I, 3, 45, 63-64, 69-72, 121, 154, 169-170, 191, 274-275
World War II, 8, 11, 13, 111, 119, 122, 124, 137, 144, 246, 253, 279
Worldwide Television News, 24
World Wide Fund for Nature, 19, 27, 141
Wortley, Stewart, 167
Wright, Hamilton M., 28, 65, 211
WTN, *see Worldwide Television News*
WWF, *see World Wide Fund for Nature* (former World Wildlife Fund)

Y

Yat-sen, Sun, 206
Yeats, William Butler, 47
Yellow Peril, 11, 52, 115, 135
Yugoslavia, 201-204

Z

Zaire, 44, 47, 60
Zambia, 236-237
Zar und Zimmermann, 4
Zeman, Z. A. B., 112, 194, 196
Zemurray, Samuel, 246, 248
Zhirinovsky, Vladimir, 129
Zimbabwe, 204
Zimmermann, Arthur, 180
Zionists, 129, 133